The Consequentiality of Communication

The Consequentiality of Communication

edited by

Stuart J. Sigman
State University of New York, Albany

P90
.C657
1995

Lawrence Erlbaum Associates, Inc., Publishers
365 Broadway
Hillsdale, New Jersey 07642

Cover design by McKevin Shaughnessy

Library of Congress Cataloging in Publication Data

The consequentiality of communication / edited by Stuart J. Sigman.
        p. cm.
     Includes bibliographical references (p.) and index.
     ISBN 0-8058-1269-5 (acid-free paper). — ISBN 0-8058-1765-4 (pbk.)
     1. Communication—Philosophy. I. Sigman, Stuart J.
   P90.C657   1995
   302.2'01—dc20   94-22939
                                                        CIP

Printed in the United States of America
10   9   8   7   6   5   4   3   2   1

Contents

About the Contributors

Wayne A. Beach (PhD, University of Utah) is Professor in the Department of Speech Communication, San Diego State University.

Vernon E. Cronen (PhD, University of Illinois) is Professor in the Department of Communication, University of Massachusetts–Amherst.

Wendy Leeds-Hurwitz (PhD, University of Pennsylvania) is Associate Professor in the Department of Communication, University of Wisconsin-Parkside.

Robert E. Sanders (PhD, University of Iowa) is Professor in the Department of Communication and the Department of Linguistics and Cognitive Science, State University of New York, Albany.

Stuart J. Sigman (PhD, University of Pennsylvania) is Associate Professor in the Department of Communication, State University of New York, Albany. He is also a Core Faculty Member of the Graduate School, The Union Institute, Cincinnati, Ohio.

Sheila J. Sullivan (PhD, State University of New York, Buffalo) is Assistant Professor in the Department of Communication at Canisius College.

Introduction: Toward Study of the Consequentiality (Not Consequences) of Communication

Stuart J. Sigman
State University of New York, Albany

Communication matters. It matters whether a word is spoken with a certain inflection, a gesture is displayed at a particular body height and with a particular intensity, an article of clothing is donned, or a bodily incision is endured at just some moment in an activity sequence. This book discusses the idea that *what* persons do when constructing messages with others has an impact on the kinds of lives they lead, the kinds of institutions and organizations they find themselves inhabiting, and the kinds of connections with other persons they make—separated across space, time, and rank.

Thus, this book is concerned with the idea that the communication process is consequential in and to people's lives. This consequentiality cannot be explained by primary recourse to cultural, psychological, or sociological variables and theorizing, however. It is the ebb and flow of the communication process itself that must be studied, and a theory of communication consequentiality apart from anthropological, psychological, or sociological theory that must be developed.

To study the consequentiality of communication, it is not necessary to study, isolate, and/or enumerate distinct consequences or effects of communication. Within the discipline of communication, there is a long and rich tradition devoted to the study of the consequences of communication or exposure to particular messages. There is just as large a tradition involved in the study of the consequences of other structures and variables (e.g., cognition, sociocultural rules, affect, etc.) on communication. But, as is argued here, such research isolates behavioral units for their effects on other units, and thus does not capture what it is about the communication

1

process (as opposed to a particular stylistic or linguistic variable) that permits such consequentiality. What communication theorists and researchers have yet to study in any detail is how it is possible for communication to have the consequences it does—that is, what it is about communication (as opposed to a particular unit or facet of behavior) that enables it to be consequential.

As detailed later, *consequentiality of communication* means that *what* transpires during, within, and as part of persons' interactive dealings with each other has consequences for those persons. Those consequences come from the communication process, not the structure of language or the mediation of particular personality characteristics or social structures. Communication is consequential both in the sense that it is the primary process engendering and constituting sociocultural reality, and in the sense that, as it transpires, constraints on and affordances to people's behavior momentarily emerge. In this view, communication is not a neutral vehicle by which an external reality is communicated about, and by which factors of psychology, social structure, cultural norms, and the like are transmitted or are influential. The communication process: (a) exerts a role in the personal identities and self-concepts experienced by persons; (b) shapes the range of permissible and impermissible relationships between persons, and so produces a social structure; and (c) represents the process through which cultural values, beliefs, goals, and the like are formulated and lived.

Thus, to study the consequentiality of communication is to envision a world composed of a continuous process of meaning production, rather than conditions antecedent and subsequent to this production. To study the consequentiality of communication is to take seriously—for purposes of description and analysis—a world sustained by persons behaving, engaged in the negotiation and renegotiation of messages, not a world of a priori (or a posteriori) cognitive states, cultural rules, social roles, or the like.

A PERSONAL ANECDOTE

A few years ago, I attended an all-day gathering—a sort of encounter session and support group—that attracted more than 30 people. While attempting to be flexible and open to the participants' emergent needs, the facilitators nevertheless had prepared a structure of exercises and experiences to cover the morning session. Thus, the morning was divided into three phases or activities: an introductory exercise involving self-disclosive talk to a partner, the listing of factors that promote or inhibit feelings of safety and trust among the participants, and a 30-minute discussion about the significance of the money contained in the donation box. What transpired during this latter event needs further elaboration, and orients us to this book's focus.

In introducing the third activity for the morning, one facilitator reached for the brightly covered cardboard box, opened the bottom seam, and allowed the assorted bills and checks contained in the box to cascade to the middle of the floor. He then proceeded to explain what meaning the money had for him, referring to it as both a resource permitting the group to do its work (payment for the meeting hall and for lunch) and a token of the participants' commitment to the group. He then asked the other group members, in round-robin fashion, to share their individual thoughts on the money in the middle of the room. The first two or three people expressed confusion over the request, and so yielded the floor to the next person. The disclosures increasingly turned to more negative views of money, until about the 10th speaker, who frankly admitted that he had had tremendous apprehensions about donating to the box when he first entered the center, and that now he felt extremely anxious in the presence of the money. The facilitator scooped up the bills and checks from the middle of the room, walked to this last speaker, and handed all the money over to him. After this speaker shared some further thoughts, the facilitator took back the money and, in midsentence, said he had an announcement to make. He apologized to the group for not having thought of it before, but he announced that everyone should and would have an opportunity to hold the money while speaking—that indeed the money could serve as a "talking stick." The money was quickly passed around to those people who had already held a turn, until it caught up with the next new speaker. The facilitator explained the importance of a talking stick to Native Americans, and suggested that in various other groups he attended the use of a talking stick (although not one physically embodied by money) was common. He apologized again to the group for not having thought about the value of a talking stick, and moreover this particular talking stick, for the exercise and discussion then ensuing. Thus, the remainder of the morning session involved the passing of the money from one participant to the next, with each person having an opportunity to share his or her thoughts on that particular money or money in general, and the money itself fulfilling its new discursive function as a turn marker or placeholder.

I offer this anecdote because it embodies the essential problem to be attacked here, and perhaps the central problem of real-time communicating: the relationship between the unplanned-for and emergent quality of most interactions and the availability of a priori behavioral resources for interaction participants. How do behavioral resources constrain the ongoing unfolding of communication events? How do actions fit into the continuous stream of behavior so that they are simultaneously seen as coherent with, and appropriate to, their existential moment of creation and location in the stream, and as coherent with, and appropriate to, the expectations, plans, grammars, and rule sets being enacted by the participants? In brief, how is it possible for a turn of phrase (or other behavior) to emerge during interaction and to shape, in an unplanned-for manner, ensuing behavioral production? In other words, *what features and activities of the communication process permit it to be consequential?*

THEORETICAL BACKGROUND OF THE CONSEQUENTIALITY CONCEPT[1]

The Brenders–Cronen controversy—concerning theories of meaning appropriate to the study of communication processes—inspired me to explore the need for communication theory to attend to consequentiality (Brenders, 1987; Cronen, 1987; Cronen, Pearce, & Changsheng, 1990). Brenders and Cronen (along with the latter's co-architect, Pearce) disagree on a number of philosophical points, the most important of which, for present purposes, are Brenders' insistence on an explanatory apparatus concerned with fixed and stable meanings of speech acts and Cronen's belief in fluid and ever-evolving meaning. Both Brenders and Cronen align their work with key ancestral lineages—Searle's (1969) speech act theory and Wittgenstein's (1958) ordinary language philosophy, respectively. What first perplexed me about their debate was the absence of some shared disciplinary vocabulary for adjudicating the two positions, and indeed the almost wholesale ignoring of the controversy in the professional journals. I find these lacunae in our disciplinary development still troubling.

One need not take sides with either Brenders' or Cronen's solution to have something to say about the general issue raised by the controversy. As I see it, the general issue is whether the process of communication plays some role in the production of meaning, and, if so, how it is able to do this. Does a discipline of communication concern itself with preserving and developing a theory of meaning production, in which meaning is predicated on a priori pragmatic conditions being met by utterances, as Brenders would have it? Or do we take up the cause of meaning as a context-dependent and context-evolving phenomenon, which is advocated by Cronen?

In other words, I believe that the Brenders–Cronen controversy represents a critical choice node for our emerging discipline, yet it has largely gone unremarked about and unnoticed. The choice is that regarding an

[1]This section is adapted from Sigman (1992). Permission to reprint by Guilford Publishers is gratefully acknowledged.

ontology of communication. The one choice is to assume that the significant "stuff" of communication transpires prior to, or at the least behind the scenes of, the behavior being displayed by communicating entities. Thus, communication involves the transmission and reception of meanings that derive from independent, determining influences (i.e., those independent of communication): the sociostructural location of the communicators; their affective states; their cognitive abilities; cultural, linguistic, and pragmatic rules; and so on. Taking this choice assumes that communication is a multiply influenced phenomenon, and it justifies the importation of explanatory concepts of a multi- or interdisciplinary nature—be these structural sociology, trait or personality theory, cognitive psychology, or the like. Also, in this view, the communication process is said to play the role of neutral medium for these other, more determinate forces.

The alternative choice, however, freely admits to multiple influences on human behavior. Nonetheless, it suggests that the process of communication has a unique influence on human affairs, and that this unique influence is not captured by anthropological, psychological, or sociological explanations. This second choice, which I contend is most appropriate for an emerging discipline of communication, requires theorizing about the consequential character of communication. This second choice defines for communication a set of practices and dynamics—interpretive procedures and "design features" (Hockett, 1958)—that transcend or augment anthropological, psychological, and sociological influences on behavior.

Recognition of the consequentiality of communication represents an understanding that something occurs in the interactional processes of message generation–reception[2] that is not accounted for by either the larger social structure in which the interaction occurs or the cognitive and affective processes that enable persons to participate in communication. In other words, the process of communication—whether that process is sustained by two people, a small group, an organization, or a telemedium and an audience—is consequential, and it is the "nature" of that consequentiality that is the appropriate focus for a discipline of communication.

In this view, the activity of behaving—the real-time process of communication—demands scholarly attention. It is here that a warrant and niche for communication theory emerges (i.e., a warrant for the close inspection of, and systematic theorizing from, communication processes). The process of communication must be approached as influential on message production and interpretation, and as nonreducible to the aforementioned social, cultural, and cognitive influences and determinants.

---

[2]Meaning is always a creation; it is never simply sent or received. Nevertheless, the meaning-creation activities of interactional coparticipants (*senders* and *receivers* in the old paradigm) may not be isomorphic, and that is what this wording is intended to capture.

I am not suggesting that attention be devoted to the consequences of communication or of particular pieces of communication behavior (i.e., the effects that purported communication variables have on other variables). This is because the study of consequences does not examine actual process; rather, it treats process as a given in order to gauge effects and results of isolated units.

In what way is a communication effect or consequence different from communication consequentiality? First, note that in referring to the former it is necessary to specify a particular unit (or units) from and about which effects are to be determined. Thus, a communication effect does not concern the process of communication writ large, but rather a particular slice (or slices) of the process. Second, and relatedly, most studies of communication effects are not concerned with communication, but rather with particular modes or channels of communication (e.g., the linguistic) and, within those channels, particular forms or styles (cf. Bradac, 1989; Bradac & Street, 1989–1990).[3] This research partakes of "'informational' [information science] conceptions where meanings are assumed to be already existing, [instead of] 'communication' explanations of processes of meaning development and the social production of perceptions, identities, social structures, and affective responses" (Deetz, n.d., p. 3). To take but one example, research on language effects fails to recognize that, at a minimum, the communication process involves the collaborative or conjoint action of multiple parties, and meaning is not sent and received, but collaboratively produced, contested, and negotiated. Thus, research on language effects fails to recognize that any effect coming from language is subject to the intrusion of, and the real-time "conveyance" by, communication (i.e., is subject to formulation as to its gist [Heritage & Watson, 1979] and to negotiation as to its meaning or import). To study communication, then, one cannot begin with studies of language variables and language effects (or other channel variables and effects). Rather, one must study situated, ongoing, and negotiated meaning-producing activities.[4]

Therefore, I use the term *consequentiality* to mean that communication evidences a dynamic structure with regard to meaning creation, re-creation, and storage. Further, this term implies a particular scholarly focus: how it is possible for the communication process to have consequences

---

[3]Note, for example, the summary description of some of this research by Bradac and Street (1989–1990): "The research on attributed power and communication is part of a broader stream of research on language and impression formation which examines connections between phonological, semantic, or syntactic features of language and persons' perceptions and evaluations of communicators who use these features" (p. 198).

[4]This assessment of the language effects paradigm should not be taken to imply wholesale rejection of such research. Far more modestly, my goal here is to distinguish communication consequences (effects) and communication consequentiality approaches.

and to exert a consequential role in people's lives. Consequentiality leads to a consideration of the procedures, dynamics, and structures of communication, not the effects (the supposed end results).

If the process of communication does not make any difference to the meanings that are generated in mass, organizational, or interpersonal contexts, then communication is not worthy of study. If meaning is assumed to be (and is studied as) determined by free-standing cognitive processes, linguistic patterns, social structures, cultural codes, and the like, then communication is at best a neutral vehicle for conveying such messagefulness—certainly it has no determining influence—and its status as an analytic interest ultimately offers a contribution back to the free-standing disciplines already engaged in the study of the aforementioned processes and structures. However, if the meaning that emerges at any one moment of communication cannot be predicated on the social structural locations or psychological features of the participants, or on a priori sociocultural grammars, then we must turn attention to the determining force played by the process of communication. The chapters in this book are devoted to the presentation of varying perspectives in the development of such a consequential approach to communication inquiry.

PLAN OF THE BOOK

I assembled four sets of authors in this book, and asked the sets to address the issue of consequentiality from within their orientation to communication. Thus, communication consequentiality is considered from the standpoint of the coordinated management of meaning (CMM; Cronen, chap. 1), a neo-rhetorical perspective (Sanders, chap. 2), conversation analysis (CA; Beach, chap. 3), and social communication theory (Leeds-Hurwitz & Sigman, with Sullivan, chap. 4). In addition, the authors provide brief rejoinders, or comparative essays, which are placed at the end of the book. These chapters permit the authors to situate their theories within the general need for a theory of communication consequentiality, and/or to provide criticism and support of the others' efforts in this regard.

At this juncture, it might be asked why I did not write this book myself. This book is intended to move the discipline of communication studies in a particular direction—toward recognition of the consequentiality of communication. It is not designed to resolve all the issues along such a path, although it does point to the kinds of topics and phenomena about communication consequentiality that can be discerned. A single-authored theory of communication consequentiality is not what is needed at this point in conceptual or empirical development because there is not, as yet, a disciplinary awareness of or interest in consequentiality. What *is* needed is for multiple authors, with differing methods and goals, to acknowledge and circle around this common problem. Thus, this book will have served its purpose when communication scholars move away from an information- and effects-based framework and move toward incorporating some view of the consequentiality of communication in their work. The precise nature of that incorporation will depend on the particular theory being employed, with a discipline-wide understanding emerging over time.

Contributing to this goal, Cronen's chapter first stakes out the territory claimed by the "received view" of social science—the one that attends to the consequences or effects of variables on each other. Cronen proposes that the received view maintains a set of *idols*—patterns and practices that social scientists employ, but which social constructionists like him find troublesome. These idols are: (a) mentalism, (b) preference for statistically redundant over emic data, (c) the failure to situate beliefs in systems of meaning and activity, and (d) inattention to communication in favor of a search for underlying mechanisms.

Cronen next explores the issue of communication consequentiality by turning his attention to experience. He argues that lived experience is patterned—that it does not separate the mind from its body, nor thought from action. Lived experience is embodied in moment-by-moment communication. To take experience seriously, Cronen proposes a number of emphases that can guide the efforts of theorists, researchers, and practitioners in understanding communication as an aboriginal or primary social process. Among these emphases, Cronen reminds us that meaning occurs through conjoint social action—it is not a mentalistic phenomenon. Moreover, the participants in this conjoint action are the particular persons they are because of this patterned and coordinated activity in which they enter and which they experience. Communication, rather than "mind," is what comprises persons. Thus, Cronen's chapter provides a rich initial vocabulary and justification for approaching communication as a primary—and in that sense, consequential—enterprise.

Sanders' chapter takes up one of the issues addressed by Cronen's largely theoretical essay in empirical terms—the relationship between communication acts and social identities (referred to as *role-identities* by Sanders). The argument is advanced through an analysis of institutional discourse, in which persons with clearly delineated or ascribed institutional identities must nevertheless achieve these identities in the face of competing demands by others. In terms of the broader discussion of consequentiality, Sanders offers a neo-rhetorical approach to interaction, which focuses on those contexts in which individuals make use of "the expressive resources and the interactional process involved in enacting role-identities when there are obstacles to doing so produced by others (inadvertently or knowingly) and/or in novel situations." In staking out this terrain, Sanders intends to go beyond Goffman's (1959) analyses of identity and identity construction. He suggests that Goffman's work is limited to those situations in which persons cooperate in sustaining the enactment of a uniform script. For Sanders, some portion of social life finds persons in conflict, either with competing institutional role and relationship demands, or with obstacles emerging from other persons' enactments (specifically, the "meaning in context" of other's behavior). Persons possess varying degrees of problem-solving competence to control the course of the interaction by establishing constraints on the presuppositions and relevance of their acts and uptake by others.

As part of his concluding remarks, Sanders proposes two alternative frameworks: one strong and one weak version of communication competence, and therefore communication consequentiality. In the weak version—one that characterizes the predominant communication paradigm, and about which Sanders has reservations—communicators find themselves obliged to inform others about their role identities. Communication is consequential to people's lives in that information or substantive content generated by their performances may be more or less isomorphic with their actual identities. In the strong version, however, persons are engaged in multifunctional behavior: while they are engaged with others in some "business at hand" (which requires coordinating their behavior with that of others), there are potential relevances that may arise concerning their or others' identities. Communication is the ongoing production of behavior and the negotiation of the entailments (coherence, relevance to presuppositions, etc.) about identity that arise from engaging in interaction. In this view, people do not simply inform others of existing role identities, but they perform behavior with the knowledge (not necessarily conscious) that particular behavior they or others perform may presuppose one or another role identity. In this fashion, identity is continuously coconstructed, not merely the subject of an "informing."

From a neo-rhetorical perspective, the consequentiality of communication resides in two features of the nonscripted character of communication. First, it is through the ebb and flow of communication—where divergent interests, goals, and interpretations may surface—that strict adherence to some prototype (for identity) may be abandoned. Second, communication processes, precisely because they need not be scripted, permit novel problem solving, as the participants adjust their behavior to meanings that are being created "in the moment." In brief, communication is not always or primarily the execution/enactment of prototypes or scripts; certain problematic situations both emerge and are resolved through ongoing communication.

Sanders' chapter thus gives rise to some consideration of the relationship between a priori templates for performance and actual, lived experience. This relationship, phrased in terms of a dialectical tension, is revisited in the chapter by Leeds-Hurwitz and Sigman, with Sullivan (discussed later).

The chapter by Beach continues a theme begun in Sanders' work—that of attention to the details of interaction as they occur, and to the trajectories leading toward and from particular details. Unlike Sanders, who uses conversational materials to address a theoretical issue, Beach remains steadfastly empirical in his endeavors. His chapter, derived from conversation analysis, attempts to situate a particular lexical item in interaction practice—the placement and occasioning of "Okay" in casual conversation. He uses this analysis to reveal features of interaction, although the chapter does not generalize beyond this analysis to universal or inherent features of interaction or communication. Thus, Beach translates the volume's overall concern with communication consequentiality into an examination of the consequentiality of "Okay." This is consistent with conversation analysis' empirical orientation to its field according to Beach: "Gaining access to the meaningful nature of participants' actions emerges from direct observations of real-time interactions, and is not necessarily facilitated by a priori theoretical starting points." This stance neither denies nor advocates the role of personality, culture, or tradition in human affairs; however, it does suggest that these be seen as occasioned (not transcendent) phenomena that are "updated" as and through "here-and-now actions."

My own reading of Beach's chapter, however, leads me to the conclusion that it is not about "Okay" at all, at least not in a certain sense. Beach's chapter is not about the single lexical item because, as he himself reveals, "Okay" does not provide any univocal or unambiguous function in interaction. Rather, the chapter reveals the use of this token to accomplish interactional work—work that emerges during and as part of real-time interacting. The analysis of "Okay" seen in this light is a case study of communication as a situated accomplishment.

What does Beach's chapter reveal about consequentiality? Beach first shows that there is an organization to communicative interactions at the level of the interaction behaviors as they are produced—an organization that does not require such "macrolevel" glosses as frequency, personality, or culture to illuminate them. This is a point similar to that recently made by Schegloff (1993). Although most social scientists assume that microbehavior is disorganized and can only be seen to be patterned in the aggregate, conversation analysis clearly demonstrates that organization exists at the microlevel, and that macrolevel analyses (frequency distributions, etc.) impose an alternative order on the data that does not reflect the order that was oriented to and produced by the communicators.

This raises the second contribution of conversation analysis and Beach's chapter to our discussion of consequentiality: The communication system is apparently set up so as to hinge on any next move in the flow of behavioral production. Any move in interaction may project differing trajectories for the participants. These are not established before the interaction began, and are not predictable from prior psychological or sociological states of the participants, but are created in the interaction. Moreover, any move in interaction may undo or redo what has just taken place; it is in the act of behaving that decisions are made, behaviorally produced, and attended to by others as to how their behavior is to be treated. Any next turn may renegotiate the meaning of any prior turn. There is a fluidity to the human communication system, and this fluidity *is* the consequentiality of communication.

Finally, Leeds-Hurwitz and Sigman, with Sullivan, argue that this fluidity associated with communication consequentiality is tempered by constraints on behavior oriented to in the moment by communicators—constraints that may precede or transcend the moment of appearance in interaction. This chapter continues Sanders' and Beach's empirical orientation by presenting a case study of ethnographic and conversational materials. The goal of the case study and the accompanying theoretical orientation is to rethink certain formulations of social communication theory—a communication perspective that the three authors have contributed to in several publications. Beginning with the classic social communication theory treatment of rules in the form of behavioral "programs" (Scheflen, 1968), the authors go on to recognize that rules explanations refer to the a priori resources with which communicators enter situations, but not to the actual process of communication (which may or may not attend to particular rules). The authors ask where the consequentiality of communication can be seen to be located, and they attempt to answer this question by comparing multiple performances of an event with that event's grammar. This comparison of the performance pieces that faithfully enact versus abandon expected components, and the accompanying analysis of the behaviors that emerge during the performance without being part of the event program, permit consideration of how communication can be consequential.

In part, the critique of the notion of programs (and, the authors contend, all rules-based theories) is comparable to the ethnomethodological rejection of rules:

I am trying to ask: When a person seems to be following rules, what is it that that seems to consist of? We need to describe how it gets done. These practices of etc., unless, let it pass, the pretense of agreeing, the use of sanctioned vagueness, the waiting for something later to happen which promises to clarify what has gone before, the avoidance of monsters even when they occur and the borrowing of exceptions are all involved. I am

proposing these as practices whereby persons make what they are doing
happen as rule-analysable conduct. (Garfinkel, cited in Heritage, 1984,
pp. 125–126)

Instead of abandoning a rules vocabulary in favor of a set of ad hoc
interpretive procedures, Leeds-Hurwitz and Sigman, with Sullivan, ask
the following questions: What is the relationship between a priori formulations of rules and their instantiations in particular circumstances? How do
rules come to be used? What does their use and nonuse reveal about
consequentiality?

The consequentiality of communication is evidenced by, and produced
in, persons' moment-by-moment attempts to resolve three tensions they
experience—the obligation to: (a) align current behavior as it emerges with
the expectations derived from a priori grammars, (b) fit one's current
behavior into the "story line" one has previously enacted, and (c) coordinate one's current behavior with that produced by one's coparticipants.
These three tensions offer multiple and potentially competitive demands
on communicators. Thus, these tensions are experienced in and during
actual moments of behaving, but it is also during and through actual
moments of behaving that communicators respond to the challenge of
these tensions and produce meaningful conduct.

These tensions are proof positive that, although programs provide a
structural or cultural competence for producing grammatical utterances
and episodes, the communication process forces persons to go beyond the
structures and rules—to engage in coordinating behavior in order to make
sense of others' behavior and in order to carry out the rules relevantly.
Although there are programs that define in some a priori sense what
communicators can and should do in particular situations, these programs
must be performed. Such performance brings with it its own dynamic and,
moreover, is not fully predicted by or adherent to the a priori programs.
Thus, the communication process is consequential in that it is a performance that involves and permits the strategic manipulation of resources to
build and work one's way through novel circumstances. Thus, a distinction is drawn in the chapter between the cultural level of analysis (one
concerned with the values and grammars of a group) and the communicational level of analysis (one focusing on what actually transpires as part of
any one moment of behaving). The broader implication of this discussion
is that communication scholars must not rest their analyses on descriptions
of communication rules because rules are resources for communication,
but not equivalent to the communication process.

As noted, the book's final section contains brief rejoinder essays. Because these chapters reiterate and sharpen many of the points contained in
the earlier chapters, they are not summarized here. Several key issues are

raised in the final section that do deserve note, however. First, the final chapters broach a number of unresolved topics—items to be placed on an agenda that acknowledges a view of communication consequentiality. One of these issues concerns the relationship between a priori and situated aspects of interaction: What contribution does each make to in-the-moment meaning production? How does each temper or constrain the influence of the other? Second, the final chapters struggle with the methodological and epistemological problems associated with a consequential view of communication: How does one acquire data on the a priori resources that communicators are assumed to "bring" to communication—data that are relevant to, yet not tautologically connected to, any one moment of real-time communication? How does one accomplish this without giving analytic primacy to cognitive, cultural, or social explanations over communicational ones? Is it possible to theorize about communication apart from the close inspection of conversational (or other communication) materials? Relatedly, is it possible to generate a theory of communication consequentiality—an understanding of general design features of the communication process—that is distinct from the description of the sequential placement and function of any particular unit of communication behavior? Finally, the relationship between informational and communicational perspectives, or weak and strong versions of communication competence and communication consequentiality, permeates this book and the last four chapters: What are the limits of communication consequentiality? Is the communication process consequential only in problematic situations? If not, in what ways do the consequential features of communication work in routine and nonroutine situations?

To conclude, I hope this introduction and the following chapters result in a rethinking of the underlying paradigm for communication research—one that currently emphasizes the isolation of discrete behavioral units and their effects in favor of one that emphasizes the consequential character of the communication process.

REFERENCES

Bradac, J. J. (Ed.). (1989). *Message effects in communication science*. Newbury Park, CA: Sage.

Bradac, J. J., & Street, R. L., Jr. (1989–1990). Powerful and powerless styles of talk: A theoretical analysis of language and impression formation. *Research on Language and Social Interaction, 23,* 195–241.

Brenders, D. A. (1987). Fallacies in the coordinated management of meaning: A philosophy of language critique of the hierarchical organization of coherent conversation and related theory. *Quarterly Journal of Speech, 73,* 329–348.

Cronen, V. E. (1987, November). *The curious case of propositions*. Paper presented to the Speech Communication Association, Chicago, IL.

Cronen, V. E., Pearce, W. B., & Changsheng, X. (1990). The meaning of "meaning" in the CMM analysis of communication: A comparison of two traditions. *Research on Language and Social Interaction, 23*, 1–40.

Deetz, S. (n.d.). *Communication 2000: The discipline, the challenges, the research, the social contribution.* Unpublished manuscript, Rutgers University, New Brunswick, NJ.

Goffman, E. (1959). *The presentation of self in everyday life.* Garden City, NY: Doubleday Anchor.

Heritage, J. (1984). *Garfinkel and ethnomethodology.* Cambridge, England: Polity Press.

Heritage, J., & Watson, D. R. (1979). Formulations as conversational objects. In G. Psathas (Ed.), *Everyday language: Studies in ethnomethodology* (pp. 123–162). New York: Irvington.

Hockett, C. F. (1958). *A course in modern linguistics.* New York: Macmillan.

Scheflen, A. E. (1968). Human communication: Behavioral programs and their integration in interaction. *Behavioral Science, 13*, 44–55.

Schegloff, A. E. (1993). Reflections on quantification in the study of conversation. *Research on Language and Social Interaction, 26*, 99–128.

Searle, J. R. (1969). *Speech acts: An essay in the philosophy of language.* Cambridge, England: Cambridge University Press.

Sigman, S. J. (1992). Do social approaches to interpersonal communication constitute a contribution to communication theory? *Communication Theory, 2*, 347–356.

Wittgenstein, L. (1958). *Philosophical investigations.* New York: Macmillan.

I

FOUR PERSPECTIVES ON
CONSEQUENTIALITY

1

Coordinated Management of Meaning: The Consequentiality of Communication and the Recapturing of Experience

Vernon E. Cronen
University of Massachusetts

The editor of this book has made a crucial distinction in the book's title. It is a very different thing to talk about the *consequentiality* of communication, as opposed to the *consequences* of communication. The etymology of the different suffixes is illuminating. The suffix *ty* (after the connecting vowel *i*) comes from Latin and indicates a state or condition, whereas the suffix *ence* indicates action or process in addition to, or to the exclusion of, a state. This distinction represents no fine semantic hassle. The choice of title indicates rejection of both the transmission model and the variable analytic tradition of research. I call the confluence of the transmission model and variable analysis the *received view* of communication. In the received view, communication is a process that has consequences of various sorts (i.e., effects subsequent to it and outside it). The reader of this chapter may be disappointed to find no claims derived from the received view of the following sort: "More communication promotes greater mutual understanding" or "Communication helps us to reach our goals." In both of these statements, the process of communication is asserted to have consequences outside itself. Such statements are, of course, counterparts of the following, which also come from the received view: "High self-esteem produces more assertive communication" and "High status in a group produces more talking turns." Taken together, the foregoing statements suggest that various prior factors in the person and situation (usually conceived as variables) determine the content and form of communication, and communication subsequently has measurable consequences for another set of variables.

In the received view, communication cannot be the site of the most important avenues of social inquiry because psychological, sociological, and cultural variables determine it. Moreover, the model states quite clearly that we only care about communication because it can have consequences for other matters that are our real concerns. By contrast, Coordinated Management of Meaning (CMM), the practical theory that Pearce and I have been developing, takes a different view of communication and the human condition. CMM is a constructionist theory of a particular sort. It is social constructionism in the tradition of American philosophical pragmatism. One undergraduate, who recognized that CMM theory did not identify communication variables that predict consequences outside communication, told his instructor that the theory was "beside the point." Indeed, from the received view, much social constructionist work seems exactly that. However, from my way of working, the received view is reminiscent of an old story about emigrants traveling by steamship to America:

> Crammed onto the lower deck of a ship were two friends from the town of Chelm. Both were very sick and very bored from many days at sea, living on little food, and packed in like sardines with little air. No one was moving around much. Then one day there was a sudden jolt and a crunching noise. An alarm sounded and a voice shouted, "The ship is sinking! Get to the life boats!" People began shouting and crying. They rushed back and forth gathering a few possessions, trying to locate their families, and pushing toward the ladder to the deck. In the midst of all this one of the passengers noticed that his friend was sitting quietly on the deck, watching and smiling. The panicked passenger said to his friend, "What is the matter with you? Didn't you hear? The ship is sinking!" And his friend replied, "So, why are you so upset? Does it belong to you?"

The calm traveler had not missed the point that the ship was sinking; he had more profoundly missed the point of the relationship between himself and the ship. He talked about the ship as an object whose value to him depended on whether he had ownership of the ship as an object. He did not think of his existence as intrinsically connected to the ship's survival. The relationship of communication to who and what we are is even more profoundly fused than that of the passenger and the ship. I think Harré (1984) was right when he argued that the primary social process is "persons in conversation." If communication is the primary social process, it is not something external to us that we are able to do as a consequence of what human beings are. Rather, it is intrinsic to our constitution as distinctively human creatures. This marks a change from the traditional epistemological paradigm focused on individuals understanding objects to people acting conjointly. In the tradition in which I work, individuals and society are not outside of communication, but are regarded as achievements in communicative practices. Dewey (1916/1966) was much ahead of his time when he wrote, in 1916, that social life is "identical with communication" (p.5). For Dewey, cultural forms, institutions, social roles and the like were lived patterns of practice. That is why he said, "society not only continues to exist by transmission, by communication, but may be fairly said to exist in transmission, in communication" (Dewey, 1916/1966, p. 4). Therefore, the kinds of selfhood and identity we have as individuals are not innate, but rather are constituted *in* and by the process of communication (Dewey, 1916/1966, 1930).

To return to the title of this book, as scholars of communication we must study the consequential character of the communication process, not the supposed correlates of this process with external variables.

PRIMARY COMMITMENTS OF SOCIAL CONSTRUCTIONISM IN THE TRADITION OF PHILOSOPHICAL PRAGMATISM

What is a social constructionist orientation? Obviously, social constructionism is not a monolithic movement. There is a neo-Marxist orientation and a phenomenological orientation, both well defined. However, outside these better defined orientations, confusion reigns. At the 1993 New Hampshire conference on "Creating Social Realities," I even heard that Freud was a social constructionist. Other participants consistently confused Cartesian doubt about physical reality with social constructionism.

Despite this confusion, there are ideas that inform a social constructionism in the tradition of *philosophical pragmatism*, although not all the contributors I identify would prefer that label. Its intellectual ancestry, of course, includes the American pragmatist philosophers, particularly James, Dewey, and Mead. Related to their work is that of the later Wittgenstein and Vygotsky, and the less behavioristic aspects of Batson's work. Contemporary social theorists within this tradition include Bernstein, Harré, Shotter, Taylor, Sampson, and the CMM group. There are important areas of difference among the foregoing ancestors and contemporaries, and I am quite aware of those differences. However, these ancestors and contemporaries provide orientations that seem related and profitable.

Minimally, my pragmatist "take" on social constructionism involves important commitments about the primary unit of social process, the appropriate unit of observation, the rationality of social life, material reality, and the kind of certainty we can expect to have.

The Primary Social Process and the Unit of Observation

Social constructionists with a pragmatist orientation agree that communication is the primary social process (Pearce & Cronen), 1980), and "persons in conversation" (Harré, 1984) is taken to be the primary unit of observation. Notice that I have treated Harré's phrase in the singular. These are not three units of observation—two or more persons and their utterances. The distinction is important because it differentiates the "constructivist" positions of Maturana (1975, 1978), von Glazersfeld (1991), Kelley (1955), and others who follow a Kantian orientation from the social constructionist work of Harré (1984), Shotter (1984), Taylor (1985), and others whose commitments are close to later Wittgenstein (1953) and philosophical pragmatism.

It is helpful here to distinguish the constructionist orientation from the constructivist one. In a constructivist orientation (Kelley, 1955; Maturana & Varela, 1988), there is a central place for the Cartesian concept of *mind*. In the spirit of Kant, constructivists inquire into the fundamental cognitive schemas that humans supposedly use to impose order on their world. Although constructivists talk about individuals as coupled by feedback, communication is primarily of interest to them to the extent that individuals perturb each other's cognitive operations (von Glazersfeld, 1991). The details of conversation become less important than the ways individuals obtain a "fit between their own condition and the messages they receive (von Glazersfeld, 1991, p. 23). By contrast, pragmatists are concerned with the details of communication. We think there is an answer to the cognitivists' question—How do individuals think?—but an answer they would not like. The answer is that people can think all sorts of different ways. How people think depends on the ways of thinking they construct in the course of social life. For the social constructionist, there is no need for mind—that mystic substance developed by Descartes, separate from body and the interactional arena. All we need are brain, communication, and the physical world.

There is, of course, a vital need for the term *thinking*, because that is what persons do as part of the activity of life. But communication does not have consequences for the way we think, who we are, and how we feel. Rather, pragmatists say the consequentiality of communication can be observed in ways of thinking, feeling, and so on that arise integral to the process of communication at the moment of action. By adopting this way of working, constructionists in the pragmatist tradition returned to Dewey's (1925/1958) distinctive way of reuniting thinking and acting.

Immanent Rationality

Pragmatism generally rejects the postmodern tendency to disparage rationality, although philosophical pragmatists are quite willing to agree that there is no singular, transcendental rationality (Cronen & Pearce, 1981), as was presumed by the Scottish philosophers of the late Victorian age (MacIntyre, 1990). Schrag (1992) observed quite correctly that French philosopher Derrida's attack on rationality has a peculiar quality shared by those who argue against rationality. Derrida's proposed means of deconstruction—*grammatology*—displays its own form of radicalized rationality. We can make the same inquiries of it that we can of any formalized academic practice. Those practices are organized by emergent situated rules, a *grammar* in Wittgenstein's terms, for rationally conducting academic conversation. These new conversations extend the range of what Plato taught—new ways to take apart and critique culturally instantiated ways of talking (see Ong, 1989).

The kind of grammar Wittgenstein described is his approach to rationality (Canfield, 1981). It is not simply a matter of creating "correct" sentences, and it is not limited to linguistic materials. A grammar of conversation has to do with the way that feelings, objects, behaviors, and utterances can be organized so that we know how to "go on" in conversation (Wittgenstein, 1953). This Wittgensteinian idea of grammar does not separate the syntactic from the phonologic and semantic aspects of language. Instead, it insists that we learn a grammar in the practice of acting with others. Thus, we may study the grammar of "love" just as we can speak of the grammar of "realism" by exploring how these utterances or behaviors can be sensibly connected to others so that persons know how to go on in conversation.[1]

It is useful to think of this grammar as made up of *rules*—a term long associated with CMM theory. Dewey preferred the term *habits*, but that word, although capturing the social nature of rational action, implies a stability that is slowly developed and slow to change. I prefer *rule* because the term is connected to the way one learns to calculate. Sometimes after

---

[1]CMM theory is a way of exploring grammars of conversation. Conversation Analysis, Social Communication Theory, Milan family therapy, and Ethnography of Communication may be described as other ways of doing so, although they do not share all aspects of the orientation described in this chapter.

many trials, but sometimes in the course of making one effort, one suddenly grasps how to do the problems. Moreover, in Wittgenstein's usage, rules may come into use and dissolve moments later as action emerges in new directions. The term *rule* also directs us to a rich set of ideas that Wittgenstein developed around it.

In the pragmatist view, not everything people do makes sense, but one must distinguish between sense and nonsense (Wittgenstein, 1953). For Dewey (1925/1958), Mead (1934), and Wittgenstein (1953), sense is created in communication, not by the adjustment of what we do to a universal grammar or logic. Making sense has to do with "coming into agreement in action" (Dewey, 1925/1958, p. 179), or knowing how to go on (Wittgenstein, 1953). This idea of coming to know how to go on was the key to Pearce's (1975) initiating the CMM project.

Although this approach to rationality is grammatical, it does not assume that everything that makes sense can be expressed in language. This emergent view of rationality treats using a rule as akin to grasping something in a situation that has future possibilities. A chess master uses the basic rules of chess (how to move pieces, what constitutes checkmate, etc.), as well as the subtle understandings of how to go on derived from extensive experience. These understandings or rules amount to more than doing the "right" thing if a past circumstance reoccurs. His or her subtle "feel for the game" gives us confidence that the chess master is in a better position to deal with a complex and new situation than the less accomplished player, but this does not mean the chess master can fully articulate the rules used. There are limits to expressibility, but rationality is not coterminous with expressibility in this perspective. Moreover, rationality cannot, in this emergent account, be judged universally by the standards of perfection, precision, or completeness. Of course, some kinds of discourse usefully call for greater efforts at precision in order to go on (Taylor, 1985). However, such precision is not the most important feature of language or rational action. There are other times in which open-endedness and suggestiveness are more valuable for going on well. James (cited in Gunn, 1987), Dewey (1922/1950), and Wittgenstein (1953) all saw living as anticipatory, with an unfinished "more is coming" quality to it. It is also crucial, for this approach to rationality, that language not have a formal unity. It is not a matter that can be neatly set apart from feeling, behaving, and making (Wittgenstein, 1953).

Realism and Certainty

Pragmatists are realists, but not objectivists. Persons in conversation are treated as material beings in a real world. The way that reality counts in our lives is not fixed, but rather constructed in joint action. To use a phrase of Shotter's (1993), the materiality of the world and our physical being in it must be treated as "sensory topics" capable of being elaborated as meaningful in the social construction process. Wherever we go on this planet, when we let go of certain objects they move downward—they do not fall up. However, whether this sort of event counts as *gravity*, *telos*, or *particle exchange* depends on the socially constructed scientific episode being played. Placement of the event in a grammar or action is what has implications for the development of particular abilities in practice. If the event is part of a Newtonian grammar of forces and particles, the extension of mathematical ability was part of that way of scientific life. By contrast, if the event is part of a theological grammar, the ability to read texts metaphorically may be extended in the course of that activity (Prigogine & Stengers, 1984).

Pragmatists reject both objectivism and relativism (Bernstein, 1985). Objectivism is rejected because it assumes one can have certain, final knowledge of the way the world "really is." But pragmatists also reject relativism. Pragmatists argue that the choice among language games is not a matter of habit or a shot in the dark. Consideration and weighing of future possibilities go on, but are not based on mechanical calculation or uniform criteria. Choice among incommensurable positions is usually based on multiple factors, including the potential usefulness of a position for carrying on in the real world of practice (Taylor, 1985). We may hold a theory of potato chips, but if that theory involves testing them by bouncing them, we will have difficulty going on with that theory. We may have an idea about how persons think and act, but when we find that we cannot go on in any coherent and useful way with others when employing those ideas, we may be advised to change them, no matter how coherent they are relative to a particular point of view.

This sort of realism—realism that is practical and neither objectivist nor subjectivist—requires setting aside the idea that the way to test our doubts about reality and truth is through Descartes' game of radical doubt. Descartes is often referred to as the father of modern philosophy. His game of radical doubt is based on the primacy of individual mind, and is at the root of our determination to play unproductive philosophical games about reality and certainty. Using the Cartesian method, one can doubt one's own physical existence because this knowledge is merely based on sense data. The assertion "I have hands" can be doubted because it is neither a clear and distinct idea independent of sensory data nor formally necessary by the criterion of noncontradiction. In the Cartesian game, it is contradictory to doubt the assertion "I have a mind" because to doubt it supposedly proves it.

However, Wittgenstein (1969) observed that "Doubt about existence only works in a language game. Hence, what we should first have to ask:

What would such a doubt be like?, and don't understand straight off"
(p. 5e). Descartes played a philosophy game of his own devising, in which
there were rules for deciding what is and is not beyond doubt. The rules of
his game, based on grammars of clarity, completeness, sensory distortion,
and absence of internal contradiction, are not the ones that scientists have
so successfully used to deal with doubt in physics, microbiology, and
neurology. Why not prefer to play those successful games?

Wittgenstein argued that having certainty was simply the situation in
any language game, in which we can say there is every reason to have
confidence in such and such, and nothing now speaks against it. Like
Dewey, Wittgenstein was not concerned with "ungrounded" propositions, but rather with useful action.

Wittgenstein (1969) put the matter quite clearly in the following comments from *On certainty*:

    para 139. Not only rules, but also examples are needed for establish-
               ing a practice. Our rules leave loop-holes open, and the
               practice has to speak for itself.
    para 140. We do not learn the practice of making empirical judgments
               and the connection with other judgments. A totality of judg-
               ments is made plausible to us.
    para 141. When we first begin to believe anything, what we believe is
               not a single proposition, it is a whole system of propositions.
               (light dawns gradually over the whole.)
    para 142. It is not the single axioms that strike me as obvious, it is a
               system in which consequences and premises give one an-
               other mutual support. (p. 21e)

Some confusion has been caused by the recent statements of Kenneth
Gergen, one of the key figures in the rise of contemporary social
constructionism. At the New Hampshire conference on "Creating Social
Realities," Gergen reiterated two themes he has expressed in a number of
public venues. He said he wished to remain "mute" on the question of
whether there is a reality outside our thoughts, and that the term *experience*
should not have a central place in constructionist vocabularies. Gergen
(1993) said that *experience* is an individual, psychological notion that is
differently explained in various cultures. With the first of these claims, I
think Gergen takes us in the direction of Cartesian radical doubt, ignoring
the centrality of Wittgenstein's (1969) arguments. With the second, he
seems to introduce a further confusion. By rejecting the centrality of
experience, Gergen mystifies the distinction of what is happening to oneself from that which happens to others. This sort of recourse to actions

without bodies would take us to a literary model of disembodied texts or discourses, and would deny any reality to pain, suffering, joy, or wonder—except as features of a text. It is hard to imagine why so many important texts exhibit grammars of pain, joy, and so on if persons had no such embodied experiences. Indeed, he joined Shotter in rejecting the text model in a recent publication (Shotter & Gergen, 1993).

What Lies Ahead

In the remainder of this chapter, I move beyond the starting places described previously and take on a task of description and analysis. I want to develop the implications of understanding human experience in terms of the consequentiality of communication—the primary social process. Therefore, what follows is an analytic, not a synthetic, enterprise. My goal is to provide a useful description that may stand in the place of the traditional reductions of experience to stimuli, information bits, cognitive schemas, and social structures. The reader may be surprised by the subjects I do not cover in detail. I do not highlight a communication-oriented analysis of culture, selfhood, gender, emotion, or power. These are matters of great importance, and I allude to them in the course of my description of communication. However, I think the careful development of those subjects depends on getting our house in order with respect to communication as primary experience.

The chapter proceeds in the following way: (a) discussion of why it is necessary to argue for the importance of experience, including an effort to clear away some idols of communication research; and (b) presentation of a set of terms for describing communication as primary experience. The terms presented are all highly interrelated, describing as they do an integrated, distinctively human way of life. The reader might regard them as something like a set of *topoi* in the classical rhetorical sense, indicating what to look for and think about in the development of communication theory and the analysis of situated action.

RECAPTURING EXPERIENCE:
A COMMUNICATION PROJECT

Experience was a central term for Dewey. He challenged traditions that dismissed experience as either too confusing and complex for study, or a shroud over hidden, orderly processes. Dewey took the "messy" stuff of life very seriously.

One of Dewey's important contributions to social thought was the way he described relationships among terms like *individuality*, *society*, and *institutions,* unifying them via the term *experience.* The term *experience* was Dewey's shorthand way of expressing the unity of thought and action and the temporality of both. "According to [western philosophical] tradition," argued Dewey (1917/1960), "experience is (at least primarily) a psychical thing, infected throughout by 'subjectivity.' What experience suggests about itself is a genuinely objective world which enters into the actions of men and undergoes modifications through their responses" (p. 23).

Do We Really Have to Argue for the Importance of Experience?

Unfortunately, we do have to argue for serious attention to experience because the Cartesian dualism that informs the received view of communication is so pervasive. Although few social psychologists today talk about Descartes, their organization of behavior into cognitive, affective, and conative dimensions is an obvious extension of Cartesian thought.[2] The inner mind is subdivided into a cognitive and an affective realm, and the body side of the dualism is retained in the conative aspect. When social psychologists add *behavioral intentions* to the mental side (a sort of updated version of the "will"), we have back together much of the received view. Individual life is divided into different sets of variables that may affect each other and change in degree, but that meet the criterion of independence for statistical analysis. When coupled with the individualistic unit of analysis, the result is the loss of anything like the quality of lived experience (Gergen, 1982; Harré & Secord, 1972).

From the point of view of research, the loss of real experience has produced a strange situation. The science of social psychology received its great impetus from the behaviorists' arguments about the need to focus on observables, whereas observables have usually come to mean paper-and-pencil tests without reference to subjects' situated experience. The relationship of cognitive and affective measures to real behavior is usually put off until a later day. When behavior is considered, it is often reduced to simple counts of behavior units. Lost is their place in a stream of action by real human agents who are trying to do something together. Thus, experience is stripped of, "what should I do next now that you have done that?"

The attempt to understand experience by variable analysis can obscure that which is no mystery at all. Not long ago, I heard the presentation of a study on emotion and communication. The presenter, who shall remain nameless, was concerned with how to differentiate *passionate love* and

---

[2]There is, of course, an even older tradition at play in that triad. That tradition is faculty psychology. Affect, cognition, and conation have a rough but evident relationship to the old faculties of imagination, reason, and will.

obsessive love. The idea was to represent each type of love by scaled items. However, intense romantic love and passionate love may be described by many of the same isolated declarative sentences. The subjects' task was to match the degree of fit between scaled items based on these sentences and their internal ideas.

Constructionists of a pragmatist bent say that we should abandon the idea that kinds of love are like sensations, leaving distinctive marks in persons' cognitive system (Averill, 1980). That is the source of the confusion. There is no great mystery here if we give up the Cartesian way of working and think about various descriptions of love as just that—commonly used descriptions of couples' experience that have a grammar. Consider the way a couple lives when one partner is what we term *obsessive.* The obsessive partner finds it hard to concentrate on work, calls the other frequently, and finds the other starting to avoid contact. The other partner may now work to create distance so as to get on with other aspects of life, only to encounter more persistent efforts by the obsessive partner. Stripping emotion out of the flow of experience and trying to distinguish what it is can only lead to confusion, and many published articles.

Social constructionists in the pragmatist tradition think there is no way to answer questions such as, "What kinds of human emotions are there?" or "What is love really?" What we can do is answer questions like these: How does what the theorist calls obsessive love have a place in cultural, community, and personal patterns of communication? How is obsessive love lived in the experience of the persons involved?

How did social science get into this state of commitment to empiricism and a Platonic tendency to seek the "real" behind observables? This is not the place for a sophisticated analysis of the development of social theory. However, I think Dewey got hold of an important part of the explanation when he recognized that substantial features of the Lockean and Kantian heritage were the result of trying to solve a pseudo problem—a philosophical muddle needing not resolution to solve it, but therapy to get over it (Dewey, 1929/1960; Wittgenstein, 1953). This muddle concerned the twin problems of the relationship between thought and action and the relationship between particular ideas and the flow of experience. The muddle was produced in two crucial moves. First, there was the Cartesian move of transferring the Greek metaphor *theater,* with spectators observing the heavens, to the realm of the mind. Mind became an internal theater in which a sort of "third eye" could survey the impressions or ideas contained within. Our English word *theory* is derived from the Greek word for theater. Aristotle used the word *theoria* to identify those arts in which the objects of study are set out before us like the action in a play in a theater—action we observe, but do not affect. The second move was that of treating the "mental contents" in mind as unitary ideas that, at their best, were clear and distinct. John Locke's ideas about a mind that registered sensory impression on the *tabula rasa* were similar in many respects to those of his Cartesian opponents. These two moves are so well instantiated that we need to discuss their consequences to clear a space for a consequential view of communication.

Four Idols of Social Research

Borrowing Bacon's famous phrase, I want to identify four idols of social research that interfere with our ability to do useful work.

1. The Idol of the Mental Theater.   If a mind is an individual's container of ideas, sensory inputs, or whatever, then two problems need to be solved: (a) How can mental contents be related to physical action? and (b) How could it be that experience does not seem like a web of beliefs and affects? Kantian philosophy (and its contemporary progeny, cognitivism, artificial intelligence, and constructivism) has its origins in trying to resolve problems intrinsic to an intellectual game, in which one must first try to get an account of the hidden operations of individual minds. These minds must somehow operate on static bits and associations they contain. In this game, it is not necessary to worry about what people "do" until there is resolution of the cognitive and affective issues (Bernstein, 1966).

Kant recognized severe limitations in the sort of empiricism that treated sense data as unitary impressions contained in the mind. He set out to understand how experience could come to have the qualities of continuity, coherence, and sequence that persons report. He concluded that if we are to understand experience, we must find its qualities in the a priori contributions of the mind. Our contemporary cognitivists, following Kant, seek to discover the schemas by which the mind (that Descartes invented) can accomplish this integrative task.

Contemporary psychologists who follow the traditional division of cognitive, affective, and conative variables attempt to achieve the recovery of something like integrated experience by studying statistical correlations of these sources of variation. However, action must then be reduced to reports of mental "intentions," thus losing all sense of coordinated action with other people and any real sense of experience. The questions that arise for the behaviorists traveling this old path are almost silly: Do thoughts cause our feelings or do feelings cause our thoughts? How are any of these matters related to what is observed? For the most part, the research that has resulted has been a welter of findings that tax the interpretative abilities of even the most clever researchers.

It is not unusual for traditionally oriented clinical psychologists to attempt to integrate the behaviorist and cognitivist perspectives. For example, they study depression by exploring correlations among measurements based on an inventory that ranks observable behaviors without reference to specific situations or the responses of others. These statements are correlated with measurements of belief in one's control over events, general optimism, and the like. How episodes of depression fit into patterns of lived experience, and the stories that patients tell about the lived interactions with others, have no important place in most of this research. Instead, the researchers want to get beneath or behind experience to fret out the connections among cognitions, emotions, and behaviors. So far, the results have been far from useful. (For a review by a sympathetic researcher, see Weaver, 1991. Also see the results of her own research in the same source.)

Kelly's (1955) psychology of personal constructs is referred to by some clinical psychologists as the "constructivist" alternative to traditional approaches because of Kelly's insistence on finding the quiddity of each person's way of making sense of the world. This, of course, is simply the mind–body dualism transposed into a person–world dualism (Dewey, 1916/1966). An avowed Kantian, Kelly thought of social action as a set of questions put to the "personal constructs" that clients come to use as a consequence of their experience. The actual movement and flow of conversation as experienced, with each person's actions and utterances contingent on the actions of another, has no important place in this work. The result has been that communication theorists who were once impressed by Kelly's constructivist idea have largely abandoned this line of work.

2. The Idol of Redundancy. Experienced clinicians who inquire into patterns of conversation know that regularity is no reliable sign of enriching interaction, and that a singular event may be pivotal for understanding the pattern of development a family (or other unit) may take. However, their insights are often dismissed as prescientific, and their writings as "not real research." Nonclinicians who do social research based on the case-study method often experience a similar reception.

The difference between statistical work and the notion of *experience* as I am developing it here is not a difference of more or less rigor. The nature of the difference is demonstrated in an exchange between Cappella (1990) and Jacobs (1990). The thrust of their exchange may be expressed this way: Statistical methodology, articulately advocated by Cappella, holds that human action can be most usefully understood as redundancy against a background of randomness. In contrast, Jacobs argued persuasively that human action is best conceived of as patterns of coherence. As Jacobs observed, the significance of one-time events and the temporal quality of much social interaction are not reducible to general tendencies expressed in aggregate data.[3]

In his book, *How Real Is Real?*, Watzlawick (1976) gave the amusing example of the problem faced by American servicemen and British women during World War II. Although the courtship patterns of the two countries were similar in many ways, the first effort of the man to kiss the woman was placed very differently in those patterns, and the grammar of the first kiss was very different. The American usually tried to kiss the woman good night after the first date. If he did not, or if she refused, it was not sensible for the American to expect a continuation of the dating relationship. However, the British woman did not expect to be kissed after the first date. If she accepted the American's attempt to kiss her, she expected further intimacy would follow. To understand this situation is not a matter of comparing how often an attempt was made to kiss, but how the attempt figured in a pattern of conjoint action, and understanding what affordances and constraints were then created for subsequent action.

The overemphasis on quantitative methods has led to losing the distinctive qualities of human communication, and thus its consequentiality as the primary form of lived experience. One is not studying a feature of communication by merely associating it statistically with something else. Statistical association is not the equivalent to native or emic meaningfulness.

3. The Idol of Beliefs.   The primacy of experience is obscured by the notion of *beliefs*. It is not that I think beliefs are irrelevant to experience. Rather, I object to treating beliefs as independent corpuscles of knowledge, or as independent propositions. This treatment of beliefs makes our confidence in them independent of and prior to communication. It obscures the place of belief assertions in patterns of activity. For example, the physicist who asserts there are six, not four, quarks is making an utterance in scientific discourse. Those who hear this know how to carry on, whether in arguments about theory or episodes of practical experimentation. We would not consider a student to be a future scientist if he or she can answer questions about the scientific community's beliefs, but cannot engage in scientific discussions or participate in research activities.

Family therapists and others who use case-study methods know how difficult it may be to understand the place of beliefs in the lived experience of clients. They know how willing persons are to give abstracted reports of

---

[3]I caution the reader that my agreement with Jacobs does not extend to his idea that case studies will, like quantitative research, lead to the discovery of lawlike statements about communication.

their beliefs in professional settings. I recall working with the Kensington Consultation Centre of London on a case, in which the husband and wife, both intelligent, well-educated people, treated the interviewer's questions as requests to report a system of political beliefs. The husband called himself a "Thatcherite" who believed that each person must pull his or her own weight, including partners in marriage. He strongly endorsed economic rationalism and the profit motive. Also among his beliefs was the idea that his wife was a good wife because she was a devoted mother. This was an important role for the woman in a home that would produce successful children. However, he wanted her to have a more financially productive job herself, working for him. The wife's beliefs were not so different from her husband's, but she criticized her husband's heavy emphasis on profits. At the same time, she enjoyed and appreciated the wealth that his success produced. Her objections to his profit orientation were usually uttered when the subject of her working for him was raised. What was the place of profit and business in their life as a couple? The reader can conjecture a number of possible ways to make sense of this. However, what we learned was not what we expected.

Questions such as, "How did you two meet?" elicited more political and social agendas. We could not figure out what attracted these people to each other or how they lived together. We decided to use an old CMM technique. The interviewer asked the husband and wife to write play scripts describing an ideal evening together (Pearce & Cronen, 1980). They accepted the task and became interested in it. There were many surprises. The wife's script included a candlelit dinner, during which her husband excited her with stories about his business dealings. The telling of such stories did not figure into the husband's script except as brief talk early in the evening. If the wife worked with her husband, this modern version of the "return of the hunter to tell his story" would not be possible. The mystery and drama could not be created the same way. A very different view of the place of business dealings in the lived experience of this couple emerged.

4. *The Idol of Hidden Mechanisms.*   Modern physical and biological science made great strides as a consequence of the idea that behind appearances there was a hidden reality of elements, molecules, atoms, and subatomic particles. That idea originally came from much older pre-Socratic sources. Although this tradition has worked well in various sciences, it has led to some strange and useless ideas in the study of human affairs.

The idea has become so common that, so long as there is an identifiable human process or ability, it is assumed there must be a hidden mechanism behind it. Some of the reifications are almost funny. In speech pathology, researchers have long observed the ability of persons to "parse" sentences.

For example, assume the following sentence: We fed her dog biscuits. Given the relevant context, a person with intact abilities should be able to tell whether some female person was fed dog biscuits, or whether some female person's dog was fed biscuits. Because there is such an ability to parse, it is assumed by some researchers that there must be a "cognitive mechanism," called the *parser*, that can be damaged (Davis, 1993). The same author says, quite rightly, that such abilities do not have a neatly localized place in the brain, so he postulates a cognitive mechanism in a sort of Cartesian mind substance.

The same move is familiar in the study of social life. When a person is able to do something like identify an object for use in a set of actions, it is concluded that there must be a "cognitive schema" for so doing. To explain the development of such a schema, there must be a still more basic cognitive mechanism that must be discovered. Harré (1984) observed that what happens here is the translation of "a personal achievement into a point in a network of conceptual relations that ramify from its thing-like status" (p. 18). Like others,[4] Harré (1984) argued that the conclusion more parsimonious with data is that our abilities are "primarily public and collective, located in talk" (p. 21).

The rush to find an underlying mechanism of some sort begins, of course, with inattention to communication. Without focus on how persons together create patterns of thought and action, we are left with the problem of how to account for an individual's abilities. Assuming that the individual is the basic unit of social observation, not communication, researchers must find within the individual some explanation for an ability—hence the retreat to ghostly hidden mechanisms.

When I say that the search for hidden mechanisms is a mistaken kind of theoretical idolatry, I do not mean to imply that understanding social interaction is simple and self-evident. What I do mean is that a properly directed study would not look for something behind social life, but would be a rigorous way to examine what happens in the experience of situated conjoint action. That would take us directly to the consequentiality of communication.

DESCRIBING COMMUNICATION:
THE "UR" FORM OF EXPERIENCE

How should we, as theorists, researchers, or practitioners, proceed in our work if we take experience seriously? I sketch an answer to this question by offering a set of descriptive terms that extend and develop the primary commitments of philosophical pragmatism introduced earlier.

---

[4]See for example Vygotsky (1962) and Shotter (1984).

Materiality and Embodiment

Experience, as opposed to metaphors such as *mind, schemas,* or *texts,* directs us to embodied persons in a real world. The reality of embodiment in a real world does not determine how reality counts in our activities; its *meaning* must be worked out in social action. Nevertheless, the physiological differences between men and women, or children and adults, interpenetrate our activities (Dewey, 1925). The ability of the body to respond when exposed to thunder or injury is crucial to what a human experience is like. Of course, these responses can be modified and woven into experience in countless ways. Dewey (1925/1958) argued that such sufferings and undergoings, whether joyful or painful, constitute the only possible metaphysics. He termed this approach a *natural metaphysics.* Santayana (1925) took him to task for this terminology, arguing that natural metaphysics is an oxymoron. A metaphysics is made up of concepts that meet this criterion: They must be analytically necessary—without them, it would be impossible to give a complete, clear, and cogent account of the world. Santayana argued that this is a task of philosophical analysis, not an empirical problem. Dewey (1927) responded to Santayana by claiming that terms meeting this criterion could not be the sort typically advanced by metaphysicians. Typical metaphysical terms, such as *space, time,* and the like, are meaningful only in particular intellectual traditions and in particular social experiences. Thus, the only features of experience meeting the metaphysicians' criterion would be those natural to our species on this earth.

The emphasis on physicality and embodiment is a good antidote for the abstractionism to which much social theory is prone today. There is an illuminating story about Dewey coming home on the subway with friends after a lecture by Russell in which Russell said that utilities should be put in public hands (Lamont & Redmer, 1959). Dewey, who was himself a socialist, was scratching his head as he held on to the strap. Then he said, "Come to think of it, I have never seen any hands that weren't private. Have you?" This point is important. In the real activity of conducting economic life, the hands of particular people will be engaged in this and that action, here and there, not some abstraction called *the people,* and not the public as a whole.

Dewey's comment has a threefold importance. First, it emphasizes communication as the primary social process. That is, understanding society must be developed from real, situated interactions of embodied persons, rather than facile appeals to forces of class, history, or institutions. Dewey, of course, thought that class, history, and institutions were important, but he saw those as constituted in situated communication practices. The failure of the Soviet system to attend to this very pragmatic point, and the resulting rise of privilege and cronyism in that system, is noteworthy.

Second, it emphasizes that no two persons can share the same location in the conversation at the same time.[5] This makes individuality possible when communication practices are developed to select out, elaborate, and encourage particular differences. Of course, each culture will do this in different ways. Thus, individuality in China is indeed emphasized, but it is a different set of emphases than individuality in middle-class North America.

Third, it implies different "person positions." One person can speak to another as a first-person speaker to a second-person respondent. However, someone can also be an onlooker, observing the conversation and commenting on it. These different positions can have different rights and obligations associated with them (Shotter, 1984). This is evident from the tendency in the West to give a privileged place to third-person observers, whose position of knowing from outside is treated as objective, and thus generally superior to knowing from the other two positions.[6]

From this orientation to embodiment and realism we begin to see the consequentiality of communication in new ways. Embodied communication is the locus of grammar, morality, individuation, and coordination. Thus, the study of these matters must start in situated communication.

Doing by Conjoint Action

Dewey (1916/1966) observed the tendency in Western thought to make a duality of thought and action, and to give a privileged place to thought and locate it in the individual's mind. Mind was a place where one could separate one's self from the mistaken traditional practices of the world, survey one's store of beliefs, and engage in creative thought (Descartes, 1637/1985). Although there are metaphors in our culture that emphasize action (e.g., *the man of action, all talk and no action*), the primacy of mind is still dominant in education as well as psychology. The ancient Athenians would have found our approach to education strange. It is organized, in practice, around the ideas of getting insight into processes happening inside individual students and improving those processes. It places little emphasis on students' ability to act intelligently in concrete situations. Consider the "essay" assignment. To whom is the essay addressed? The other students? The teacher? The world? In the Sophistic schools, such as those of Protagoras and Isocrates, a presentation (typically a speech) was clearly addressed to one's soon-to-be fellow citizens sitting in the room. The speaker practiced being an adviser in the political action of the state.

---

[5]This same point was later developed by Arendt (1958).

[6]This argument is, of course, indebted to the work of Johnson (1987), who argued for the significance of embodiment in a real world for understanding features of language that are interculturally common.

Emphasizing "doing" reminds us that experience is not something that happens to us that we later process in our minds. Persons enter into patterns of activity and become the sorts of persons they are based on their embodied actions in coordination with others. In so doing, they learn to be intelligent agents, and their intelligence is an intrinsic part of the experiences they have. Of course, intelligence requires a brain that is intact and has certain potential. But how neurological inheritance will come to matter depends on communication.

Conjoint Action and Coordination.   The primary form of action is the "conjoint activity" of two or more persons. This claim, implicit in the writing of Dewey and made explicit by Mead (1934, 1938), has been central to the development of CMM from the start (Pearce, 1975, 1989; Pearce & Cronen, 1980). Of course, persons can and do create episodes that are monologues, but these are derivations from conjoint activity (Dewey, 1925/1958). The child first learns to take a role as agent by instructing the self out loud, often in the very words that parents use (Becker, 1971). Contemporary research on the development of children in the first few months of life has focused more and more on the articulation of the child's and parents' behaviors, though which the newborn becomes a functional human being (Tronick, 1982). It has been argued by Benveniste (1979), Shotter (1989), Harré (1984), and Cronen and Pearce (1991–1992) that the very identification of the *I* as an indexical and grammatical position in social action depends on the identification of a *you*. One comes to be a certain person in the social world through one's interaction with others.

Turning to adult interaction, Shotter (1986) observed that, in their activities together, people can create—as an unintended consequence—a shared context that cannot be traced back to the wishes or desires of any individual prior to the conversation. Little in the social-science literature is as funny as studies that attempt to predict "outcomes" of behavior based on the sheer number of occurrences of a certain type of behavior, or the sophistication of available "cognitive plans," without regard for the constructed context. I may know 300 ways to end a telephone conversation, but I cannot use any of them if the other party says certain things and has a kind of relationship with me that prohibits the use of them and obligates me to carry on.

Conjoint action helps us understand how rules hold together the coherence of talk without that coherence breaking down at every turn due to differences in persons' understandings. Wittgenstein (1953) argued that thinking one is obeying a rule is not the same as obeying a rule. If someone simply thinks he or she knows a rule for connecting bits action coherently, that person also probably has the ability to come up with some creative rationale by which most anything can be argued to be in accord with any rule. Hence, the ability to engage in human communication cannot simply depend on a personal knowing. It depends on others responding to us—so as to create conjoint action. One knows that one is using a rule well when one can go on with others in coherent action.

By focusing on conjoint action as the natural "acting into" the activities of others, the whole issue of "intersubjectivity" is set aside as wrong-headed. Intersubjectivity assumes two separate agencies, each both a "subject" and somehow "subjected to" phenomena produced by another. If we assume this perspective, the problem is a daunting one. How can we know what another mind is thinking? In contrast, the conjoint action focus says that the way people think is created in patterns of interaction with others. Communication is prior to the question of individual thought. The idiosyncrasy of a person's way of thinking is a matter of neurology/physiology, position in the social discourse, and acting into patterns in which unique ways of acting are attended to, and elaborated in episodes of conjoint action. To understand another is not a matter of looking inside them, but of acting with them and considering other patterns of interaction in which they engage. Thus, individual uniqueness is a social creation, not the dualistic opposite of sociality. The consequentiality of communication does not lie in displaying or restricting individuality, but in making it.

The Moral Character of Conjoint Actions.   Conjoint action is, by its nature, the domain of morality. Aristotle organized the arts in a way radically different from the Enlightenment tradition. When he distinguished the arts of *praxis* from *theoria* and *poeisis*, he discussed the implications of a subject matter that was not "out there" in the theater of nature or mind. *Praxis* means, roughly, action. However, as Bernstein (1971) pointed out, Aristotle's more technical use of the term in the *Nichomachean Ethics* gives it a distinct political and moral character. Arts such as economics, political science, ethics, and (I would add) communication[7] are political in a broad sense: They are concerned with how people act together to create ways of life. These arts are related to moral studies because they are concerned with creating a good life—there is no legitimate reason to study the family, culture, or social institutions unless we are concerned with creating a good life for people.

Aristotle was right to think that the separation of moral concerns from the science of social studies is wrong-headed.[8] The rules used in conversation are intrinsically moral matters about what can, must, or must not happen next. That is why CMM rule formulations are always written in

---

[7]Of course, Aristotle called rhetoric a practical art. However, our discipline, communication, is of much wider scope, including activities such as family patterns of communication. Moreover, as this chapter suggests, communication is the primary practical art and the primary social process. Thus, all other kinds of arts must be derivative from the primary one.

[8]Arendt (1958) developed a similar point in her book *The Human Condition*. The writings of Bernstein (1971, 1985, 1992) are similarly addressed to this point.

terms of moral force. One of the few cross-cultural claims that we can make about human action is that every society has prohibitions against doing some things, requirements to do others, and ranges of legitimate alternative choices. Similarly, there are conditions in which what is legitimate, required, or prohibited may be unsettled and open to negotiation.

It is significant that another cross-cultural universal is the presence of sophisticated language. It is in language that moral claims are made and moral accounts given. Elsewhere (Cronen, 1991) I described a case in which a father with an anorectic daughter justified his actions and those of his family this way: He said that his anorectic daughter was not responsible for what she did because "She has a disease." Her actions, he claimed, placed requirements on him to do what a father is supposed to do. Then he said that he could understand why other members of the family acted the way they did toward him; their actions were understandable in light of his obligatory action. Notice that the father provided a moral account. One daughter is not to be held accountable—her acts are "caused" by disease. His own actions are obligatory, and he is to be held accountable only insofar as he carries out his role-based obligations. Other family members, however, were described as acting with much more latitude of choice and thus, presumably, more responsibility than he or his anorectic daughter. The "sick" daughter was not held responsible, nor is she treated as a full-fledged agent who could be held accountable for her actions. The father was also beginning a description of his own situation as being "stuck" with little room for choice in a difficult situation.

All cultures make some differentiations concerning the responsibility of actors for the actions or events that transpire. However, the way these matters are worked out varies greatly across cultures and are closely connected to language. For example, White (1992) observed how the "middle voice" of classical Greek has become attenuated in contemporary European languages. The middle voice is a form that indicates neither a choice clearly under the control of one actor, nor an effect to which a person is simply subject. Rather, it refers to the actions that are contingent on the doings of others, circumstances, time, and the like. The result of our attenuated use of the middle voice, said White, is that our moral vocabularies strain toward fixing responsibility on an individual.

It could be argued that, in the domain of scientific work, the appropriate standards are accuracy and probability, not obligation or prohibition. However, I think that Harré (1986) argued rightly that scientific communities are fundamentally moral communities with well-established understandings about what is obligatory, legitimate, and prohibited in their practices. These moral understandings are the foundation by which scientific claims about accuracy and facticity are legitimized. Perhaps one of the clearest examples of how we commit to a moral order when we engage in a practice that seems to work by nonmoral standards was offered in a cartoon drawn by Walt Kelly. In that cartoon, Pogo 'Possum is playing checkers with his friend, Albert the Alligator. Pogo is vigorously jumping most of Albert's checkers in a single turn while Albert looks on unconcerned. Pogo then says something to the effect of, "I got all but two of your checkers in one move." Albert casually replies, revealing a hand of playing cards, "Perhaps son, but I've got three kings."

Thus, the rules of coherence that form in the coordination of everyday life are fundamentally moral matters, not simply matters of probability or formal inclusion. The consequentiality of communication looms large when we recognize that communication is the locus of the creation of moral communities, and that moral matters are intrinsic to what it means to be living a human life.

The Unity of Experience

The practices in which we engage are not physical or emotional ones as *opposed* to intellectual ones. For Dewey, a discussion among colleagues and students, the activity of a laboratory, and the silent engagement of a person with a text are all kinds of action. We must learn how to engage in them, and—by various kinds of engagement—we may develop the ability to participate in such practices very well. These doings are situated: We read a certain book at this time, after doing those things, when particular other events are going on in our lives.

It would be a bad misplacement of emphasis to say that Dewey was trying to enrich the concept of *intelligence* with the notions of *temporality* and *action* His purpose was not enriching the concept of *intelligence* with the idea of *action*, but producing intelligent action. I want to encourage the development of theory with this same emphasis: providing a way of intelligently joining into the activity of the world so as to enrich it.[9]

The unity of experience extends beyond treating intellect as an ability to engage in practices. Intrinsic to the "unity of experience" idea is that our practices include emotion, pain, warmth, cold, light, darkness, softness, roughness, and the rhythms of sound and motion—all that is present in embodied human activity. The way one's partner's hand feels in one's own is part of the experience of intimate moments. An interview of clients by clinicians is experienced as language, as well as patterns of movement, eye contact, and sound. Similarly, getting an exciting idea in a discussion includes the ability to feel a kind of excitement. Rather than separating these matters from mind and action, Dewey set the agenda of understanding how experience is organized as a unity of identifiable elements whose

---

[9]Pearce and I refer to CMM as a practical theory because it has this emphasis.

nature and significance are derived by their participation in a pattern of practice.[10]

It is important that the emphasis here be clear. It is not enough to say that the features of experience have relationships to each other. That kind of account harkens back to the older, more mechanical, cybernetic approach that spoke of parts of a system exchanging information with one another in an organized way. That was a great step forward in many ways, but not a sufficient step. It is not simply that emotions, beliefs, and utterances are "there" and have a pattern of systemic relationships with one another. This older cybernetic view is what keeps social constructionism stuck in the traditional psychological view from which it means to liberate us (Pearce, 1994). This is revealed by looking at the agenda that many social constructionists have set. They want to understand *remembering* as a social construction, *perception* as a social construction, and so on. This way of working retains the original psychological agenda, which assumes the foregoing to be quasi-autonomous processes hooked up in a pattern. Instead, unity of experience means we will never understand much about perception or the like outside the analysis of situated conjoint action.

Therefore, the consequentiality of communication is a call for reversing the old agenda. The first priority must be to develop useful ways to understand and critique patterns of human communication. Our understanding of perception, recall, emotion, and identity will never be useful unless we develop it as part of some better ways to understanding the primary process of which those traditional concerns are identifiable aspects (Dewey, 1925).[11]

Episodes and Forms of Life

Although persons in conversation constitute the primary unit of social observation, the episode may be called the basic unit of social analysis (Pearce, Cronen, & Harris, 1982). The idea that social action is organized into episodes has become widely accepted. Harré and Secord (1972) de-

---

[10]I do not claim every aspect of experience is integrated with all others at every moment. Rather, the way experience comes to be unified in action allows for relatively separate change in some component, which then may influence other aspects of experience at different times. Without modifiability of some aspects of experience, no change would be possible because no event is likely to affect every aspect of experience at once. The principle in biology is termed *mosaic evolution* (Gould, 1989).

[11]It is the author's suspicion that Shotter, for one, holds the view that no unified theory-like approach is appropriate for social constructionism because, although he starts with the view that conjoint action is the primary process, he emphasizes the old agenda, trying to solve this problem and that left by traditional psychology. Of course, the situation must seem like one that requires a bag or kit full of devices to be used for various problems.

scribed an *episode* as a "natural division of social life" (p. 147). They did not mean that particular kinds of episodes exist in nature, but rather that humans—wherever we find them—organize their activity into episodes with distinctive rules for acting and understanding. Wittgenstein's (1953) idea of a "language game" embodies the same ideas. Bateson (1972) called *punctuation* the ability to grasp the start of an episode or change from one episode to another. I prefer the term *episode* to *game* because its academic lineage carries the ideas of individuality and different positions within conversation. The rules that constitute an episode are not static, although they may be relatively stable. *Rules,* in the sense I am using the term here, are normative, but need not be widely used and may not endure more than a few moments as interactions develop.

Adopting the episodic unit of analysis takes us to the temporal dimension of communication. It denies the practice of counting acts as a sufficient way to understand human action. The idea of assigning an intrinsic quality to some kinds of acts, and using the quantity of those as an indicator of the quality of communication, can be the source of some fun by composing hypothetical scenarios. For example, when a researcher tells you that more caring, affiliative responses make a relationship better, think about this sort of scenario:

"A Nice, Caring Episode"

Her: The house is on fire, that son of ours is making drugs in his room again!

Him: Yes, but you look so beautiful tonight. Let's forget the house and Billy and go out for dinner and dancing.

Her: The house is on fire! The fire department is coming and the police are coming for Billy!

Him: You are really a wonderful, caring person. You are concerned about the house and our son. I love you and appreciate your caring.

Her: The fire is reaching the kitchen! The gas stove might blow, run!

Him: Here, I brought you flowers. Don't you want to put them in water?

An episodic emphasis is also a good correction for the tendency to carelessly generalize from particular kinds of episodes to the exclusion of others. I recall a meeting on communication and culture, in which Korean women were described as reticent in comparison with North American women. Professor Young Y. Kim and I asked whether that referred to discussion at home with a spouse, in a seminar, bargaining with a street vendor, and so on. Korean women are among the most assertive and skilled bargainers you can find, and some of their interactions with husbands may strike North Americans as too direct and assertive. The point is not how much assertiveness or how many assertive episodes, but contextual relevance. Indeed, the terms *reticent* and *assertive* must be used with caution here because we are dealing with different grammars of practice. To understand what is happening in Korean experience, one must understand the rules of emergent episodes and the way episodes of different kinds are related to create "forms of life" (Wittgenstein, 1953).

The episodic emphasis must not be construed to mean that each episode is an independent monad. To do so would contradict the realism-embodiment emphasis. As Strawson (1959) argued, no way of life that could be recognized as human could exist without assuming that persons as physical beings endure in time and space across episodes.

The Temporality of Episodes and the Intentionality of Language.   Experience taken seriously is both an undergoing and an acting in the world. Dewey (1916/1966) called it a "striving" that is already "pregnant with connections." This emphasis on striving illuminates the temporality of episodes, extending it beyond the simple notion that the past influences the present. If our primary problem is what to do, then experience is a projection into future possibilities.[12]

The notion of *temporality* is not sufficient, however, unless we further specify what is entailed in the pragmatists' use of it. James (cited in Gunn, 1987) said in his article, "Is Radical Empiricism Solipsistic?", that our commonplace terms such as *with, and, then,* and the like give our thinking a quality of pointing to something beyond. "Call it self-transcendency or call it pointing, whichever you like," James wrote, "It makes no difference so long as real transitions toward real goals are admitted as things given *in* experience and among experience's most indefeasible parts" (cited in Gunn, 1987, p. 114). Likewise, Dewey (1916/1966) argued against the idea that experience can be understood by simply treating it as matter of how the past creates the present:

> So far as anything beyond the bear present is recognized by established doctrine, the past exclusively counts. Registration of what has taken place, reference to precedent, is believed to be the essence of experience. Empiricism is conceived of as tied up with what has been, or is "given." But

---

[12]Based on what has been said about temporality and conjoint action, it follows that we must be careful about how we use the word *context* with reference to episodes in a consequential view of communication. Because experience is temporal and includes projection into future possibilities for action, the term *context* should not be treated as something fixed like a frame. We should use the term in a way close to its etymological origin. According to the *Oxford Etymological Dictionary*, our English word *context* comes from the Latin *contextus*. It is formed on the stem of *contextere*, meaning "weave together." The active weaving together of various strands into a coherent pattern is much more like experience. Threads that are woven together in a certain way at one time both open different possibilities for the progress of the work and close off others. The weaver may stick to a clear plan, or may let new ideas emerge as the work develops.

experience in its vital form is experiential, an effort to change the given; it is characterized by projection, by reaching forward into the unknown; connection with a future is its salient trait. (p. 23)

If the pragmatist view of experience is taken as a basis for discussing our human possibilities, then we come to see experience leading us to, in James' words, "A more to come" (cited in Gunn, 1987, p. 114).

Episodic Temporality and the Constitution of Persons' Intentions. Saying that language has an intentional quality is not the same thing as saying that a person has intentions. However, we learn how to have intentions in the process of communication. A baby "acts into" the actions of others. It is by this acting into (to borrow Shotter's felicitous phrase) that a baby enters into a world of meaning and action, not merely a world of behavior and motion. A child may be made to bow every time he or she meets a certain person by pressure on the neck muscles, and thus bowing may become automatic. However, according to Dewey (1916/1966), this would not be an act of deference on the child's part until the child understood what was going on and performed the act in light of its meaning. To have an idea of a thing (such as bowing) "is not just to get certain sensations from it. It is to be able to respond in view of its place in an inclusive scheme of actions: It is to *foresee the drift and probable consequences* of the action of the thing upon us and our actions upon it" (Dewey, 1916/1966, p. 30).

Consider a parent and baby playing the game of "grab the finger." In this game, the parent is telling a story about the action, as well as giving the baby intentions as features of that action. The baby will grab the finger when it is placed in the baby's hand. Many mothers and fathers know that grabbing when a finger is placed in a baby's hand is a reflex. However, the parent gives the baby an intention by first saying, "Are you trying to get my finger?", then, "Oh you've got it." It is in the course of acting and telling a story that intentionality is created (Shotter, 1984).

Intentionality requires having an idea of the consequences that our acting has in the world. A child's actions become meaningful through participation in episodes of communication. Dewey (1916/1966) used the example of a hungry infant to further clarify his point. When an infant cries, he or she is at first simply reacting to his or her own physical condition and is controlled by that condition. But soon the infant begins to make a back and forth reference to what he or she is doing and experiencing, what others do, and how the doings of others modify his or her own experience. Now the infant is no longer simply reacting to his or her own hunger. "His whole attitude changes. He takes interest, as we say. He no longer reacts just to his own hunger, but behaves in the light of what others are doing" (Dewey, 1916/1966, p.31). Thus, in such simple episodes, the child comes to live in a world of meaning and intentions—as a participant in what Pearce (1975) first called the Coordinated Management of Meaning (CMM). The consequentiality of communication does not lie in the mere fact that persons communicate to achieve their intentions. More profoundly, communication is the process in which human intentionality is created.

Episodic Coherence Without Essence. Following the tradition of science from Pythagoras to Newton, we are tempted to understand social phenomena by finding their underlying "essences," or the most basic elements of which they are constructed. Such fundamental substance behind appearances supposedly makes a thing what it is.[13] With our intellectual heritage, this approach seems natural and universally useful. However, what makes up episodes and forms of life—including relationships to other persons, institutional practices, professional commitments, selfhood, and cultural tradition—may not be usefully achieved by essentializing methods. For example, what makes for a relationship includes many matters large and small that come together in grammars of action. Some connections may disappear from everyday practice only to be revived in new forms. New practices may be introduced at any time, sometimes without much ado and sometimes with momentous consequences.

Those of us who have worked with or closely studied families have learned that a form of life may be easy to change if problematic episodes are closely connected to the grammar of one or two problematic stories. Families that are resistant to change often have many interlocking stories about relationships with each child, with spouse, with families of origin, with work, with community expectations, and the like. Changing one or two stories has little impact on problematic patterns of interaction. The point here is not that patterns of experience held together by multiple connections are necessarily problematic, only that they are stable.

A few years ago, Bill Moyers conducted a television interview with a reconstructionist rabbi. Moyers asked what the essence of Jewish tradition was. The rabbi responded that it did not have an essence. Moyers said it must have some common thread. He suggested the "chosen people" theme, only to have the rabbi tell him that reconstructionists like himself reject that idea. Belief in one god was suggested, only to have the rabbi note that there have been and are many Jews who strongly identify with the

---

[13]Some interpretations of factor analysis are examples of this esssentialist way of thinking. Some researchers argue that the factors—mathematically derived vectors through n-dimensional space—stand for the common essence shared by variables loading on the factor. When this interpretation is carried to the extent of treating the mathematically created factors as the most important reality, we have Platonism masquerading as empiricism.

tradition, but do not believe in God. After several other thoughtful attempts, Moyers asked what keeps the tradition going. The rabbi answered that there are thousands of threads that interconnect here, which are of no consequence there—they appear, disappear, and reappear in another time, place, and form.

From this orientation, we see the consequentiality of communication from still another angle. Communication is not a phenomenon based on a singular transcendental logic, but is the locus of action, wherein different kinds of connections emerge to be extended, critiqued, changed, or discarded.

The Reflexivity of Thought and Action

Dewey rejected the idea that thought is a kind of substance set off against the material world. That idea makes the relationship of thought to the body and the world a riddle and a theoretical muddle. Instead, he argued for what today we would term the *reflexivity* (as well as the *unity*) of thought and action.

Dewey first argued for the reflexivity of thought and action in his critique of the reflex arc in 1896, and it was in the context of that argument that his claims were made most clear. It is worth our time to look closely at this critique because it applies equally to any account of mind that posits preexisting mental "software." Dewey (1896) argued that the idea of the reflex arc reduced behavior to a set of "jerks" impelled by prior stimuli (p. 360). The reflex arc, he said, was another case of the "psychologists' fallacy" first described by James (1890/1950 p. 196).[14] The psychologists' fallacy occurs when terms that make sense to describe a completed product are inappropriately used to describe the processes that produced it. Regarding the reflex arc, we can only describe a stimulus as a stimulus and a response as a response, said Dewey (1896), post hoc by assuming their common relationship to an inclusive coordination that marks each off as stimulus and response. If there is no such outcome, the events cannot be described as stimulus or response. The only way that the so-called arc could come to exist and be sustained is by feeding the products of its activity back into itself so that it is both product and process. Sociologist Giddens (1976) called this kind of relationship between the abilities of an organism and its activities the *duality of structure,* and the process in which one creates the other *stucturation.*

Shotter (1981) observed that whether one calls the activity of knowing a

---

[14]In this discussion of Dewey's critique of the reflex arc, I follow Shotter's (1981) work very closely and am much indebted to it.

product or a *process* depends on the direction from which one is looking. If one looks back, retrospectively, one sees structure (i.e., that which has been specified). If one looks forward, one sees process (i.e., a productive process). Unfortunately, the prospective, forward-looking view is usually forgotten in favor of a way of working that allows us to write down the supposed character of a finished product. What Dewey was looking for, and what CMM theory also seeks, is a way to think well about the unfinished, in-process character of experience. The creators of the reflex arc forgot that the ability to identify something as a stimulus and response depends on a simultaneous temporal succession of events that projects into the future as a way of acting.[15]

Dewey (1896) offered the following redescription of the reflex arc:

> The stimulus is that phase of the forming coordination which represents the conditions which have to be met in bringing it to a successful issue: the response is that phase of one and the same forming coordination which gives the key to meeting these conditions, which serves as instrument in effecting the successful coordination. (p. 370)

Notice the import of this argument for the relationship of thinking and acting: The stimulus is specified only when the response to it becomes more specified. Until that happens, the larger emergent pattern that gives them meaning is still vague. Thus, Dewey said that experience was always a "value in the running."

The Reflexivity of Stories Lived and Told.   Reflexivity and episodic punctuation together suggest another important distinction to be made about human experience. Consider again an infant engaged in a game of "grab the finger." The infant is engaged in living the story of playing this little game. What is happening has the character of learning to use rules, and thus learning the meaning of things. What, then, is the meaning of *grasping*? Its meaning in this little episode lies in the way grasping points to what may happen next. In Wittgenstein's terms, the baby is beginning to learn the *grammar* of *grasping, tugging,* and *letting go* in this game. The coherence of this story lived, or episode, is formed in the playing of it.

There is more going on in this episode. The child is told a story about the game before, after, and/or during play. When the coherence of the game is broken, the parent may say, "Oh, oh, you're not getting my finger, you

---

[15]Sixty-six years after Dewey's (1896) article appeared, Dulany (1962) provided a test of some of these questions about the reflex arc. Dulany found that what could reasonably be interpreted as stimuli and response in studies of verbal conditioning depended on the larger pattern of activity that a subject engaged in with the experimenter.

have to get it so I can get it free." This sort of running narrative is important to the baby's learning. The baby is both living the story and being told a story about what is happening.

Many cultures encourage telling stories about lived experience from a very early age. Some cultures engage in more direct instruction than others, and different cultures emphasize different ways of telling stories. It is common in European culture for fathers and mothers to ask in the evening, "What did Susie do today?" The parent then goes right on saying, "Susie went for a ride in the car with mommy and then. . . ." Of course, the telling of a story is part of a lived story.

It is important that we not think of the stories people can tell as all separate and sealed off, although some may be quite unrelated to others. The grammar of one story may be important for another (Cronen, 1994). For example, in a study of change in a therapeutic setting (Cronen, Pearce, & Tomm, 1985), the husband told a story about worth, and how worth is fragile and must be sustained in each encounter. The grammar of this story, which had roots in the husband's family of origin, became part of the husband's relationships with work subordinates and his wife. The grammars of these stories were crucial to the way he described what was happening in specific episodes of conflict, and to the way those episodes were carried on in lived experience. When another person offered an idea, the husband's ability to act in the episode was informed by grammatical abilities strongly informed by the old family story about worth, and how comparative worth is at stake in every interaction. The other person had to be defeated. Taken together, the husband's stories about worth, relationships, and the conduct of episodes constituted an important part of his grammatical abilities.

The relationships among stories do not mean that they and their grammatical relationships are used the same way in all situations. Some episodes may have no relevance. Other episodes may have previous additional stories that are relevant and connected. In the previous example, when that husband's wife offered an alternative suggestion to his own, a story about how one must never destroy the worth of one's spouse became relevant for him. It, too, was organized by the grammar of the struggle for worth. The obvious result was the initiation of unfinished conflicts with his wife, which he could never allow himself to win or lose.

Understanding the relationship of stories lived and told requires the idea of reflexivity. For the husband, the recurrent lived conflicts he experienced with his wife reflexively confirmed the truth of the story about the fragility of worth. Thus, stories told are both product and process.

So far I have emphasized the connection of stories lived and told. However, the difference is also very important. Every telling is done under particular lived circumstances. These tellings give us some idea, but only a partial idea, of the original lived experience. They give only some insight into the rich array of abilities beyond, but including, language that form in the course of that experience. The telling of stories may also conceal the inability to articulate the story's grammar into rules for sophisticated and artistic action in real situated action. A marriage partner may tell stories about loving and caring for his or her spouse, but not have the ability to use those stories in artistic and subtle ways that coordinate well with the spouse. We must not assume that the ability to tell a story is identical to sophisticated ways of using it.[16]

Discursive Formations in the Reflexive Process. There is a term that describes the special character of some stories lived and told that I find increasingly useful. Its value was brought to my attention by Peter Lang, one of the coprinciples of the Kensington Consultation Centre, London. That term is *discourse.* Following P. Lang (personal communication, July 6, 1993), I employ the term here in a way roughly akin to Foucault's (1972) usage in *The Archaeology of Knowledge and the Discourse on Language.*[17] Foucault used the term *discourse* to describe stories of a particular character. In my use of this term, a story can be regarded as a discourse if it includes a formalized set of grammatical relationships among utterances that is well instantiated in a group of users. The formalizations include the kind of relationships persons have with each other. The relationships that make up the discourse are widely known and available, carrying great authority and strong feelings for certain people. For example, Foucault said that modern medicine can be described as the formalization of certain sets of relationships among persons such as doctors, nurses, patients, hospitals, researchers, and so on. Some of the stories that "in-form" the abilities of persons have the character of discourses, and that gives them a kind of authority with respect to other stories both live and told. Thus, they work similarly to the commonplace of sophistic rhetoric.

The idea that stories told may be discursive formations opens another interesting line of investigation. We can consider what is happening when someone in a family says, "You can never trust anyone, you have to be on the alert every minute." Family members who hear this may know it is part of the discourse of father and the community, regardless of whether it is he

---

[16]The neurological evidence is helpful. Damage to the right hemisphere can leave intact the ability to tell a story about action while destroying the ability to use that story for coherent action. For example, right hemisphere damaged patients may retain the ability to tell a routine story about how to prepare food, yet when confronted with a can, can opener, pot, and stove, they may be quite unable to weave the elements together to successfully heat the contents of the can (M. Cronen, 1989).

[17]I am grateful to Lang for calling to my attention the usefulness of this term. His theoretical and clinical applications inform this analysis.

who utters it. If someone else utters it, then the person is not speaking his or her own voice alone, but also in the voice of the father and community— a voice that may carry great authority for some members of the family.[18]

Reflexivity and the Unfinished Quality of Stories.   To say that experience is unfinished does not, however, mean that it is simply free-flowing. In some cases, the process of communication may be described as the elaboration and extension of traditions, or even the reification and simplification of traditions. However, the reflexivity focus suggests that reifications and reinstantiations are not to be taken as simply natural, but as ongoing achievements (although sometimes dubious ones) in conjoint action.

Consider this example from a dissertation by Bean (1989). The study was concerned with heart attack patients who failed to follow doctors' prescribed regimens. One of the cases concerned a police officer who had a heart attack, after which he engaged in repetitive episodes of argument with his wife over what he could eat for breakfast. Clearly, fried eggs, lots of bacon, and buttered toast were no longer permitted. Arguments over breakfast typically began with his demanding a "real breakfast" for a "real man." He challenged his wife about whether she was going to act like their kind of people, or do what outsiders say. At the point of the interview with Bean, the policeman told stories about what made people like himself different from the hospital staff or other helping professionals. The stories prominently included ways of eating. Inquiring into how the problem over food started, Bean learned that the policeman had a visit from his chief in the hospital, which he considered a great honor. However, the chief was rather brusquely ushered out by a nurse who had to perform some of her duties. This episode was a great embarrassment to the policeman. After that embarrassing episode, the policeman began to talk in terms of *us* and *them* and *respect*. This way of talking was probably elaborated at his meeting with the dietician. Clearly, the policeman had the ability to say some things about differences between professionals and working people prior to the episode of his chief's visit. However, it seems likely that the coherence of the story he told Bean—in which food figures very significantly—began to come together in a new and more formalized way after the chief's visit and during the conversation with the dietician. The policeman acted into the particular events at the hospital, trying to establish a place of respect in distinction from those who had badly treated his chief in front of him. These lived episodes reflexively developed the ability and need to tell more coherent and detailed *us and them* stories.

These newly created stories became part of the policeman's ability to

---

[18]Important implications for the analysis of powers emerge from the notion of discursive formations, and the affordances and constraints created in conjoint action.

respond to his wife. When his wife began cooking a breakfast that followed the dietician's instructions, he accused her of acting like *them*. To act like *them* is to enter into a grammar of practice, in which people like himself do not seem to have a place of respect. The wife is urged to prove she is a good wife by their community standards. However, the wife is being asked to do what a good wife must not do by their community standards—knowingly feed her husband food that may kill him. The result was a pattern of daily struggle at breakfast time. These episodes of daily struggle reflexively reconstituted and developed the story that there is a great difference between people like himself and the professionals, and that he must struggle to hold his family together in opposition to a way of life that does not respect people like him.

The problematic story, which began to form from bits of culturally available stories, was further elaborated in daily interactions at home. In those elaborations, the kind of food served became a more prominent feature. The argument was over breakfast, so the episode required developing the story by acting into talk about food, the dignity of working people, and on whose side his wife was. His wife's position in the conversation prevented her from either refusing ever to cook what he wanted or giving in to him. Her obvious discomfort seemed to further prove how problematic it is to let outsiders get into another's pattern of life. The arguments perpetuated the reflexive process, in which the story lived and the story told co-evolved.

The idea of *incompleteness* helps us understand the limits of a "technologized" or goal-oriented approach to communication research. In the case of the policeman and his wife, the husband's goals of defining the boundaries between *us* and *them*, and attaining his wife's commitment to their way of life through food, were not necessarily set prior to the episodes at the hospital. These goals emerged in the course of action as aspects of the episodes created (Cronen, Chen & Pearce, 1988). A technologized approach to communication that purports to study how communication is used to attain certain prior goals misses much of what is consequential about communication—because communication is that process in which goals are created and reformulated.

Reflexivity, Mystery, and Wonder.   Searle (1969) argued, "It is in principle possible to say exactly what I mean" (p. 19). CMM theory could not disagree more. Searle's claim is more than the result of misguided idea about language. It harkens back to the "Cartesian anxiety" (Bernstein, 1983) about failing to have foundational knowledge that is fixed and final. From the pragmatists' orientation, experience always points beyond the present to new possibilities. Elaboration, as well as change, are achievements in conjoint communication where no one can know with certainty what the future holds. Therefore, there must always be an element of mystery in human action. The unity of experience also specifies that what is important in communication cannot be entirely reduced to words, and surely not to well-formed propositions.

Pearce and I began our 1980 book by saying, "The most human of human characteristics is that of wondering, and the objects of wonder most characteristically human are human characteristics" (p. 1). We then cited Koestler's (1978) observation that wonder is a meeting of the tragic and the trivial planes of existence: "By living on both planes at once, the creative artist or scientist is able to catch a glimpse of eternity looking through the window of time. Whether it is a medieval stained glass window or Newton's formula of universal gravitation, is a matter of temperament and taste" (p. 164).

Although the future is neither fully predictable nor fully in any one person's control, what we do points into that future. Recognition of this may lead to terror as well as wonder. A technologized view of life suggests that something must be wrong any time we are unsure of our goals or the means to attain them. Dewey's (1929/1960) critique of Enlightenment philosophy was organized around the problems associated with this dread of the uncertain and the resultant "quest for certainty." In his book by that name, Dewey entitled the sixth chapter "The Play of Ideas." It is a perfect title because there Dewey contrasted different ways of looking at commonplace objects and scientific propositions. His point was that human thought is an aspect of action, and that action in the world has the marvelous quality of being unfinished. For example, formal inquiry is a particular kind of experience in which wonder and mystery so enthrall us that we must go further in our work, regardless of where it takes us. For this reason, Dewey's approach to educational reform was to replace the emphasis on recording wisdom in a neat notebook with the sense of wonder that comes from acting in the world in such a way that new questions and possibilities are created. Rote learning was to be replaced by students' reflexive engagement. Our present concern is with U.S. schools' failure to teach science (or anything else) well. This concern reveals that we have failed to help young students develop the sense of mystery and wonder that is potential in human experience and necessary for the development of thoughtful action.[19] Aristotle (1966a) said, "Men began to philosophize, now as in the beginning, because of wonder" (p. 692).

The same claims about mystery and wonder can be made for everyday experience. The typical response to the mysterious, ever-changing quality of our lives has been to divide it into stages so that we can neatly place our

---

[19]The responsibility for this is not simply the fault of the schools. Family, community, economic, and cultural factors are playing at least as large a part.

activities into their proper context. This will supposedly help us cope with mystery and wonder by dispelling them as merely apparent. The pragmatists' view takes pride in the creation of mystery and wonder, and treasures that which is in process and unfinished, as well as that which is fixed and final. The communication discipline's stress on "mutual understanding," which Pearce and I (1980) have been criticizing for so long, is rooted in this same fear of the unknown future. The mutual understanding idea assumes that a relationship can be assessed if we stop time and make a static assessment of points of good and bad fit in the stories that partners tell. By contrast, in the pragmatists' orientation, a good relationship can thrive on difference if the partners find a way of living that is a creative and enriching use of differences.

Substantializing and Realizing Thought and Meaning

Bateson (1972) argued that mind is social. That claim is similar to Dewey's ideas about thought and action. Recall that in Dewey's critique of the reflex arc, he argued that a stimulus is not fully formed until it becomes part of "forming coordination."[20] In Dewey's work, thinking cannot be described as fundamentally a matter of re-presentation. It is neither the case that a separate Cartesian category called the *mind* contains ideas that are then re-presented by communication, nor that stimuli are received and matched against ideas that the mind contains.

A representational view maintains the spirit of the mind–body split by describing hidden representational processes in the individuals that act on the phenomena encountered. This problematizes the possibility of a relationship between thought and the material world. However, it is Rorty's (1979, 1989) position that our experience (including our language, thoughts, and practices) could never be out of touch with the phenomena of the world. Experience is in the world, and thus inextricably bound up with conjoint action in the world.

Consider what a representational view requires. There must be criteria for coding and decoding thoughts and words (Edwards, 1985). This is so because it would be necessary to "re-present" an internal idea with the right symbols and decode symbols into the right ideas. Now consider the case of having a pain. Clearly, when we have a pain, we do not wonder if we really do. If mental representations were involved, it could be doubted whether the sensations really meet the criteria. Pain is not represented in cries or words. It is simply presented or avowed (Wittgenstein, 1953). Similarly, when we look for a towel to dry our hands, we do not stop to consult the criteria for towels—we know what to do with a towel (Edwards,

---

[20]The models of CMM therapy can be described as "forming coordinations."

1985). If we are confused about whether we are looking at a towel for use or only for display, we know what to do. We play a little criteria matching game that might help us decide. However, this, is quite different from the employment of mystic mental criteria. There is nothing hidden about the way people can work to distinguish a display towel from one that is for use.

In contrast to the individual-representational view, the social-presentational view of thinking is based on the common observation that, through communication, persons develop abilities. When we speak, we do not usually (although we may) first rehearse what we are going to say. In fact, when consultants or researchers are discussing a case together, one member of the group may respond to another in a way that the person would not have done except for the flow of conversation. Often that response is a better contribution than the person would have made outside that episode. The same goes for nontechnical, everyday conversation. Most of us have had the experience of thinking we knew just how to write something, only to find that when we had to actually work out the words there was much more thinking to do. Indeed, much good thinking occurs in the process of writing or telling something to another.

Where then is thought? Is it something happening to the brain,[21] in the technologies of articulation (writing, gesturing, speaking, etc.), in the physical–temporal situation, in the comments of others, or in others' responses to us? Obviously, all the foregoing are involved. Wallace (1971) argued that thought and utterance are part of a unified process of communication, and are responsive to the exigencies of a situation. More recently, Shotter (1990), following Bakhtin (1981) and Vygotsky (1962), called this *knowing at the boundaries.*

I propose calling this the *substantializing* of neurological processes into utterances, gestures, or internal rehearsals. Rehearsals are, of course, another technology of action, not a necessary precondition. This way of describing thought and action preserves the feeling we get when we think we might be onto an idea, but cannot "get hold" of it. The idea is not fully formed inside waiting to get out.[22] Rather, I prefer to say someone is working on substantializing their thoughts and feelings.[23] Of course, substantializing can have the character of a fabrication—a successfully rendered work of art, or a new machine. Here, too, we may hear the

---

[21]It is not something happening inside the brain because the brain is not a container of ideas. Thinking is a change in the brain's chemistry.

[22]Word-finding difficulties are close to the traditional view. This common problem may be described as a problem of substantialization close to the end of the process.

[23]Averill (1980) argued that getting into an emotional role is another example of what I have called *substantialization*.

inventor or artist say, "I just can't seem to get it right yet, but I feel I'm close."

The representational description of thought is not consistent with the common experience of finding we can sometimes do much better than we expected (and sometimes much worse) when we act into the activities of others. Consistent with the unity of experience, it is important to also recognize that substantializing is not a purely intellectual phenomenon discrete from feelings, rhythms, and attentional orientation, which are integral to thoughtful action.

I think it is useful to reserve the word *realizing* for an aspect of experience related to substantializing. We substantialize thought into utterance at a moment of action. However, the meaning of what we have done is not realized (made a reality of conversation) until others respond in some way. It is in conjoint action that the meaning is realized, although never completed. Development of the grammatical ability to act coherently depends on others. Of course, conjoint action is never fully finished, and we may come to explain the meaning (i.e., use) of an utterance differently at a future time. This holds true for fabrications as well. Once created, their meaning must be realized in social interaction. Thus, I would prefer to say that we substantialize our thinking at the moment of action, but action is realized as meaningful as conversation develops.[24]

This substantializing–realizing orientation takes the consequentiality of communication in an important direction: It makes communication not a process of encoding and decoding, or representing and sending, but the material location in which brains and actions become human experience.

The Historical–Cultural Character of Experience

Heretofore I have emphasized the material, situated, and reflexive character of conjoint action. However, to understand any case of conjoint action in a way consistent with what has been argued so far requires a focus at once historical and cultural. A person acts into ongoing practices that have both idiosyncratic features particular to the interaction, and historical–cultural features that are part of those abilities and practices. For example, traditional social psychologists are rarely aware of their historical roots, so they may vehemently deny that they are Cartesians. Still, they use a grammar of practice that is much indebted to Descartes' treatment of mind and Ideas.

In the historical–cultural development of practices, persons learn some

---

[24]I am indebted to Linda Harris for ideas about *realizing* that she discussed with me some years ago.

basic forms of grammar that are woven into a variety of stories lived and told. For example, there are grammatical forms in psychology and communication that lead to descriptions of individuals as sealed-off entities (Geertz, 1973). The Cartesian orientation clearly has historical roots in problems peculiar to the cultural, institutional, and political situation of the late Renaissance. These problems included finding a space for the introduction of new ideas that might be in contradiction to the authority of Aristotle or the church. I do not mean to say that ideas are only of use to those who share the culture in which the ideas originated. I only argue that there are no ahistorical, acultural ideas.

This historical–cultural focus allows a fuller understanding of the unity of experience. Consider the typical social psychology topics of *perception* and *attention*. Dewey (1925/1958) observed that, in typical psychological research, seeing a chair, for example, is reduced to qualities of sense attending the act of vision. When this happens, we lose the chair of experience. The chair of experience was purchased, is used to sit in when particular episodes take place, and has a place in the history of the family. It also has a place in forms of life unique to particular kinds of families in their dealings with various institutions. For example, Archie Bunker's famous chair had to be understood as having a place in the hierarchical organization of a homeowning, working-class family.

The Aesthetics of Experience

Dewey emphasized those never finished activities through which we articulate our actions to those of others, calling them the *instrumental* aspect.[25] However, Dewey also emphasized the *consummatory* aspect of experience. By *consummatory* he meant a sense of completion and perfection that may come in an episode. This consummatory aspect plays an important role in the way we live together. The classical Greeks understood this well, and used public money to erect works of art providing an environment in which their ideals were manifest.

The way Dewey developed his ideas about communication and aesthetics tells us much about the centrality of communication from a pragmatist's orientation. Communication becomes the primary process within which art and its appreciation are made possible. Dewey developed the aesthetic side of his philosophy most fully in the books *Art As Experience* (1934a) and *A Common Faith* (1934b). The aesthetic and consummatory side of Dewey's

---

[25]I am not very satisfied with the term *instrument* because today it implies a technology with preestablished ends, rather than the notion Dewey intended—that ends are emergent and changed in practice.

work is important because it strikes at a concern for developing ways to encourage desirable patterns of practice. Dewey thought that the distinction between science and art, like that between practice and theory, was overdrawn and wrongly made. Bernstein (1966) observed that Dewey's analysis of art showed that "the 'artistic' as production, and the 'aesthetic' as fulfillment and consummation are concepts integral to all experience" (p. 152). Therefore, it is a mistake to pit aesthetic concerns against intellectualism or practicality. Dewey (1934b) put the matter in these words:

> The enemies of the "aesthetic" are neither the practical nor the intellectual. They are the humdrum: slackness of loose ends, submission to convention in practice and intellectual procedure. Rigid abstinence, coerced submission, tightness on one side and dissipation, incoherence and aimless indulgence on the other, are deviations in opposite directions from the unity of experience (p. 40).

Dewey could make such a claim because he thought of the aesthetic as fulfillment and consummation within experience, not of experience. Such moments could be had in the appreciation of such artistic products as literature, painting, sculpture, or music. They could also be had in the experience of developing an elegant theory, hearing a well-phrased argument, lovemaking, or a touching moment of conversation. Thus, the aesthetic in experience is identified by degree, not by kind.

Experiences that we term *aesthetic* have a feeling of completeness—a coming together or a final feeling that is immediately enjoyed (Dewey, 1929/1960). Indeed, Dewey (1934b) argued that it was the task of aesthetics to restore "continuity between the refined and intensified forms of experience that are works of art and the everyday events, doings and sufferings that are universally recognized to constitute experience" (p. 3). The idea of communication as a vehicle for something else blinds one to the fact that communication—whether written, oral, signed, or gesticulated—has rhythm, pitch, force, and so on. We lose sight of the idea that when we communicate we feel different ways. It feels differently when struggling to substantialize our thoughts than it does when listening to a lover's voice in a romantic episode.

At first glance, what has been said here seems at odds with Dewey's emphasis on what is in process and unfinished, and his desire that we learn to appreciate those things as much as we do that which is finished and complete. However, closer consideration shows that there is no contradiction here. The feeling of completeness and consummation is a moment in the course of experience. Bernstein (1966) said, "There is a difference between a quality of finality [in experience] and a final quality" (p. 148). Moments of consummation are always resolutions of specific

tensions in real experience and may give way to new tensions in unfinished activity. A Christian may find a powerful aesthetic moment in the
contemplation of *sancta* specific to that faith, but that is because those
sancta have a specific place in bringing resolution to tensions the Christian
may experience in the course of a life informed by the Christian view.
Having such an experience is not a proof of the faith or a moment of truth,
argued Dewey (1934a), but rather a moment made possible by a tradition
that informs the daily event of that person's lived experience.[26] Notice
Dewey's emphasis on the interpenetration of the instrumental and the
aesthetic. Outside the flow of experience, the symbols have no intrinsic
meaning and have no particular effects. A Jewish person raised on grandparents' stories about pogroms—in which priests carrying crosses led
rioters through the streets—is going to have different feelings than a
Christian would when passing a cross.

Thus, Dewey was careful to distinguish the aesthetic quality in experience from "knowing" or "proving." He developed a critique of classical
thought, in which he argued that the Greeks had been mistaken to think
that achieving such a feeling in experience was attaining a kind of knowledge or proof. Dewey said the Greeks were right to appreciate the aesthetic
quality possible in life, but they conflated this appreciation with instrumental activity. The result, argued Dewey (1934a), was to begin the deni-
gration of experience in Western thought by treating it as below the
contemplation of an object of art. Aristotle (1966b) argued that the life of
contemplation was a higher form of life than engagement in practical
affairs.[27] This confused the relationship between the aesthetic and rational
elements of experience by placing one above the other, rather than seeing
one as created within the other.

By learning to create consummatory moments in experience, one can
further develop the ability to have such experiences (Gunn, 1992). However, it should not be assumed that all experience entailing an aesthetic
aspect is enriching. Classical and jazz trumpeter Wynton Marsalis has
commented on the sad state of popular music. He says the commercial
media have presented such an impoverished, simplistic array of music
that the ability to experience and appreciate subtleties is being lost. Marsalis
implies, rightly I think, that the result is encouragement of a coarse and
crude way of life. Like other aspects of experience, the aesthetic points

---

[26]The reader should observe that this view is opposed to the Kantian view of aesthetics, in
which aesthetics is assigned to a separate faculty different from knowing or willing.

[27]What Aristotle actually said is that the life of contemplation offers the *happier* life, but
happiness, as Aristotle defined it, is the end for the sake of which a human life is lived. Earlier
in the *Nichomachean Ethics*, Aristotle stated that politics is the higher art because it defines the
extent to which each art may be pursued.

beyond itself, opening possibilities.[28] However, that pointing beyond is not into the void, but into real activities of others. If the aesthetic leads only to simplistic experiences of repetition, the ability to have such moments of finality and completeness is not further developed. An illustration of what is meant here may be found in the art produced under authoritarian regimes. The huge neoclassical sculptures encouraged by the Hitler government provided moments of consummation, and to have such moments one needed to be part of the discursive experience of the Nazi movement. However, having these moments of consummation did not lead to an ability to produce or experience new or subtle forms of art.[29]

Artistic failure may be an element of problematic communication patterns. A few years ago, Pearce and I worked with the Milan team of Gianfranco Checchin and Luigi Boscolo, and with Karl Tomm of the Calgary Medical School, on a case involving a family with an anorectic daughter. One thing we all observed about the case was that some members of the family found a sense of joy in displaying rapid-fire exchanges, in which everyone's positions on important matters changed from moment to moment. At times, one particular family member would clap hands, laugh out loud, and say to the therapist, "See—see how we are!" One of these consummatory moments even gave rise to the title of an essay by the Milan team based on the case. While discussing how the family business was affected by their problems, the mother declared, in a voice that sounded a note of discovery and excitement, "We used to have an anorectic family, now we have an anorectic store!" (Boscolo, Cecchin, Hoffman, & Penn, 1987, p. 183). Those of us discussing the case were saddened by this for several reasons, not the least of which was sorrow over how repetitive the pattern of interaction was, and what a stultifying set of activities sufficed for the art of living together. We could find little else in their activities as a family that led to moments of consummation.

The Diversity of Experience

One of the unfortunate consequences of the received view is that we have come to think that all differences are ultimately amenable to compromise by reducing them to common coin. There now is a general public belief that all matters of difference can be sensibly addressed by questions such as the following: How much difference? Which is right? How many ___ will you swap for ___? Such notions assume that all differences ultimately can

---

[28]Such experience cannot simply open possibilities in some abstract sense. Learning to appreciate jazz probably does little to enhance the ability to appreciate Shinto ritual.

[29]The implications of this argument for the crude banality of rock 'n' roll music (so beloved by Marxist critics in communication) are not lost on the author.

be reduced to a common measure and adjudicated by a common standard. That assumption, in turn, assumes that there is some common substance, such as "affective value," behind appearances. We see this assumption clearly when positivists deal with cultures that are very different from their own. They assume that the differences among cultural ideas about identity, for example, can be understood by finding where cultures should be placed along a continuum from *individuality* to *sociality*. More sophisticated versions of positivism place a culture or a cultural practice in an N-dimensional space (Hofstede, 1980, 1984). However, the assumption of an underlying common yardstick is still present in that work.

Contemporary pragmatist philosopher Bernstein (1985) has proposed a useful rough-and-ready way to think about kinds of differences in experience. His proposal is based on three terms: *compatibility, commensurability,* and *comparability. Incompatibility* refers to differences to which a common yardstick and common standards of satisfaction can be applied. For example, the feverish disputes over theories of attitude that preoccupied social scientists in the 1960s and early 1970s were usually compatibility problems. Advocates of Fishbein's theory and Anderson's theory could compare results of their respective studies with relative ease (see Anderson & Fishbein, 1965). They shared a definition of *attitude* and how to measure it. They also agreed as to how the two theories could be pitted against each other, and what the criterion for decision was to be.[30]

By contrast, an example of *incommensurability* would be the present chapter compared with work by behaviorist scholars of communication. Behaviorists criticize CMM theory for not satisfying the criterion of producing predictive general propositions about communication; they think the difference between the two is a matter of compatibility. To take an example of incommensurability from a different field, consider the differences between Newton and Einstein's physics. Results produced in the tradition of Newton's physics can only be roughly compared with Einstein's, and only in local space time. Newton's physics is based on absolute time and space, with a sharp difference between those two concepts. Einstein's view is incommensurable because it is based on uniting the two concepts, arguing that they bend and slow down near powerful gravitational masses.

The example from physics illustrates that, although positions are incommensurable, this does not mean we are left with what some philoso-

---

[30]Despite all of this agreement and careful study, no resolution occurred. Each side usually found support for its own position and could create a coherent account of why other studies were not consistent. Those who insist that we must not lose the idea of a common yardstick for fear of sacrificing the ability to resolve theoretical disputes should look closely at the history of attitude research in social psychology.

phers have called a criterionless "radical choice." Although two traditions may be incommensurable, that does not mean they are incomparable. The resources of cultural traditions are multiple and rich, and so it is always possible to create means of comparison. Throughout this chapter, I have compared my view of experience and communication to received views in a variety of ways. When we encounter a new set of practices, we can always begin by thinking, "It's sort of like this and very different from that."

Because language has no essence, we can create multiple comparisons that get us started when engaging with a different form of life. I do not think that any experiences are inherently incomparable. This is because humans share a common earthly home and a common physiology, and they can develop the ability to find family resemblances among things and actions. My rejection of inherent incomparability is also based on conjoint action. We can work to bring our actions into articulation with that of others, although we begin by muddling through. Thus, we can begin to create experience that serves us in making comparisons and then explore the family resemblances we find. As Wittgenstein (1953) put it, where explanation leaves off, action takes over.

It is important to caution the reader about the trap of thinking that diversity is only a problem to be overcome. Arendt (1958) argued that diversity of perspective is necessary for individuality. The only way we can know who we are is in distinction from others. We act conjointly with others, who treat us as identifiable loci of action. In this way, the *I* becomes an indexical expression, locating us for ourselves and others in the social world (Harré, 1984).

In the first part of her argument, Arendt developed the idea that the *you* is prior to, and a requirement for, the *I*—a theme more recently taken up by Shotter (1989), Harré (1989), and Cronen and Pearce (1991–1992). However, Arendt's argument went further. She said the ability to recognize and live in a common world also depends on diversity of perspectives. We create this common world by virtue of the fact that we coordinate with others who are not mirror images of ourselves. Arendt did not hold the Cartesian position—that each person is a unique subjectivity—but she argued that it is possible to create episodes of communication that work to produce disattention to differences and discourage the elaboration of differences if noted. In such cases, said Arendt, we can become imprisoned in a singular subjectivity. A common world depends on difference as well as individuality.

The postmodern orientation has developed a perspective in which diversity is celebrated and unity is disparaged. Haug (1987) argued that the need for consistency simply ornaments inconsistencies. However, this line of thought about diversity seems to obscure the difference between stories lived and stories told. Of course, there is great diversity among the stories one tells. However, the value of the diversity is a "value in the running." How is diversity, even contradiction, lived? Does it lead to productive tensions that take the form of creative ways of life, or merely to confusion or stagnation? The worst part of the postmodern turn, from a pragmatist's point of view, is that it seems to simply celebrate diversity and stress that any unity can be deconstructed. As Burman (1990) observed, celebration of diversity without focus on coordinated social action can lead to obviating any possible coherent political action. Why adopt any form of unified action if it, too, can be deconstructed?

The importance of unity and diversity can be better understood when we think about the cultural and historical quality of communication and the unfinished, nonessentialized character of it. A few years ago, I argued that there is no way to know a priori when an artifact or practice of one culture can have a great and perhaps highly beneficial impact on another (Cronen, 1991). I noted the impact of Picasso's chance encounter of African masks and the impact that had on Western art. The multiple roots of jazz is another case I cited. However, I should have also cited the disastrous impact of the introduction of steel axes to a Stone Age culture. The negative example would have better highlighted the importance of conjoint action. Just as the flexibility and unfinished quality of human communication allows us to benefit from all sorts of cultural encounters, the question of whether there will be benefit or disaster depends on the way conjoint action proceeds to create forms of life.

THE CONSEQUENTIALITY OF COMMUNICATION: AGENDA AND IMPLICATIONS

There are some radical changes that lie before readers who want to give serious attention to the pragmatic orientation: You are invited to think about distinctions between individuality and sociality as mutually creative activities, rather than as different entities. Thus, you may often need to clarify ideas by using verbs and gerunds to replace nouns. For example, you may discuss the activity of identifying, rather than having an identity, and you may discuss emotion as an emergent ability to do something, not merely as a state of being. You may need to reject the static metaphor of the *eye* that surveys the objects of knowledge in favor of Dewey's preferred metaphor of the *hands* that grasp, manipulate, and do (cited in Lamont & Redmer, 1959). You may have to emphasize the active, temporal character of life, rather than the static, universalized propositions about it. Conjoint action may have to be given the primary emphasis usually given to individual thought. Thought and action become a unity because thought becomes a feature of action. Aesthetic features of life have to be treated as vital aspects of everyday experience, not something other than or outside everyday experience.

Embarking on such a course of action requires thinking about theory in a very different way from the received view. The point of a social theory cannot be revealing hidden laws of behavior or conversation. From a pragmatist orientation, a theory should be practical in the sense that it informs our ability to describe, interpret, critique, and influence real communication processes. The test is use. CMM is one example of a practical theory, but it is not the only way to refine the foregoing commitments into research practices.

It is not just the behaviorist and cognitive traditions that are at odds with this pragmatist outlook. The reduction of persons to texts in the narrative tradition, and the tendency of critical cultural studies to examine only fabrications (e.g., videos, films, and consumer products), are also brought into question. So, too, are the conversation analysts' focus on stories lived to the exclusion of stories told, and those ethnographic practices that treat language as a code. As the editor of this book put it, the strong implication of the orientation developed in this chapter is that "we can't study communication the way scholars traditionally do. Communication is an embodied experience and practice, and what we as scholars have to understand are those lived embodied practices" (S. Sigman, personal communication, December 10, 1993).

The imperative to create communication theory that guides researchers' participation in social–political–cultural life comes from the old Greek idea that, in practical arts, we are engaged in the moral process of trying to make life better. This classical sensibility is at one with the pragmatists' idea that creativity, individuality, aesthetic moments, political virtue, and the like are achievements in the process of communication. If we care about them, we must attend to the lived communication episodes in which they are created.

We must not think of the relationship of communication to our political, personal, relational, and cultural situation the way the traveler thought of the relationship of himself to the sinking ship. Communication is consequential because it is intrinsic to being human, not merely something individuals decide to do. To study communication from the orientation I have suggested is to inquire—in a situated, historical–cultural way—into how we are cocreating who we are and what are we doing, and with a view as to how we might do better.

REFERENCES

Anderson, L. R., & Fishbein, M. (1965). Prediction of attitude from the number, strength, and evaluative aspect of beliefs about the attitude object: A comparison of summation and congruity theory. *Journal of Personality and Social Psychology, 3,* 437–443.

Arendt, H. (1958). *The human condition*. Chicago: University of Chicago Press.

Aristotle. (1966b). Nicomachean Ethics. In R. McKeon (Ed. and Trans.), *The basic works of Aristotle* (pp. 927–1112). New York: Random House.

Aristotle. (1966a). Metaphysics. In R. McKeon (Ed. and Trans.), *The basic works of Aristotle* (pp. 681–926). New York: Random House.

Averill, J. (1980). A constructivist view of emotion. In R. Pluchik & H. Kellerman (Eds.), *Theories of emotion* (pp. 305–339). New York: Academic Press.

Baker, G. P., & Hacker, P. M. S. (1984). *Language, sense & nonsense*. Oxford, England: Basil Blackwell.

Bakhtin, M. M. (1981). *The dialogical imagination*. Austin, TX: University of Texas Press.

Bateson, G. (1972). *Steps to an ecology of mind*. New York: Ballantine.

Bean, W. S. (1989). *Compliance and noncompliance with cardiac rehabilitation: A family systems, communication perspective*. Unpublished doctoral dissertation, University of Massachusetts, Amherst, MA.

Becker, E. (1971). *The birth and death of meaning: An interdisciplinary perspective on the problem of man*. New York: The Free Press.

Benveniste, E. (1979). *Problems in general linguistics*. Miami, FL: University of Miami Press.

Bernstein, R. J. (1966). *John Dewey*. Independence, OH: Ridgeview Publishing.

Bernstein, R. J. (1971). *Praxis and action*. Philadelphia: University of Pennsylvania Press.

Bernstein, R. J. (1985). *Beyond objectivism and relativism: Science, hermeneutics, and praxis*. Philadelphia: University of Pennsylvania Press.

Bernstein, R. J. (1992). *The new constellation: The ethical-political horizons of modernity/postmodernity*. Cambridge, MA: MIT Press.

Boscolo, L., Cecchin, G., Hoffman, L., & Penn, P. (1987). *Milan systemic family therapy*. New York: Basic Books.

Burman, E. (1990). Differing with deconstruction: A feminist critique. In I. Parker & J. Shotter (Eds.), *Deconstructing social psychology* (pp. 208–220). London: Routledge & Kegan Paul.

Canfield, J. V. (1981). *Wittgenstein: Language and world*. Amherst: University of Massachusetts Press.

Cappella, J. M. (1990). The method of proof by example in interaction analysis. *Communication Monographs, 57*, 236–240.

Cronen, M. P. (1989). *Production and comprehension of indirect requests by persons with right hemisphere dysfunction*. Unpublished doctoral dissertation, University of Massachusetts, Amherst, MA.

Cronen, V. E. (1991). Coordinated Management of Meaning theory and postmodern ethics. In K. J. Greenberg (Ed.), *Conversations on communication ethics* (pp. 21–53). Norwood, NJ: Ablex.

Cronen, V. E. Coordinated Management of Meaning: Theory for the complexities and contradictions of everyday life. In J. Siegfried (Ed.), *The status of common sense in psychology* (pp. 183–207). Norwood, NJ: Ablex.

Cronen, V. E., Chen, V., & Pearce, W. B. (1988). Coordinated Management of Meaning: A critical theory. In Y. Y. Kim & W. Gudykundst (Eds.), *International intercultural annual: Vol. 12. Theories of intercultural communication* (pp. 66–98). Beverly Hills, CA: Sage.

Cronen, V. E., & Pearce, W. B. (1981). Logical force in interpersonal communication: A new concept of "necessity" in social behavior. *Communication, 6*, 5–67.

Cronen, V. E., & Pearce, W. B. (1991–1992). Grammars of identity and their implications for discursive practices in and out of academe: A comparison of Davies and Harre's views to coordinated management of meaning theory. *Research on Language and Social Interaction, 25*, 37–66.

Cronen, V. E., Pearce, W. B., & Tomm, K. (1985). A dialectical view of personal change. In K. Gergen & K. Davis (Eds.), *The social construction of the person* (pp. 203–224). New York: Springer- Verlag.

Davis, G. A. (1993). *Survey of adult aphasia and related language disorders* (2nd ed.). Englewood Cliffs, NJ: Prentice-Hall.

Descartes, R. (1985). *Discourse on method and the meditations* (F. E. Sutcliffe, Trans.). Hammondsworth, Middlesex: Viking Penguin. (Original work published 1637)

Dewey, J. (1896). The reflex arc concept in psychology. *Psychological Review, 3,* 357–370.

Dewey, J. (1925). A naturalistic theory of sense perception. *Journal of Philosophy, 22,* 596–605.

Dewey, J. (1927). Half-hearted naturalism. *Journal of Philosophy, 24,* 57–64.

Dewey, J. (1930). *Philosophy and civilization.* New York: Minton, Balsh.

Dewey, J. (1934a). *Art as experience.* New York: Minton, Balch.

Dewey, J. (1934b). *A common faith.* New Haven, CT: Yale University Press.

Dewey, J. (1950). *Human nature and conduct.* New York: Henry Holt. (Original work published 1922)

Dewey, J. (1958). *Experience and nature.* New York: Dover. (Original work published 1925)

Dewey, J. (1960). *The quest for certainty.* New York: Putnam. (Original work published 1929)

Dewey, J. (1960). The need for a recovery of philosophy. In R. J. Bernstein (Ed.), *John Dewey on experience, nature and freedom* (pp. 3–69). New York: Liberal Arts Press. (Original work published 1917)

Dewey, J. (1966). *Democracy and education.* New York: The Free Press. (Original work published 1916)

Dulany, D. E., Jr. (1962). The place of hypotheses and intentions: An analysis of verbal conditioning. In C. W. Eriksen (Ed.), *Behavior and awareness* (pp. 102–129). Durham, NC: Duke University Press.

Edwards, J. C. (1985). *Ethics without philosophy: Wittgenstein and the moral life.* Tampa: The University Presses of Florida.

Foucault, M. (1972). *The archaeology of knowledge and the discourse on language.* New York: Harper & Row.

Geertz, C. (1973). *The interpretation of culture.* New York: Basic Books.

Gergen, K. (1982). *Transformation in social knowledge.* New York: Springer-Verlag.

Gergen, K. (1992). Social constructionism in question. *Human Systems, 3,* 163–182.

Gergen, K. (1993, February). *Science as social construction: Problems and prospects.* Paper presented at Loyola University, Chicago, IL.

Giddens, A. (1976). *New rules of sociological method.* London: Hutchinson of London.

Gould, S. J. (1989). *Wonderful life: The Burgess shale and the nature of history.* New York: Norton.

Gunn, G. (1987). *The culture of criticism and the criticism of culture.* New York: Oxford University Pres.

Gunn, G. (1992). *Thinking across the American grain.* Chicago: The University of Chicago Press.

Harré, R. (1984). *Personal being.* Cambridge, MA: Harvard University Press.

Harré, R. (1986). *Varieties of realism.* Oxford, England: Basil Blackwell.

Harré, R. (1989). Language games and texts of identity. In J. Shotter & K J. Gergen (Eds.), *Texts of identity* (pp. 20–35). London: Sage.

Harré, R., & Secord, P. F. (1972). *The explanation of social behaviour.* Totowa, N. J.: Littlefield & Adams.

Haug, F. (1987). *Female sexualization.* London: Verso Press

Hofstede, G. (1980). *Culture's consequences: International differences in work-related values.* Beverly Hills, CA: Sage.

Hofstede, G. (1984). Hofstede's culture dimensions: An independent validation using Rokeach's value survey. *Journal of Cross-Cultural Psychology, 15,* 417–433.

Jacobs, S. (1990). On the especially nice fit between qualitative analysis and the known properties of conversation. *Communication Monographs, 57,* 241–249.

James, W. (1950). *The principles of psychology* (Vol. 1) New York: Dover. (Original work published 1890)

Johnson, M. (1987). *The body in the mind: The bodily basis of meaning, imagination, and reason.* Chicago: Chicago University Press.

Kelly, G. (1955). *The psychology of personal constructs* (Vols. 1–2). New York: Norton.

Koestler, A. (1978). *Janus: A summing up.* New York: Random House.

Lamont, C., & Redmer, M. (Eds.) (1959). *Dialogue on John Dewey.* New York: Horizon.

MacIntyre, A. (1990). *Three rival versions of moral inquiry: Encyclopedia, genealogy, and tradition.* Notre Dame, IN: University of Notre Dame Press.

Maturana, H. R. (1975). The organization of the living: A theory of the living organism. *International Journal of Man-Machine Studies, 7,* 131–332.

Maturana, H. R. (1975). Biology of language: The epistemology of reality. In G. A. Miller & E. Lenneberg (Eds.), *Psychology and the biology of language and thought* (pp. 26–63). New York: Academic Press.

Maturana, H. R., & Varela, F. J. (1988). *The tree of knowledge: The biological roots of human understanding.* Boston: The New Science Library.

Mead, G. H. (1934). *Mind, self, and society.* Chicago: University of Chicago Press.

Mead, G. H. (1938). *The philosophy of the act.* Chicago: University of Chicago Press.

Ong, W. J. (1989). *Orality and literacy: The technologizing of the word.* London: Routledge & Kegan Paul.

Pearce, W. B. (1975). *An overview of communication and interpersonal relationships.* Palo Alto, CA: Science Research Associates.

Pearce, W. B. (1989). *Communication and the human condition.* Carbondale: Southern Illinois University Press.

Pearce, W. B. (1994). Recovering agency. In S. Deetz (Ed.), *Communication yearbook 17* (pp. 34–41). Thousand Oaks, CA: Sage.

Pearce, W. B., and Cronen, V. E. (1980). *Communication, action, and meaning: The creation of social realities.* New York: Praeger.

Pearce, W. B., Cronen, V. E., & Harris, L. M. (1982). Methodological considerations in building communication theory. In F. E. X. Dance (Ed.), *Human communication theory* (pp. 1–41). New York: Harper & Row.

Prigogine, I., & Stengers, I. (1984). *Order out of chaos: Man's new dialogue with nature.* New York: Bantam.

Rorty, R. (1979). *Philosophy and the mirror of nature.* Princeton, NJ: Princeton University Press.

Rorty, R. (1989). *Contingency, irony, and solidarity.* Cambridge, England: University of Cambridge Press.

Santayana, G. (1925). Dewey's naturalistic metaphysics. *Journal of Philosophy, 22,* 673–688.

Schrag, C. O. (1992). *The resources of rationality.* Bloomington: The University of Indiana Press.

Searle, J. R. (1969). *Speech acts: An essay in the philosophy of language.* Oxford, England: Oxford University Press.

Shotter, J. (1981). *"Duality of structure" and intentionality" in an ecological psychology.* Unpublished manuscript, University of Nottingham, England.

Shotter, J. (1984). *Social accountability and selfhood.* Oxford, England: Basil Blackwell.

Shotter, J. (1986). Realism and relativism, rules and intentionality, theories and accounts: A response to Morss. *New Ideas in Psychology, 4,* 71–84.

Shotter, J. (1989). Social accountability and the social construction of "you." In J. Shotter & K. J. Gergen (Eds.), *Texts of identity* (pp. 133–151). London: Sage.

Shotter, J. (1990). *Knowing of the third kind.* Utrecht, Netherlands: Utrecht University Press.

Shotter, J. (1993). *Conversational Realties.* London, Sage.

Shotter, J., & Gergen, K. (1993). Social construction: Knowledge, self, others and continuing the conversation. In S. Deetz (Ed.), *Communication yearbook 17* (pp. 3–33). Thousand Oaks, CA: Sage.

Strawson, P. E. (1959). *Individuals: An essay in descriptive metaphysics.* London: Methuen.

Taylor, C. (1985). *Philosophy and the human science: Philosophical papers (Vol. 2)*. Cambridge, England: Cambridge University Press.

Tronick, E. (1982). *Social interchange in infancy*. Baltimore, MD: University Park Press.

von Glazersfeld, E. (1991). Knowing without metaphysics: Aspects of the radical constructionist position. In F. Steier (Ed.), *Research and reflexivity* (pp. 12–29). Beverly Hills, CA: Sage.

Vygotsky, L. S. (1962). *Thought and language*. Cambridge, MA: MIT Press.

Wallace, K. (1971). *Understanding discourse*. Baton Rouge: Louisiana State University Press.

Watzlawick, P. (1976). *How real is real?* New York: Random House.

Weaver, D. A. (1991). *Pessimism—related cognitions and depressed mood: A logitudinal study of psychiatric patients*. Unpublished doctoral dissertation, University of Massachusetts, Amherst, MA.

White, H. (1992, April). *Writing in the middle voice*. Paper presented at a lecture given at University of California at Santa Barbara, Santa Barbara, CA.

Wittgenstein, L. (1953). *Philosophical investigations*. New York: Macmillan.

Wittgenstein, L. (1969). *On certainty*. New York: Harper & Row.

2

A Neo-Rhetorical Perspective: The Enactment of Role-Identities as Interactive and Strategic

Robert E. Sanders
State University of New York, Albany

This chapter is about the enactment of institutional role-identities as a product of the give-and-take of social interaction, not a product of individual performance. The core of the chapter is an analysis of filmed enactments of the role-identities of supervisor and subordinate in a particular workplace. The issues, topics, and claims developed here, and their relevance to the theme of this book, the "consequentiality of communication," arose inductively from these data. For that reason, the topic of consequentiality is not explicitly addressed until the closing discussion.

ENACTMENTS OF ROLE-IDENTITIES AS INTERACTIVE

Having claim to a role-identity binds a person sociologically to others who have claims to reciprocal—complementary or competing—role-identities (as salespersons are bound to customers and vice versa, or family members are bound to each other). Thus, description of a person's enactment of a role-identity typically includes the person's own conduct (especially toward role-reciprocal others), but also how others treat the person (especially role-reciprocal others).

There is an interactive connection between one's own conduct and others' treatment of one that is fundamentally communicative (Sanders, 1987). A person's communicative acts constrain what is available for others to say or do (including how they treat the person), and others' acts constrain what is available for the person to say or do (including conduct

67

which the person's role-identity calls for). Accordingly, within the limits of their technical knowledge and institutional commitment, the manner and success of persons' enactments of role-identities depend on what their own communicative competence, and the communicative competence of the other parties involved, allows and disallows to be said and done during role-relevant interactions. This is the matter that this chapter is principally about, on which the data and analysis discussed herein are intended to shed light.

A common notion of everyday life is that different persons who have claim to the same role-identity, even within the same organizations and cultural groups, often enact their[1] role-identity in markedly individual ways, yet without necessarily diverging from the institutional definition of their role-identity (i.e., its rights and responsibilities). This rules out that role-identities are only nominal devices for assigning category memberships, or that they have the force to uniformly "script" persons' conduct. Instead, because enactments of role-identities are individualized, and yet are often consistent with the institutional definition of the role-identity, there is a tie that role-identities have to people's conduct that must be complex and indirect, as follows. Having claim to a role-identity does not make any specific conduct or treatment from others obligatory, but instead places a burden on persons to devise ways to uphold the institutional definition of the role-identity in each of the various interactions in which they participate. This leaves the individual responsible for how to do this under the circumstances (except in highly regimented organizations). Enactments of role-identities—ways persons conduct themselves and promote certain treatment of themselves by others in living up to their role-identities—must therefore depend on certain contingencies that bear on the course of person's interactions with role-reciprocal others: each person's motivations, understandings of his or her rights and responsibilities, relevant knowledge and experience, and the corresponding qualities of role-reciprocal others with whom they interact. Such contingencies predict the individual differences that are commonplace in enactments of role-identities.

Thus, the reality of institutional role-identities lies as much in their enactment as in their institutional definition. This indicates a bidirectional relationship between the institutional definition of a role-identity and its enactment: The institutional definition of a role-identity can just as well be constructed or transformed by the way it is enacted, as it can "preexist"

---

[1]It is argued later that it is counterfactual to say that a person does not "have" a role-identity, but only has "claim" to a role-identity that is contingent on the way he or she acts and is treated. In this chapter, the phrase "[he, she, or they] have claim to a role-identity" is not treated as asserting anything different from locutions such as "[he, she, or they] have a role-identity," and "[his, her, or their] role-identity."

and structure the enactment. There could also be a corresponding bidirectional relationship between the qualities of persons and interactions, and the enactment of role-identities: The qualities of individuals and interactions can just as readily be constructed by the way a role-identity is enacted as those qualities can "preexist" and structure the enactment.

THE "NEO-RHETORICAL" PERSPECTIVE
ON ENACTING ROLE-IDENTITIES

Although the data came first and the topics and conclusions of this chapter came second, the analysis did not start in a vacuum. The starting point was a "neo-rhetorical" perspective on language and social interaction, which I have detailed and applied elsewhere (e.g., Sanders, 1987, 1989, 1991). From this perspective, the analysis of social interactions focuses on details of turns at talk, and the interrelationship among turns, that are instrumental for overcoming rhetorical problems posed by the interaction for one or more of the parties involved.

For the purposes of analysis, a social interaction is considered rhetorically problematic if at least one person orients to it as such, as follows:

- The content or acts of the person's turns at talking recurrently conflict with other(s)' turn, by functionally being different from or "disregarding" what would most meet the "demand" of or conjoin supportively with the content or act(s) produced by the other(s).
- The person has preferences[2] about how the interaction will conclude or what it includes.
- The content or acts of other parties' turns at speaking do not make relevant, or do make irrelevant, what the person prefers about how the interaction concludes or what it includes.

In cases where interactions seem to be rhetorically problematic for a person, one can characterize the person's turns at speaking as rhetorical—

---

[2]Analytically, whether someone can be said to have preferences about the course of an interaction depends on meeting two conditions (with the analyst possibly addressing those conditions in reverse order). First, there has to be a reason to consider that the person, P, has something at stake, something to win or lose, depending on the course of the interaction. It may be attributed to P that he or she has something at stake based on what P and/or others explicitly say during the interaction, or based on background information about P or the immediate circumstances, or based on psychological or sociological verities such as the needs people generally have, or on the generic needs people with P's specific role-identity have. Second, at least one party to the interaction, whether P or some other, must orient to others' turns at speaking as potentially jeopardizing the want(s) or need(s) that are attributed to P.

as fashioned to constrain the course of the interaction to overcome the rhetorical problem—insofar as:

- The person does not (could/would/should not) unilaterally impose on the other parties involved, through the exercise of power or force, how the interaction concludes and/or what it includes.
- The person's turns at speaking are fashioned—whether knowingly or not[3]—in a way that constrains the participation of others, and thereby the course of the interaction, so as to favor the person's (apparent) preferences.[4]

What is *not* of interest from this neo-rhetorical perspective is to debate whether specific interactions are rhetorically problematic, or whether participants knowingly engaged in them as such. What *is* of interest is to detail the ways that turns at talk are fashioned in such interactions so that the participation of others is constrained, and thereby so is what the interaction includes and how it concludes. Thus, the concern is with what resources of social interaction could knowingly be used by individuals in solving rhetorical problems in interactions, leaving aside the question of whether they are knowingly being used in that instance (Heritage, 1990–1991; cf. Sanders, 1990–1991). Such an analysis sheds light on what indi-

---

[3]The perspective here is *neo*-rhetorical because there is a need for caution whenever one claims a person in interaction knowingly fashioned his or her turns for the sake of constraining others in regard to how the interaction concludes or what it includes, no matter how "artful" or "artless" the person's turns seem (Heritage, 1990–1991). Traditional rhetorics are about an "art of discourse" as a distinct practice that persons engage in knowingly. But participation in interactions is often so extemporaneous that it generally is a matter of inference in specific cases (for participants as well as analysts; Sanders, 1983), based on circumstantial indicators and recurrent qualities of content, style, or timing, whether any specific turn at speaking was fashioned artfully to constrain others.

[4]Rhetorically problematic interactions are not necessarily ones where all of the interested parties have apparent preferences and produce speaking turns that favor their own preference. Although this often happens (e.g., Sanders, 1983, 1991), it is not always the case. Some participants in interactions may not exhibit any clear preference about the course of the interaction, and yet they may produce turns at talk that are counter (possibly by happenstance) to what someone else seems to prefer. In one such case I have studied, the person apparently realized in midstream that she had done this, and then seemed to fashion her turns at speaking to "repair" the problem she had created, although she actually made matters worse (Sanders, 1987). In addition, a participant who apparently does have a preference about the course of the interaction that conflicts with another's preference nonetheless may fashion turns at speaking that do not constrain the other against following the dispreferred course, and may even constrain the other toward that course (as in the case of the female supervisor in Interaction 3 analyzed in this chapter). How widespread such occurrences are, and whether they indicate that individuals may differ in the extent of their communicative competence, are important empirical questions.

viduals must "know" about communicative acts and social interactions, i.e., what their communicative competence must include (and possibly what is lacking if they fail), to "artfully" fashion their utterances and behavior to have an influential or effectual part in social interaction.[5]

Applying this neo-rhetorical perspective to the enactment of role-identities does not contradict the central proposition of this chapter—that the enactment of a role-identity is an interactive process—even though from this perspective individuals are seen as independent agents who are competent to fashion their turns at speaking to influence the course of interactions according to their preferences. By definition, interactions are ecologically entwined progressions of turns at speaking;[6] From the neo-rhetorical perspective, however, each turn may be fashioned by individuals to constrain the course of the interaction to promote their own wants and interests, but within the limits of having to be progressively responsive to the other's turns at speaking. In that case, the course of a social interaction might be consonant with the preferences of one or more participants insofar as those preferences are unopposed, but could just as well be

---

[5]Speakers in face-to-face interaction often have to identify within the moments of a few turns at talking, often in the microseconds between turns, that there is a rhetorical problem (that the interaction is taking a course contrary to their preferences for what it includes or how it concludes), and thus fashion the first of a possible series of communicative acts calculated to change (if incrementally) the course of the interaction. An adequate theory of communicative competence has to capture the ability of people to do this. This involves considerably more than what others have examined under the heading *communicative competence*—for example, the community's standards and norms for participation in interaction ("speaking rules") of ethnographic interest to Hymes (1964, 1974), or the "skills" exhibited in the speaking of "effective" versus "ineffective" speakers of pedagogical interest to Spitzberg and Cupach (1984). The notion here centers on "knowledge" of the formal properties of interactions and communicative acts on which projections of their future course must be based, and used to fashion coherent, rhetorically apt turns at speaking at the speed exhibited in face-to-face interactions (Sanders, 1987).

[6]I refer here to *interconnections* within and between several levels of analysis, beginning with minimal structural units within interactions such as adjacency pairs, repair sequences, and so on. At the other extreme, the components of interactions are interconnected as constituents of activities (Levinson, 1992) or interactional genres that are structurally ad hoc and fluid, organized partly by the meaning relations among their components. We usually refer to these activities with terms such as *discussion, gossip, quarrel, interview, consultation,* and so on. Although little has been done to identify what distinguishes such activities from each other, or what defines their boundaries, the direction toward doing so is implied in many studies as a combination of two main ideas. First, people orient to interactions in generic terms: as conventional *speech events* or *activities* (e.g., Hymes, 1974; Schank & Abelson, 1977). Second, such generic activities comprise one or more episodelike structures (along the lines of Edmondson's, 1981, proposal), each defined and bounded by an initial act that "proffers" a certain matter to be acted on and a closing act that resolves it. Interactions (e.g., speech events or activities) may comprise one or more such structures, with multiple structures ordered either consecutively or, following Reichman's (1985) analysis, embedded within each other.

dissonant with the preferences of all participants if there are conflicting preferences that are not somehow reconciled. Interactions can take an unexpected, and even unwanted, course because of the synergy between the participants' individual rhetorical efforts to promote their respective wants and interests, as arguably happened in the third of the interactions analyzed herein.

When there is a rhetorical problem during a social interaction, it is usually specific to that interaction—emergent for all practical purposes from the interaction, and therefore unanticipated. Exactly what preferences a person has that become jeopardized by the course of an interaction, and specifically what remedies of utterance and behavior might alter its course, are inherently matters of local circumstance, contingent on the give-and-take of the interaction.[7] However, some rhetorical problems have a generic dimension formed by an impersonal, institutional exigence. It turned out, from the analysis of the supervisor–subordinate interactions given here, that such problems can arise in the enactment of role-identities. Their generic, institutional dimension facilitates the identification of the wants and interests of interacting persons, and what is at stake for individuals and institutions if enactments of role-identities do not conform to institutional expectations.

In two of the three interactions examined later, the respective supervisors and subordinates participated in a way that interfered with each other's enactment of his or her role-identity. This problem was responded to in one interaction with the subordinate in particular, and the supervisor to a lesser degree, having fashioned turns at speaking sufficient (all else being equal) to constrain the interaction to favor the enactment of their own role-identity, despite obstacles created by the other. In the other interaction, marked coordination problems about the business at hand persisted, resulting in apparently deficient enactments of the supervisor and subordinate role-identities; neither subordinate nor supervisor fashioned turns at speaking in ways that were responsive to or sufficient to overcome the obstacles each created for the other's enactment of his or her role-identity.

The following section provides a conceptual overview of the enactment of role-identities that accomplishes a shift away from the usual focus of role theory on individuals to a focus on interactions, and from a focus on

---

[7]Speakers in face-to-face interaction do not have the luxury of analyzing rhetorical problems in unhurried contemplation, and fashioning discourse in response well in advance of the occasion, as traditional rhetors generally do. As stated in a preceding note, speakers in face-to-face interaction often have to instantly identify that there is a rhetorical problem—that the interaction is not taking a preferred course—and immediately fashion a communicative act calculated to change the course of the interaction.

expressive resources for routinized enactments of role-identities with others who cooperate to a concern with expressive resources for enacting role-identities in novel situations with others who do not cooperate. This is followed by a theoretical discussion of two aspects of communicative acts—relevance relations, and presupposition—that turned out, on preliminary analysis of the data, to be critically important for the way role-identities were enacted. The analysis of the three interactions between pairs of supervisors and subordinates is then presented, particularly the aspects of their communicative acts that matter to the enactment of their role-identities, and may be consequential for the relevant institution as well. The chapter concludes with a discussion of the consequentiality of communicative acts for the social arrangements among people.

THE INSTITUTIONAL BASIS OF THE ENACTMENT OF ROLE-IDENTITIES

Goffman's (1959, 1967) analysis of social conduct is an important starting point for analyzing what is involved in the enactment of role-identities. His rich and influential analysis represents role-identities as constitutive of persons as social beings, rather than facades. However, his analysis conceals what is of central interest here—that enactments of role-identities generally depend on the course of social interactions as worked out between persons each pursuing his or her own wants and interests, not (as Goffman assumed) independent co-acting individuals whose performances mesh despite themselves because of their institutional relationship. Thus, a brief overview of Goffman's ideas and a refinement of key elements is needed to provide a foundation for the present analysis of actual enactments of role-identities.

Goffman's analysis implies at least the following five "axioms."[8] (a) Unless people have a social identity in any instance, they are ciphers to others in regard to how the person should be treated and what treatment can be expected from him or her. (b) Persons acquire social identities within the framework of particular social institutions[9] (i.e., any social

---

[8]It does some violence to Goffman's work and the way he thought about it to characterize his thinking as "axiomatic" in any strict sense (see his remarks in Verhoeven, 1993). Nonetheless, many of Goffman's observations and concerns are founded on a core set of ideas that are axiomatic in the loose sense that they serve him as first principles.

[9]The term *social institutions* here refers broadly to all frameworks in which groups of people act conjointly by virtue of their common membership in a social unit that predates and survives specific episodes of conjoint action, and whose definition and existence are recognized in a society by virtue of having a name. This includes: *formal organizations*, where goals, procedures,

identity is an institutional role-identity).[10] (c) Persons can only acquire a role-identity at a given time from among the possible role-identities of the institution within which they are acting.[11] (d) A person has to appear, speak, and behave in certain ways, and be treated in certain ways by others, to be credited with the role-identity he or she has claimed. (e) Persons who have claim to a role-identity that act and are treated accordingly reaffirm and renew the social reality of the institution within which their role-identities exist.

The fourth of those axioms—that persons have to conduct themselves and be treated in certain ways to enact the role-identities they claim— captures the central idea of Goffman's (1959, 1967) early texts, especially his concepts of *creating fronts, performance,* and *facework.* However, that axiom is more troublesome than Goffman's analysis indicates. If role-identities have to be enacted in particular ways, one would expect that persons who have claim to the same role-identity would conduct themselves in the same way, and be treated alike by others.

The question is, what do the terms *in the same way* and *alike* mean here? On the one hand, it seems inherent in the concept of *role-identity* that

---

and official responsibilities are codified, and where participants are relatively unchanging across episodes of action; *informal organizations and groups,* such as families, clubs, amateur athletics, and political movements, where such matters are not codified, and which vary as to the relative permanence or fluidity of participants across episodes of action; and *established customs, procedures, and rituals,* where people (possibly different people on each occasion) recurrently assemble temporarily to conjointly produce some episode, such as class reunions, legal proceedings, and religious ceremonies.

[10]Goffman might not have wanted the matter stated quite this categorically. But the spirit of his analysis is that identities are social in the most important (i.e., sociological) sense if they can be recognized and oriented to in society. The question is whether there can be any noninstitutional, extrasocietal frameworks, which are still in some sense "social," in which people have identities. The only obvious candidate is interpersonal relationships, in which it might be argued that persons have "private" social identities—a social standing and significance to the relational partner alone. It seems a matter of definition, rather than observation, whether such private identities are actually independent of the broader society, or are modeled and standardized within extrinsic social ideologies, such as societal stereotypes about mateship and family, religious teachings, and popular culture. However, if the reader prefers to think that some such noninstitutional social identities do exist, understand that they fall outside the scope of this chapter.

[11]For present purposes, it is unnecessary to closely examine how actors mutually know in what institutional framework they are. It generally seems to be a jointly achieved construction, based on the physical setting the people are in and/or the shared reason they have for being with each other. However, sometimes it is sufficiently equivocal what the institutional framework is that it needs discussion. For example, if married spouses are both employed in the same organization and one encounters the other with a third employee, it may be equivocal whether the spouse$_2$ and third person are together for business reasons—so that the spouse$_1$ has no privileges to join them except as a colleague—or whether the spouse$_2$ and third person are engaged in a nonbusiness, social episode—where the married couple is then husband and wife to each other, and the spouse$_1$ has whatever privileges to join the spouse$_2$ and third person that their marital relationship affords.

people who have claim to the same role-identity will act and be treated in certain ways, insofar as each can be said to have successfully enacted that role-identity, and this was Goffman's point. On the other hand, as already noted, common experience indicates that any two persons with a claim to the same role-identity—whether parent, doctor, friend, client, and so on— are likely to enact the role-identity in distinctive ways, yet often with equal degrees of institutional sufficiency. It seems more the rule than the exception that there will be individual differences between people who have claim to the same role-identity in the specifics of their conduct and treatment by others.

Goffman (e.g., 1967, in "Where the Action Is") was duly sensitive to the reality of individual differences, but not in regard to the enactment of role-identities (the staging of performances). His stated program was to go as far as possible in explaining individuals' public conduct solely in terms of what was incumbent on them to do their assigned part in maintaining the social order, without reference to any psychological basis for their public conduct. Thus, Goffman's analysis attributes any problems that are created or encountered in enacting role-identities solely to individuals' ill will, error, or defect, and this is reflected in his ideas about what can be done to remedy them.

However, Goffman's approach can only be sustained if there is a direct relationship between the institutional definition of a person's role-identity and the way he or she actually acts and is treated. The point here is that the relationship is indirect and complex. This is evident from the diversity of ways in which role-identities are enacted, as well as from the fact that people have claim to role-identities even when they do nothing to enact them, or they enact them in a way contrary to what the role-identities make incumbent on them (if this were not so, it would make no sense to assess the sufficiency with which persons enact their role-identities, as we routinely do, nor coherent to refer to someone as a *bad* teacher, parent, clerk, scientist, etc.). Goffman's analysis does not examine (a) problems in enacting role-identities and possible remedies that arise from individual differences, (b) conflicts of interest specific to the immediate circumstance, and (c) constraints on the acts that can relevantly occur because of the course the interaction has taken. The intent in this section is to refine Goffman's analysis in this regard, not overturn it.

The key is to reformulate the relationship between the institutional aspects of a role-identity (its rights and responsibilities, and the basis for one's claim to that role-identity) and the way people with that role-identity act and are treated. The relationship between the two has to be stated to reflect the following. First, there must be an institutional basis for having claim to a role-identity apart from whether the person acts and is treated accordingly. Second, the institutional definition of a role-identity—its rights and responsibilities—must be socially binding sufficiently that it is used as a standard for assessing the quality of a person's conduct and treatment by others, and that it generally coincides with preferences individuals exhibit for what acts they produce and how they are treated, yet is not binding in a way that precludes individual differences or marked deficiencies in its enactment

Having Claim to a Role-Identity

As noted earlier, a person's claim to a role-identity cannot depend on the way he or she acts and is treated. Rather, because a person has claim to a role-identity only with a specific institutional frame, his or her claim says something about the person's standing in relation to others within the relevant institutional frame, not about his or her conduct and treatment by others.

Acquiring Role-Identities in Formal Organizations. In institutions that involve formal organization, the basis for a person's claim to a role-identity is obvious: Role-identities are formally assigned to people. Although persons may earn their role-identities by acting and being treated in ways that display personal qualities commensurate with the rights and responsibilities of a role-identity that is then assigned to them, it does not always happen that way. Moreover, there is no assurance that, even if a person earns a role-identity by virtue of his or her past conduct and treatment by others, he or she will thereafter act and be treated accordingly. Rather, once a role-identity is formally assigned to someone, the person has claim to that role-identity until and if he or she is officially divested of it. When a person who has claim to a specific role-identity does not look or act the part, that may be confusing to those who do not already know the person's assigned role-identity and offensive to those who do. However, in and of itself, that does not disqualify the person's claim to that role-identity.

Acquiring Role-Identities in Informal Organizations and Groups. The more complicated case analytically involves informal organizations and groups (IO/Gs; e.g., the informal organization within a formal one, families, clubs, friendship circles), where there is an apparent paradox in regard to the issue here. The absence of formal authority prevents role-identities from being officially assigned.[12] In that case, role-identities must be distributed informally among the participants, perhaps on the model of "leaderless" discus-

---

[12]We have to regard participants as nonetheless having role-identities in these cases: (a) on the grounds of Goffman's logic that persons are ciphers to each other unless they have social (role-) identities, and (b) because IO/Gs are functional units that would tend toward a division of effort that would functionally amount to different role-identities.

sion groups (Fisher & Ellis, 1990), where role-identities, associated with a division of functional responsibilities as defined by the group's task, are interactively acquired. But if we say that persons acquire role-identities in IO/Gs by "earning" them, through the exhibition of qualities of conduct and treatment by others that are commensurate with a task-relevant responsibility, we have to be careful to sidestep an empirically questionable implication of that idea. Without further elaboration, that idea implies that role-identities would more likely be enacted sufficiently in IO/Gs, in which they are earned, than in formal organizations, in which they are assigned (whereas there is nothing remarkable about finding deficient enactments of role-identities in IO/Gs; e.g., bad caregivers in families, bad help-services volunteers, bad club members, etc.).

This implication can be avoided, at least pending an empirical resolution of the matter, if we posit that role-identities in IO/Gs are earned not necessarily by "merit," but by default, through a process of elimination among the pool of candidate persons involved. This would result given that, within the frame of an IO/G, there are a few possible role-identities, and the particular individuals participating in the institution in a given instance have to be distributed among those possible role-identities. Then if an individual's conduct and his or her treatment by others conformed to one of those role-identities more than anyone else's involved, that individual would probably have claim to that role-identity by default, the question of merit aside. Hence, it is just as likely in IO/Gs as in formal organizations that a person who has claim to a role-identity will, or will not, act and be treated accordingly.

The Institutional Definition of Role-Identities

As noted, two conflicting requirements have to be satisfied by the way institutional definitions of role-identities are formulated. On the one hand, the definition must be sufficiently prescriptive and binding so that persons' enactments of their role-identity are subject to evaluation, and they can be held accountable for deficiencies in their enactments. On the other hand, the definition cannot be so prescriptive and binding that there are any specific acts or behaviors required in the conduct of someone with that role-identity, or in the treatment (to be secured) from others, given the variety of ways in which people with the same role-identity conduct themselves and are treated.[13]

---

[13]A qualification is in order. The line of argument underway here does not apply to institutions such as the military, insofar as they are highly regimented and, as such, hold participants accountable for specifics of how they enact their role-identities. Institutions probably vary in this regard along a continuum from *highly regimented* to *egalitarian collectives;*

Both of these requirements for institutional definitions of role-identities can be satisfied by representing those definitions as prototypes of the role-identities or, more precisely, prototypes of their enactment (Lakoff, 1987; Rosch, 1978, 1981). Prototype theory arose from an empirical analysis of the psychology of categorization, where the core idea is that a *category* is formed around salient exemplars (prototypes) that exhibit certain distinguishing properties or qualities. It is a matter of degree whether pertinent objects of experience fall within such a category or fail to, as a function of how closely their properties or qualities approximate or how far they diverge from the properties or qualities of exemplars.

If we characterize a role-identity as a category of participation in a social institution, then prototype theory makes it possible to avoid defining a role-identity in terms of specific acts or behavior required in the conduct of persons with that role-identity, or their treatment by others. Rather, an institutional definition of a role-identity as a prototype (more precisely, a prototype of its enactment) would be based on a set of exemplars of its enactment, whose distinguishing properties or qualities would be that they uphold certain rights and responsibilities, as a function of both the person's conduct and the way he or she is treated by others (or allows himself or herself to be treated).

There is some indirect evidence—from the way performance evaluations are generally conducted in the workplace—that it is not a theoretical refinement, but an empirical reality, that institutional definitions of role-identities take the form of prototypes. First, if institutional definitions of role-identities take the form of prototypes, then judgments of the sufficiency of enactments of role-identities must be a matter of degree, not categorical. Second, if institutional definitions of role-identities take the form of prototypes, then judgments of the sufficiency of enactments of role-identities must concern whether prototype rights and responsibilities are upheld, which is a matter of the effect of the person's conduct and treatment by others across interactions over time, rather than the acts and treatment that are produced in any instance (except in highly regimented organizations, and for taboo behaviors such as public lewdness, violence, etc.). Both of these predictions are empirically borne out by the way performance evaluations are conducted in the workplace. Performance items are usually graded on scales; overall evaluations are stated in terms

---

but even in ones that generally are not highly regimented, there may be restricted areas where certain specifics are obligatory (e.g., certain details of decorum and procedure in courts of law). However, institutions so highly regimented as to contradict the argument here seem the exception (at least in Western, postindustrial societies). Regimentation (not its absence) is the marked condition in ordinary discourse and it is generally newsworthy when regimented organizations are discovered to not be so highly regimented after all (e.g., the publicity given to U.S. soldiers' misconduct during the Vietnam War).

of a mix of strengths and weaknesses; and evaluations generally are based on a review of a person's enactment of a role-identity over a span of time on multiple occasions, not made "on the spot" regarding a single instance.

Thus, the institutional aspects of role-identities are prototypes that represent the rights and responsibilities that sufficient enactments have to uphold, not scripts that make certain acts and treatment by others obligatory. Given this, it falls to individuals to devise acts and secure treatment by others—within the limits of the business at hand and the course of the present interaction—that most approximate the prototype for enacting their role-identity. In that case, the analysis of the enactment of role-identities must expand its scope beyond a traditional concern with the institutional aspects (how role-identities are acquired, and what rights and responsibilities are involved), and even beyond such concerns as Goffman's with expressive resources for enacting role-identities when others cooperate and there is an established script. In addition, we must be concerned analytically and practically with the expressive resources and interactional process involved in enacting role-identities when there are obstacles to doing so produced by others (inadvertently or knowingly) and/or in novel situations.

EXPRESSIVE RESOURCES FOR ENACTING ROLE-IDENTITIES

Given that role-identities are defined in terms of rights and responsibilities within specific institutional frames, then they must be enacted by fulfilling those responsibilities and being accorded those rights. This suggests that in the normal course, there must be ways for the enactment of role-identities to be a by-product of engaging in the business at hand, not an explicit component of the communicative acts produced during an interaction: "Ordinarily, maintenance of face is a condition of interaction, not its objective" (Goffman, 1967, p. 12). In that case, the principal expressive resources for enacting role-identities must be ones that are embedded within communicative acts, and display—rather than state—orientations to oneself or the other as having certain rights and responsibilities, or that constrain the course of the interaction in such a way as to include or conclude with an exercise of one's rights or fulfillment of one's institutional responsibilities.

For example, suppose a supervisor calls his or her staff together to discuss work issues, and one of the staff members comes and joins the group as requested, but says on arriving, "Now what?" with an impatient tone. The staff person has not actually done anything disobedient or insubordinate. However, the question and tone of the utterance implicate a judgmental attitude, tacitly laying claim to the staff person's right and competence to judge the supervisor and downgrading the supervisor's status to that of someone subject to the subordinate's judgment—each arguably contrary to the prototypes (in at least some organizations) for enacting the role-identities of both subordinate and supervisor. Such an instance poses a rhetorical problem for the supervisor insofar as the supervisor's preference is to avoid being treated in a way that downgrades his or her status or inappropriately upgrades the subordinate's. The problem for the supervisor is how to fashion turns at speaking to redress the offense and/or constrain the interaction to inhibit its recurrence, especially because redressing that offense explicitly, when the subordinate's surface utterance does not make it relevant to do so, could have an unwanted "meaning in context" of being a defensive or paranoid act.

Analysis of the transcripts reveals two principal aspects of communicative acts that figure in the participants' turns at speaking to enact their role-identities. The first of these is *relevance relations* among communicative acts, as discussed earlier. What a person's communicative acts make relevant or irrelevant affects the meaning in context of what is said or done afterward, and thus "allows" or "disallows" the acts of others and vice versa. The second aspect of communicative acts that figures in the enactment of role-identities is *presuppositions*. Communicative acts can differ in terms of whether they presuppose (among other things) certain rights and responsibilities that are central to the role-identities of the people involved. This section of the essay provides an overview of relevance relations and presuppositions, thus laying the technical foundation for the analysis of the transcribed interactions.

Relevance Relations

The meanings of utterances and nonverbal displays in context cannot be explained solely in terms of the meanings that their intrinsic qualities give them (e.g., their form and component parts). The intrinsic qualities of utterances and nonverbal displays are constant, but their meanings in context are not. Instead, their meanings in context are based on how they are relevant (Sanders, 1987; Sperber & Wilson, 1986).

Sperber and Wilson conceived of *relevance* as a matter of individual cognition—a matter of whether utterances and nonverbal displays make any difference to the interpreter's assumptions (cognitive model) about the world. Insofar as they do they are relevant (to the interpreter), and their meaning is what they convey to the interpreter or call attention to about the world that makes a difference to the interpreter's held assumptions.

In contrast, my work (Sanders, 1987) defines *relevance* as a matter of meaning relations among the component tokens of a discourse or interaction—most centrally, for present purposes, a matter of how communicative acts contribute to the progress and coherence of the whole. Thus, the relevance of communicative acts is a public, rather than a private, phenomenon. In this view, the relevance of communicative acts is a function of which among their possible meanings coheres them with other acts to form a whole; reciprocally, the "meaning in context"[14] of an utterance or nonverbal display is analyzed as being the "specific interpretation" that makes it relevant—contributes to the progress and coherence of the whole—to what has been said or done previously and/or subsequently in the interaction. This predicts that the way an unfolding interaction has been cohered up to a given point constrains how the next communicative act will be relevant and thus interpreted, but that it can happen instead that the possible meanings of the next communicative act may only be relevant if prior acts are reinterpreted and cohered differently. It is this interactional view of relevance that applies to the issues here.

The analysis of relevance, in terms of meaning relations among the components of interactions, has implications about communication strategy (Sanders, 1987). Given that the "meaning in context" of a communicative act depends on which among its possible meanings makes it relevant in the interaction, it follows that only communicative acts that are relevant, and relevant on a specific basis, warrant having a specific "meaning in context" attributed to them. At any point in any interaction, then, there are limits on what communicative acts a person can produce that would have any "meaning in context," and even fewer with an intended or desired one. Consequently, the communicative acts that each person produces in an interaction may change what acts relevantly follow, or may change the basis of relevance, and thus the "meaning in context," of any following acts and thereby may change the disposition of others in the interaction to produce or avoid certain communicative acts. This aspect of the relevance relations among communicative acts can be exploited for tactical purposes—acts can be fashioned to constrain what it would be meaningful or desirable for others or oneself to subsequently say and do in the interaction.

By affecting the coherence and attributed meaning of communicative acts, the relevance relations among acts functionally allow or disallow (make more or less probable) what people go on to say or do in an interaction, regardless of whether the acts are knowingly produced for the sake of having that effect. The application of this theoretical frame to the enactment of role-identities is this: Even if one has the expertise and commitment needed to do so, being able to coherently enact one's role-identity in a way that approximates the template for it depends on what is

---

[14]"Meaning in context" is used throughout this chapter for the sake of brevity, but should be understood as having the technical sense alluded to here. To indicate this technical sense, the locution "meaning in context" appears in quotation marks throughout.

made relevant interactionally in terms of one's own conduct and the way others treat one. Deficient enactments of a role-identity thus arise from either or both of two contingencies:

1. If one's own acts make treatment by others relevant, which diverges from the prototype for enacting one's role-identity, and one is treated accordingly, then one has tacitly enacted one's role-identity in an institutionally deficient way.

2. If others' acts fail to make conduct of one's own relevant, which approximates the prototype for enacting one's role-identity, or if others make relevant conduct of one's own, which diverges from the prototype, and one acts accordingly rather than trying to reform the interaction, this too tacitly enacts one's role-identity in an institutionally deficient way.

Presupposition

Although presupposition has been broadened considerably beyond its original sense in formal semantics, and I broaden it further here, it is important to preserve its technical aspect. A *presupposition* is a claim or proposition, inferred from the rules of a communicative act, that the conditions exist that satisfy the rules of the act (i.e., for a communicative act to occur, be formed, and be produced as it was presupposes that certain conditions exist). Persons who produce communicative acts are accountable if the acts' presuppositions fail.

Presuppositions are distinct from such constructs as *background knowledge, preconceptions,* and so on. These refer to the personal cognitive frames that the recipients of communicative acts impose, which give the acts special meanings. These personal frames have no principled tie to the specifics of a communicative act. Nor would the person who produces an act generally be held accountable if the special meaning that is conveyed by an act, through the imposition of some such cognitive frame, is not borne out or does not cohere in the present context.[15]

---

[15]The exception to this is when the cognitive frame (e.g., background knowledge) imposed on a communicative act is not personal, but communal, as in the case of cultural knowledge. If special meanings conveyed on that basis do not cohere in the present context, then the membership in the community of the person who produced the act, or his or her character, may be called into question. This is illustrated by Philipsen's (1975) depiction of the confusion about a nonnative's character that natives of a community experienced when the nonnative produced talk as a response to aggression, rather than physical force—acts that had special meanings for community members, but did not cohere in those terms, or cohered in negative ways, in the immediate context. But in such instances, the person who produced the act is not held accountable for the kind of qualitative defects that he or she would be if a presupposition failed.

Presupposition and Sentence Meaning. To recap the origin of presupposition in formal semantics, consider that we can parse the semantics of sentences into: (a) components (related to the verb) that specify some property of objects or a relationship between objects, and (b) components (related to noun phrases) that specify those objects that have that property or relationship (Fillmore, 1971). We can then say that a sentence *asserts* as true or false that specified object(s) have the specified properties or relationship, and *presupposes* the existence of the object(s) that the sentence is about. Thus, the sentence "Joe's daughter likes ice cream" presupposes that a person exists who is Joe's daughter (the object that the sentence is about) and asserts that the asymmetrical relationship of "liking–being liked" exists between that object (the daughter) and a second object (ice cream). The truth value of a sentence is a function of the assertion, of whether the specified object has the asserted property or relationship.

The technical problem that arose about this was what truth value a sentence has if an object about which something is asserted does not exist (e.g., if, in the sentence "Joe's daughter likes ice cream," there were no daughter). The debate was whether an assertion about an object that does not exist is false, or whether its truth or falsity is moot and the sentence has some third value—neither true nor false (Kempson, 1975; Wilson, 1975).

Presupposition and Language Pragmatics. Lewis (1979) shifted the ground of the debate from semantics to pragmatics. He took the position that a concern with the truth value of sentences whose presuppositions fail is narrow and overlooks a great deal because it disregards what he called "the kinematics of presupposition." Rather than assuming, as per formal semantics, that there is a static, known reality that people refer to as they produce and interpret sentences, Lewis proposed that persons' realities are changed over the course of a conversation. There is often ambiguity, vagueness, variability, or indefiniteness in beliefs about the objects that sentences are about. Hence, on the strength of something akin to Grice's (1975) Cooperative Principle, if a sentence is produced that presupposes that such objects exist or have certain qualities, hearers are led to effectively alter reality and make it be so, bearing out the presupposition.

Lewis' (1979) article was written in the context of a wider interest in presupposition from a pragmatic, rather than a semantic, perspective, much of it explicitly tied to Grice's (1975) idea of conventional implicature (e.g., Atlas & Levinson, 1981; Kartunnen & Peters, 1979). The basic idea is that a sentence presupposes not just that some object exists, but—by virtue of its phrasing—that the speaker believes it, and believes that other objects and conditions exist relevant to what the sentence asserts.

For example, Sentences 1a and 2a assert the truth of the state of affairs described in Sentences 1b and 2b. At the same time, to phrase Sentences 1a and 2a to include the italicized words presupposes (that the speaker believes) that the relevant conditions exist that are described in Sentences 1c and 2c. That Sentences 1c and 2c are pragmatic presuppositions is "tested" by considering that their truth or falsity makes no difference to the truth or falsity of Sentences 1b and 2b.

1a. Martha *realizes* that she's smarter than Jack.

1b. Martha accepts as true that she's smarter than Jack.

1c. Martha is smarter than Jack.

2a. I *managed* to get the dishes washed.

2b. I got the dishes washed.

2c. It was difficult to get the dishes washed.

Presupposition and Speech Acts.   We can extend the construct of *presupposition* from the constative aspects of utterances discussed previously to the performative aspects.[16] Aspects of the form and content of sentences presuppose, and thus tend to make be (the speaker's beliefs in) certain existential conditions regarding what the sentence is about. Similarly, certain (speaker beliefs about) social conditions are presupposed (especially concerning qualities of the speaker–hearer relationship, and qualities of the persons involved), and thus are often made to be by the performance of speech acts, barring any well-formed beliefs to the contrary on the hearer's part.

By definition, speech acts are the institutional meanings that utterances have when they are produced under certain conditions (Searle, 1969). Insofar as an utterance is interpreted as a particular speech act, the idea here is that occurrence of that act presupposes that (the actor perceives that) the conditions exist and the rules are satisfied, thus giving the utterance its institutional meaning. For example, if an utterance is interpreted as a directive, the rules by which an utterance counts as a (felicitous) directive include that the speaker has the authority relative to the hearer to direct the other to do something, and that what the hearer should therefore do is feasible. For an utterance to be produced and interpreted as a directive presupposes that those conditions for felicitously producing that act exist: The speaker thereby potentially makes be, and makes visible that he or she believes it to be, that he or she has the authority to direct the hearer, and that it is feasible for the hearer to do what the speaker wants.

---

[16]Lewis (1979) did also discuss the presuppositions of performatives, but in terms of the existential claims that are involved in some performatives, not the social underpinnings of speech acts, which are of interest here.

It is controversial, however, to say that the occurrence of a speech act presupposes that its rules are satisfied, because this means it might not be so (i.e., that an utterance could count as, or be interpreted as, a specific act without satisfying all of its rules). Searle's (1969) own discussion ran the other way. He saw only one possibility: For an utterance to be produced as, and be interpreted as counting as, a specific act, the conditions that are specified in the constitutive rules must actually exist. This argues against extending the notion of presupposition to speech acts.

However, Searle's analysis overlooks the difficulty of reliably interpreting utterances as speech acts, considering the variability of the way speech acts can be expressed and the covert or subjective quality of the conditions specified by constitutive rules (Bach & Harnish, 1979; Green & Morgan, 1981; Sanders, 1987). Assuming that speech acts are interpreted reliably, and for now we have more intuition than evidence that they are, we have to posit that utterances are interpreted as speech acts on the basis of more than the constitutive rules of the act (e.g., the structural role of the utterance in an episode [e.g., Edmondson, 1981] and the kinds of acts a speaker is disposed to produce given the person's role-identity and background knowledge about him or her [Sanders, 1987]). The weight of these various factors might then warrant counting (or not counting) an utterance as a certain act, even when (some) rules are not clearly satisfied. If so, when a speech act occurs—when an utterance is interpreted as a particular speech act—it thereby presupposes that (the speaker believes that) the conditions exist that satisfy the rules (i.e., presupposes, rather than entails, it because they might not).

Searle's (1976) taxonomy of speech acts specified in more detail what amount to generic presuppositions that classes of speech act make. The taxonomy distinguishes five types of illocutionary force that utterances can have. Searle's characterizations of these five types are summarized next to highlight the conditions that each type of act presupposes.

1. *Assertives.* The content of utterances with such force is a belief predicated on the speaker that some physical or social condition exists. Assertives comprise acts such as stating, boasting, and complaining. Assertive acts differ from each other with respect to the speaker's interest in making his or her belief known to the hearer. (The speaker's [conventional] interest in having the hearer's knowing his or her belief, and the institutional rules and role relations on which that interest is based, are thus presupposed by any utterance that is understood as an assertive.)

2. *Directives.* The content of utterances with such force is a future act predicated on the hearer. Directives comprise acts such as requesting, commanding, and begging. Directives involve future deeds that the speaker

does not expect the hearer to undertake in the normal course, and that the speaker wants undertaken. Directive acts vary with respect to the relative power of speaker and hearer. (Hence, the relative power of speaker and hearer, and the institutional or task requirements on which expectations are based that the hearer will not do the indicated act in the normal course, are presupposed by any utterance that is understood as a directive.)

3. *Commissives.* The content of utterances with such force is a future act predicated on the speaker. Commissives comprise acts such as promising, threatening, and resolving. Commissives involve future deeds that the speaker intends to be publicly committed to undertaking, and that the hearer does not expect the speaker to undertake in the normal course. Commissive acts differ with respect to what the hearer's interest is in having the deed be undertaken. (Hence, the hearer's interest in the speaker's undertaking of the deed, and the institutional or task requirements on which expectations are based of what the speaker would do in the normal course, are presupposed by any utterance that is understood as a commissive.)

4. *Expressives.* The content of utterances is the speaker's subjective orientation toward some social or physical condition. Expressives comprise acts such as thanking, apologizing, regretting, welcoming, and disapproving. Expressives involve the speaker's orientation to conditions for which either the speaker or hearer is responsible. Expressive acts differ with respect to the speaker's interest in making known to the hearer his or her subjective orientation to that condition. (Hence, the speaker's or hearer's responsibility for the cited condition, and the institutional basis for the speaker's interest in making known his or her orientation to that condition, are presupposed by any utterance that is understood as an expressive.)

5. *Declarations.* The content of utterances is a change in a social rule or role predicated on the speaker's authority. By the fact of and at the time of their occurrence, these acts explicitly change current social conditions. Declarations comprise acts such as appointing, pardoning, overruling, and consecrating. All declarations involve rules or roles that are contingent on the rulings of an authority, and can only be performed by individuals with such authority. (Hence, the dependence on authority of cited rules or roles, and the authority of the speaker, are presupposed by any utterance that is understood as a declaration.)

As these summaries indicate, acts' presuppositions can "make be" what the interests are of speaker and/or hearer in a given matter, and what their institutional rights and responsibilities are—toward the matter at hand

and toward each other. If such presuppositions fail—if institutional realities cannot or will not be adjusted to bear out what an act presupposes—there are only a few ways for people in interaction to explain the failure. This would call into question either the speaker's knowledge or experience in regard to the institution, or his or her character or communicative competence within the institutional frame of the act.

In short, when the presuppositions of a person's acts are upheld, they either affirm or transform the institution that framed the act. When the presuppositions fail, the person's success in enacting his or her role-identity and participating effectively in the relevant institution are at risk. This is of particular relevance to the issues of interest here.

Presupposition and Turn-Taking.   Although it has not been discussed in these terms, much work on "talk-in-interaction" tacitly depends on this idea: What people orient to (respond to) as acts are introduced in sequential progressions is what the act's placement in the sequence presupposes. One topic in this regard is of particular importance in the analysis of the transcripts provided later—turn taking, based on work in conversation analysis (especially Sacks, Schegloff, & Jefferson, 1974).

Sacks et al. proposed that the orderliness of turn taking in conversation is a function of three rules for selection of next speaker, and that the rules are ordered so that each subsequent one is a default if the prior one is not applied. The rules and their order of application are as follows: At each turn-relevant transition place, the next speaker is: (a) selected by current speaker, or if not, (b) the first person who speaks next, or if not, (c) the current speaker who resumes or continues.

If taken at face value, without reference to the discussion in the last portion of the Sacks' et al. (1974) article, these rules seem to be a dead end for three reasons. First, except for the ordering of their application, these rules exhaust what can possibly happen at a turn-relevant transition place, and thus they are trivial as rules. Second, it is unspecified what a turn-relevant transition place (TRP) is: If TRPs are defined broadly enough, the idea is trivial because the next speaker cannot fail to be selected at a TRP; if TRPs are defined narrowly, they are counterfactual because, for any narrow definition of a TRP, there will be numerous instances where speakers usurp the floor at other places. Third, the ordering of the rules is empirically questionable: Next speaker is sometimes not the one that current speaker selected; next speaker sometimes self-selects at the same time that current speaker continues (leaving undecidable whether next speaker is "wrong" that there was a TRP, or current speaker is "wrong" for having applied the third rule out of order, current speaker continues).

The thrust of the Sacks et al. conceptual discussion following presentation of these rules, however, is that they should not be regarded as statements of how people do turn taking. Instead, they are statements of the rules that turn taking presupposes are satisfied. As people take turns, "reality" is adjusted to bear out these rules. For example, Sacks et al. made the point that a TRP is a joint construction of the participants in conversation, not an objective feature of conversational turns. If next speaker begins in the grammatical middle of current speaker's utterance, and current speaker stops at that point, they have jointly oriented to that point as a TRP, and by doing so have made it be a TRP. By the same token, if a person takes the floor at a given juncture, and others who might speak or have started to speak give way, this presupposes that the former's taking the floor is the default option at that point, making moot any prior rules that might have applied and selected someone else.[17]

Turn-taking rules vary with the institution, especially with the task at hand and the special privileges of certain speakers in that institutional frame to have the floor (e.g., because of rank or responsibility). Restrictions may also be created on possible TRPs, and the application of the rules for selecting of next speaker may be altered in that way. In formalized settings, the floor is allocated according to certain protocols, or it is in the purview of an official of the proceeding to have standing authority over the allocation of turns at speaking (especially in courtrooms, classrooms, and other official proceedings). Greatbatch (1988) observed that, during interviews, the turn-taking protocol is that the interviewer has the floor as long as he or she wishes—until the interviewer states the question the interviewee is to answer, thus relinquishing the floor. Schegloff (1988–1989) and Clayman and Whalen (1988–1989) showed that a televised interview of George Bush by CBS newsman Dan Rather gave the impression of having degenerated from an interview into a verbal "brawl" because Bush did not adhere to the turn-taking protocol for interviews. Coupled with Rather's effort to reassert the protocol and then his abandonment of it, their turn-taking practices cumulatively presupposed and made be a different activity from interviewing and different role-identities than they "officially" had—to Rather's disadvantage (the professional interviewer) more than Bush's (the politician under fire).

In summary, if someone takes or holds the floor and others cooperate,

---

[17]In this respect, the rules for turn taking are similar to Grice's (1975) maxims. Although the maxims seem to specify how people (should) compose their utterances, they are actually statements of what people presuppose about the content of others' utterances (that the utterances are intended to be relevant; are intended as expressions of what the speaker believes to be true; and are as unambiguous, clear, and informative as the speaker believes is possible or needed).

that presupposes a privileged claim to the floor. Likewise, controlling access to the floor in ways that are institutionally the prerogative of a person with a specific rank or responsibility, and being "allowed" to do so by others, presupposes that the speaker has that rank or responsibility.

THE DATA: ENACTMENTS OF ROLE-IDENTITIES IN THE WORKPLACE

The three transcribed interactions analyzed in this section are taken from Wiseman's (1975) documentary, *Welfare*. The documentary spans a work-day in a social-services center in New York City, and is composed of a variety of interactions between staff members and clients, staff members among themselves, and clients among themselves. The transcribed inter-actions analyzed here have two things in common: they are between supervisors and subordinates (exclusively so in two cases, primarily so in the third), and they are interactions about current work problems. In two cases, the interaction was initiated by the subordinate; in the third, it was probably initiated by the supervisor, but the film does not show it.

The analysis of the three interactions is intended to empirically ground the central claims of the previous conceptual and theoretical discussion: that the enactment of role-identities is an interactive process, that it may also be rhetorical, and that role-identities tend to be enacted tacitly by means (in these interactions, and presumably more generally) of relevance relations and presupposition.

An analysis of the enactment of role-identities must be organized around the institutional definitions or prototypes involved—in this case, those for supervisor and subordinate. This is not simply a matter of defining the terms *supervisor* and *subordinate*. Rather, it is an empirical question. The prototypes for enactments of supervisor and subordinate (hereafter $PROTO_{sup}$ and $PROTO_{sub}$ respectively) undoubtedly vary across organizations and institutions, local customs, national cultures, and so on. In lieu of directly finding what the prototypes pertaining to these data actually were for that organization and those participants at the time (recall that the interactions were filmed in 1975), I have devised provisional ones, based on: (a) how those role-identities were enacted in the one interaction that does not seem rhetorically problematic, (b) the apparent expectations of participants in the interactions that do seem rhetorically problematic, (c) other supervisor–subordinate interactions in the documentary, and (d) my own institutional experience. In this organization, these role-identities have the distinctive aspect that subordinates (especially caseworkers) gen-erally have their own professional expertise and responsibilities, which are incumbent on them to uphold and incumbent on supervisors to respect.

Supervisors have more experience, and thus can function as sources of advice or guidance if asked; they also have authority over the delegation of work, subordinate actions outside the subordinate's immediate jurisdiction, the distribution of work, worker absences and leaves, the quality of the work environment, and so forth. Provisionally, $PROTO_{sup}$ and $PROTO_{sub}$ are as follows:

1. *Supervisors*, in interaction with subordinates, prototypically are enjoined to do the following: respect subordinates' professional jurisdiction, provide resource and procedural support for the exercise of their responsibilities, exert leadership, give direction, give instruction and explanation, give permission or authorization, delegate work and responsibility, make decisions, solve problems, and resolve disagreements.

2. *Subordinates*, in reciprocal interaction with supervisors, therefore are enjoined to do the following: take responsibility for their professional jurisdiction, seek procedural and resource support from supervisors, respect supervisors' authority, seek and take direction, seek and take instruction and explanation, seek permission or authorization for actions beyond their own jurisdiction, take on assigned work or responsibility, and uphold supervisors' decisions, solutions to problems, and resolutions of conflict.

The interactive aspects of the enactment of these role-identities are indicated fragmentarily as the analysis proceeds. However, the point can be made in summary fashion beforehand. In each interaction, the degree to which the supervisor provided direction is the degree to which the subordinate deferred to it and vice versa; the degree to which the subordinate took control of the interaction is the degree to which the supervisor did not provide direction and vice versa. There was rough equivalence for each one of an interacting pair in their degree of approximation of or divergence from the prototypes for enacting their role-identities.

The enactment of role-identities seems to have involved rhetorical problems in two of the three interactions (Interactions 2 and 3). In both, the subordinate's problem seems to have been to surmount the supervisor's preference, or opposition to the subordinate's preference, for how to act on the matter at hand, without diverging from $PROTO_{sub}$ so much as to be insubordinate. The supervisor's problem in both cases seems to have been to achieve resolution of a matter on which their judgment was being resisted by the subordinate, yet without infringing on the subordinate's jurisdiction or giving direction precipitately (without understanding and respect for the subordinate's approach), thereby not diverging from $PROTO_{sup}$ so much as to be ineffectual or incompetent.

Note that there were individual differences in responsiveness to these problems. The subordinates in both interactions were more rhetorical than the supervisors in enacting their role-identities (i.e., they more extensively fashioned turns at speaking in ways responsive to the cited problems). Further, the subordinate in Interaction 2 in particular, but also the supervisor, responded to those problems more effectively than did their counterparts in Interaction 3, in the sense that the former pair achieved what the latter pair did not: (a) They coherently produced communicative acts consonant with the prototype's for enacting their role-identities, despite constraints in the interaction against it; (b) they produced communicative acts that constrained the course of the interaction in a way that favored the enactment of their role-identities approximating the prototypes; and (c) they resolved their coordination problems and completed the business at hand.

The order of presentation of the transcribed interactions is from least to most rhetorically complex, and from the interaction in which the enactment of role-identities most closely approximates the prototypes to interactions in which enactments of role-identities are progressively more discrepant from those prototypes. The analysis of the three interactions is presented in two stages. First, the full transcripts of Interactions 1 and 2 are given, along with an explanatory gloss of their content, followed by a comparative analysis of the differences in the way the respective supervisors and subordinates enacted their role-identities. Second, the full transcript of Interaction 3 is given, along with an explanatory gloss, and then it is analyzed in comparison with the first two.

Interaction 1: Prototype Enactments of Role-Identities

In Interaction 1, the subordinate is a caseworker who went to his supervisor to get confirmation that he correctly understood the status of a client who had come for help to meet housing costs after an expected benefits check had not arrived. The client's case evidently had been transferred recently from the city's jurisdiction to the jurisdiction of the Social Security Administration, giving it the status of a "conversion case." The caseworker was uncertain why the client had been referred back to the city agency for "home relief"; if hers were a conversion case, she would not be eligible for home relief from the city.

T1: Welfare (36:56–38:06).[18]   The female supervisor, FS_1, is seated at her desk; the male caseworker, MW_1, comes to the desk and stands in front of it as they both look through the file he places in front of her. The camera is

---

[18]The beginning and end of segments in the documentary are indicated with reference to the minutes and seconds of elapsed time after the first video frame following the title.

behind and to the right of MW$_1$, shot over his shoulder at FS$_1$, except for opening and ending shots of MW$_1$ from behind FS$_1$.

```
 1. MW₁:    She claims she's been on assistance here since
 2.         Ma:rch. (1.5) She was living, she was– (0.8) she
 3.         has this– (0.2) uh, rent receipt from the Hotel
 4.         Marque:z, dated one, two, seventy fou:r:
 5. FS₁:    mm↓hm
 6.         (0.5)
 7. MW₁:    So apparently it's a con↑version, but here they
 8.         have her as–
 9.         (1.0)
10. MW₁:    C'n you make this out ↑here? ((looking at file))
11. FS₁:    ess ess aye ((SSI)) benefici ⌈ ary
12. MW₁:                               ⌊ (yes,) which means that
13.         she was– a conversion
14.         (0.3)
15. FS₁:    which ⌈ means   that    she    was    a   con⌉ver:sion,=
16. MW₁:          ⌊ so how could she– (0.3) cuz everythi–⌋
17. FS₁:     ⌈ ye:s.
18. MW₁:   =⌊ (For them) to give her: a hundred do:llars
19.         (2.0)
20. MW₁:    eh– she obviously is a con↑ver ⌈ sion ↓case ⌉
21. FS₁:                                  ⌊   It's a   ⌋
22.         conver:sion⌈ æ:::            ⌉=
23. MW₁:              ⌊ Nothin' we can ⌋ =⌈ ↑do
24. FS₁:                                 ⌊ either that or they
25.         would've assumed (in error) that she was, and it
26.         doesn't seem like it since she's been in receipt
27.         of assistance ⌈ since March ⌉
28. MW₁:                  ⌊ But I don't ⌋ understand=
29.         ((pointing to a paper in the file))
30.         =is they're saying needs home re↓lief.=
31. FS₁:    =Well, apparently, they just, eh::, are ho:ping that
32.         she can get some help here or wanted to get rid of
33.         her either one. ⌈ .hhh (0.1) Becuz uh: ⌉
34. MW₁:                   ⌊ (Yuh:) I– I was won ⌋ dering if
```

```
35.              they were inferring ((≡ implying?)) that– (.) her
36.              eligibility had been uh::m (0.8) (a– a–) deni:ed, for
37.              assist– but they ⌐ (wouldn't) ⌐
38. FS₁:                         └ did she  ┘ give us the phone number?
39. MW₁:    No, no ⌐ (      )
40. FS₁:           └ No, they never give us ⌐ phone numbers ⌐ to call.
41. MW₁:                                    └ (No they don't) ┘
42. MW₁:    She's at– (.) now:: she's at the Hotel Va:sque:z.
43. FS₁:    Oh– (0.2) yeah well she'll have ⌐ to put  ⌐ through=
44. MW₁:                                     └ (uh huh) ┘
45. FS₁:  =the change of address with them and we can not help
46.              her here, it looks as if she's a conver:sion case=
47.          =⌐ (        )
48. MW₁:    ⌐ └ She is is a conversion case, obviously, yes.
49.              (0.5)    Well, I'll inform her of this.
```

Interaction 2: Subordinate Leads Supervisor

A caseworker has come to his supervisor about a problem. He found that an action to close a client's case was in error. Until late in the interaction, the supervisor apparently thought the caseworker need not be concerned because the client had not yet had a "fair hearing" on the matter (a fair hearing is evidently for appeals of agency actions). The caseworker apparently thought the matter should not involve an appeal—that it was a procedural error to take the action in the first place, and that he (the caseworker) should take the file to the responsible unit/person to have the action voided.

T2. *Welfare* (101:44–102:30).   MW₂, the male caseworker, and MS₂, the male supervisor, are standing at a desk or table, shoulder to shoulder, at about 45° to each other, much of the time looking down at the case file MW₂ has brought over as they talk. The camera is across the desk from them.

```
1. MW₂:    No Tom, you're mis,understa:nding ⌐ ↓me. ⌐
2. MS₂:                                       └ Yes ┘ I know
3.              what your (idea) is=
4. MW₂:    =She got ↓thi:s.
5.              ((showing document in file))
6. MS₂:    ↑Ri↓ght ↑ri↓ght.
```

```
 7. MW₂:    She called the num↑ber?
 8. MS₂:    And she should⌐'ve gotten a fair hearing.⌐
 9. MW₂:             └ she        GOT       ┘ THIS
10.         co:nference?
11. MS₂:    yuh.
12. MW₂:    The conference said her case would be clo:sed,
13.         so they're sending her this notice saying
14.        ⌐ yes, your case is gonna be closed.⌐
15. MS₂:   └ yuh,  but  she    didn't in  fact ┘ have a
16.         fair hearing. It was a conference, right?=
17. MW₂:    =Well– my question is ↓this,=she sa:ys that she
18.         gave them the information they ↑wan↓ted.
19. MS₂:    But I mean ⌐did sh–⌐
20. MW₂:              └ and if ┘ you look in the record,
21. MS₂:    Yeah! But I'm asking you did sh– =
22. MW₂:    =you will see that in fact she did.
23. MS₂:    Yuh! But I'm not–
24. MW₂:    So I wonder why they're closing the ↑case.
25. MS₂:    O:h, tha::, OK. (0.3) U::h This is u:h
26.         ((MS₂ is scanning a file document for information))
27.         from uh– u::h, from u::h George Drew's office.
28.         (0.8)
29. MW₂:    Horowitz worked on the,
30. MW₂:   ⌐Should I go up and give Horowitz the (      )?⌐
31. MS₂:   └Well sh– (0.2) alright, ↓ya:h, ge– go up and ask┘
32.         =Hightower (.) go up and ask ⌐Horowitz=
33. MW₂:                                 └↑huhh.hhh
34.         ((MW₂ is neatening and closing the file))
35.         =why they're=
36.         ((MW₂ starts turning away, MS₂ makes eye contact))
37. MS₂:    =clo⌐sing her⌐
38. MW₂:        └Fabulous.┘
39. MS₂:   ⌐ case.
40.      =└ ((MW₂ has started walking away behind MS₂))
41. MW₂:°   ((not looking back)) °Thanks Tom.°
42. MS₂:    Right. (1.5) That was a whole, ba::– (0.1)
43.         ((to MW₂ who does not look back)) ↑Thanks, ↓Noel.
```

44.   (0.5) ((MW$_2$ is now out of sight around a corner))
45.   Thanks, Noel.

Enactments of Role-Identities in Interactions 1 and 2

The overall impression of the enactments of the supervisor and subordinate role-identities in Interactions 1 and 2 is that they are almost opposites of one another. MW$_1$ oriented to his supervisor as an authority, and deferred to her; MW$_2$ oriented to his supervisor as "not understanding," and undertook to correct or instruct him. Reciprocally, FS$_1$ oriented to MW$_1$ as needing explanation, a "ruling" and direction. MS$_2$ oriented to MW$_2$ as someone to be listened to—someone to whom MS$_2$ owes "thanks." These orientations are manifest in several ways.

Relevance Relations.   Both MW$_1$ and MW$_2$ recurrently gave information in their turns at speaking. However, although these are the same speech acts on the surface, they are different communicative acts based on their relevance to the progress and coherence of the interaction. In MW$_2$'s case, the information was made relevant by MS$_2$'s "misunderstanding" him (Line 1); In MW$_1$'s case, it was made relevant by his own uncertainty about how to understand the discrepancy between what the client's file showed and the referral for home relief. Hence, the way MW$_2$'s information-giving was relevant gives it the "meaning in context" of an act such as giving correction or instruction regarding MS$_2$'s misunderstanding. Because MW$_1$'s information giving was relevant to his displayed uncertainty about his own understanding, its "meaning in context" (e.g., a request for confirmation or instruction) is correspondingly different from that of MW$_2$'s information giving.

Thus, MW$_2$'s enactment of his role-identity was almost the reciprocal of MW$_1$'s. To seek instruction or explanation, as MW$_1$ was arguably doing, is fully consonant with PROTO$_{sub}$. To instruct, as MW$_2$'s information giving did, is discrepant from PROTO$_{sub}$, and in fact more consonant with the reciprocal PROTO$_{sup}$.

The different "meanings in context" of the information giving by each subordinate, in turn, make relevant different acts by their respective supervisors. To be presented with the subordinate's expressed uncertainty about a client's status, as in FS$_1$'s case, makes relevant such acts as acknowledgment or correction of the information, explanation and instruction, a ruling, and/or direction. All of these are consonant with PROTO$_{sup}$, and FS$_1$ produced most of them: confirmation (Lines 15 & 17: "which means that she was a conver:sion, ye:s"), explanation (Lines 31–33: "they just, eh::, are ho:ping that she can get some help here or wanted to get rid of her either one"), and a directive and a ruling (Lines 43 & 45–46: "she'll have to put through the change of address with them and we can not help her here").

In contrast, for MS$_2$ to be given information to correct his misunderstanding makes relevant such acts as "disagreement" and "counterargument," "concession or compliance," or "disallowing" the information and ruling by fiat. Consistent with this, MS$_2$ protested that he understood (Line 6: "↑Ri↓ght ↑ri↓ght"), checked his understanding and/or disputed MW$_2$'s (Lines 15–16: "but she didn't in fact have a fair hearing; it was a conference, right?"), conceded to MW$_2$ (Line 25: "O:h, tha::, OK."), and acknowledged being indebted to MW$_2$ (Line 43: "↑Thanks, ↓Noel"). Although these acts may be consonant with the aspect of PROTO$_{sup}$ involving respect for subordinates' jurisdictions, they diverge from the aspect involving exertion of leadership. MS$_2$ only produced one act that involved the exertion of leadership—a directive—and that only occurred after MW$_2$ made it relevant (at Lines 31 ff.), so that it was flawed (the further analysis next).

Presupposition and Speech Acts.[19]   PROTO$_{sup}$ and PROTO$_{sub}$ have various speech acts as components. However, it is not necessarily the acts per se, but the social conditions that these acts presuppose, that links them with those role-identities. Each of those component acts presupposes an asymmetry of rights and obligations consistent with the relationship between supervisor and subordinate. Consider acts linked to PROTO$_{sup}$: To give direction presupposes that the speaker is authorized to do so, and that the hearer would not otherwise act as directed (needs direction); to resolve disagreements and make decisions presupposes that the speaker is both authorized and competent to do so; and to give instruction and explanation presupposes that the speaker is knowledgeable or experienced on the matter, and that the hearer is less so. The converse of these asymmetries is presupposed by acts linked to PROTO$_{sub}$: To seek and take direction presupposes the speaker lacks authority and/or competence to act independently, and that the hearer has both; to seek and take instruction and explanation presupposes that the speaker lacks knowledge or experience, and/or that the hearer has more knowledge and experience; and so on.

On that basis, the acts that each person's utterances count as (through relevance relations as discussed earlier) either approximate the prototypes

---

[19]The following analysis relies on bald assertions about what various acts presuppose. These assertions have their basis in the overview above of the generic presuppositions of each of Searle's (1976) types of speech act. Further refinement and justification of assertions about what these acts presuppose is undoubtedly possible, but unnecessary for present purposes—to show how enactments of specific role-identities diverge, and to show that they are enacted interactively and tacitly.

for enacting their role-identities (for MW_1 and FS_1) or diverge from them (for MW_2 and MS_2). MW_1's information giving has the "meaning in context" of seeking confirmation, explanation or instruction, direction, and so on—all presupposing that MW_1 lacked certain knowledge or experience, and/or that FS_1 had more knowledge and experience. By the same token, FS_1's confirmations, explanations, directives, and "rulings" all presuppose that she had greater authority, knowledge, and experience than MW_1. In both cases, these presuppositions approximate the prototypes for enacting their respective role-identities.

Contrary conditions to those presupposed by MW_1's and FS_1's acts seem to be presupposed by MW_2's and MS_2's. For MW_2 to judge that MS_2 was misunderstanding him (and presumably was not disposed for that reason to approve what MW_2 apparently wanted), and then to correct or instruct MS_2, presupposes that MW_2 had greater knowledge and/or experience. For MS_2 to protest that he understood, check for the rightness of his understanding, thank MW_2 for his help, and so on presupposes, at minimum, that MS_2 was not privileged and, to some degree, that MS_2 was dependent on MW_2's help.

This characterization of what is presupposed by the acts in Interaction 2 needs to be qualified, however. Going back to the relevance relations involved, MW_2's instruction of MS_2 can be regarded as a tactical orientation to, and thus acknowledgment of, MS_2's authority. If we infer that, from the outset, MW_2 intended and wanted to take the file to Horowitz to have the action to close the case voided, his instruction of MS_2 is instrumental to making relevant a positive, rather than a negative, response by MS_2 to a request from MW_2 for authorization—where MW_2's implicit concern with getting MS_2's approval of the request displays an orientation to his supervisor's right to give or deny approval. MS_2's participation in the discussion indicates that he is comparably oriented to his authority to approve or deny what MW_2 wants to do.

In Line 30, MW_2 asked for permission to take the file in question to the person responsible for the error, Horowitz—an act that presupposes that he was subordinate to MS_2. In Lines 31 ff., MS_2 directed MW_2 to take the file to Horowitz and find out why she closed the case—an act that presupposes that he had authority. Thus, MW_2 and MS_2 produced acts at that point that seem consonant with the prototypes for enacting their role-identities, and (but for the earlier qualification) at odds with the overall pattern of meaning and presupposition in their interaction. However, both of these acts are flawed, especially MS_2's directive.

MW_2's act of asking permission only partially conforms to $PROTO_{sub}$. The act, in its own right, presupposes that MS_2 had the authority to grant permission as noted previously; both MW_2's and MS_2's orientations during the interaction are consonant with this. However, the act was produced only after MW_2 instructed MS_2 about the case—in short, after he had taken care that permission would be given by getting MS_2 to concur about what was wrong. Thus, MW_2's instruction of MS_2 displays the former's orientation to MS_2 as not having the knowledge and experience consonant with his role-identity to understand that permission should be given. By delaying the request for permission until he had corrected MS_2, and thus ended MS_2's unwillingness to grant it, MW_2's act of asking permission conforms only partially and superficially with $PROTO_{sub}$.

With regard to MS_2's directive in Lines 31 ff., note that directing someone to do something is at odds with that person's asking permission to do it. To have given MW_2 a directive to take the file to Horowitz presupposes that he would not have intended or wanted to do it in the normal course. Yet MW_2's request for permission presupposes the opposite—that he did intend and/or want to do it. Although the two acts co-occur, so that MS_2 did not ignore MW_2's act per se, MW_2 had previously indicated his want and intention to have the action voided just by the effort he devoted to instructing MS_2 about the matter. Thus, MS_2's directive was hollow, and its antecedents give it the meaning in context of giving permission. For that reason, and because the two acts occurred simultaneously (Lines 30–31), MW_2 can and did respond to MS_2's act as giving permission, not a directive. Thus, MW_2 closed up the file and turned to walk away while MS_2 was still telling him what to do because he already knew what to do. Furthermore, MW_2 expressed appreciation for MS_2's act while it was still being produced (Line 38: "Fabulous") and afterward (Line 41: "Thanks Tom"), both of which are relevant in response to getting permission, not in response to a directive. Giving permission does conform to $PROTO_{sup}$, whereas producing a hollow directive that functions as giving permission does not.[20] Thus, MS_2's directive conforms to $PROTO_{sup}$ in the same partial and superficial way that MW_2's request for permission conformed to $PROTO_{sub}$.

Presupposition and Turn Taking. The turn taking in Interaction 2 is notably divergent from $PROTO_{sub}$ and $PROTO_{sup}$. Once this is shown, only brief attention needs to be given to the turn taking in Interaction 1—for the sake of contrast.

What is most notable about the turn taking in Interaction 2 (especially in Lines 7–16 and 17–24) is that it was the subordinate who held the floor and

---

[20]It is equivocal whether MS_2 took his own directive at face value or understood it as giving permission at MW_2's urging. At the end of the interaction, he called out his thanks to MW_2 twice. This would be relevant either to the directive as a directive (to thank MW_2 for going to do the task that MS_2 had assigned him), or to the directive as approving MW_2's request for permission (to thank him for a job well done in identifying the problem and the solution).

would not yield to his supervisor, despite the latter's repeated efforts to take the floor. MW_2's consecutive turns at speaking in each of those portions combine to form a virtual monologue across the various attempts at speaking made by MS_2, as follows (with the points where MS_2 spoke marked with an asterisk):

> She called the num↑ber? * She GOT THIS co:nference? * The conference said her case would be clo:sed, so they're sending her this notice saying * yes, your case is gonna be closed. * Well—my question is ↓this, she sa:ys that she gave them the information they ↑wan↓ted * and if you look in the record, * you will see that in fact she did. * So I wonder why they're closing the ↑case.

There are only two indications in the component turns of MW_2's monologue that MS_2 spoke at all. In transcript Line 9, MW_2 raised his voice when he talked over MS_2 to continue speaking ("She GOT THIS"). At Line 11, MW_2 used the shift marker "well," plus contrastive emphasis on "my," to continue speaking past a question that MS_2 asked ("Well—my question is ↓this"). Moreover, with two exceptions (discussed later), the content of MS_2's attempted turns at speaking in those portions of the interaction was disregarded entirely (except in the sense that MW_2's multiturn utterance responds to the misunderstandings in what MS_2 was trying to say).

The rules of turn taking posited by Sacks et al. (1974) are that, under ordinary circumstances, the option "current speaker continues" beyond a TRP applies only if current speaker does not select a next speaker and another speaker does not self-select. MS_2's efforts to take the floor as next speaker ordinarily would have precedence in that case over MW_2's retention of it, and this is particularly so considering their nominal asymmetry in rank. Yet MW_2 spoke in disregard of a direct question (Line 17)—the one time MS_2 completed a substantive turn at speaking—and spoke over or cut off MS_2's efforts to take the floor four times (Lines 9, 19, 22, 24) before his act of asking permission. MW_2 also spoke over MS_2's directive twice (Lines 30 and 38), and walked away while MS_2 was finishing it. The presupposition of this is that MS_2 had no claim to the floor except to express acceptance of MW_2's point and to give permission, which runs contrary to the rules of mundane conversation, let alone their differences in rank. For MW_2 to control the floor and, in addition, to deny MS_2 access to the floor when he bid for it are both discrepant from $PROTO_{sub}$.

Of course, this divergence from the prototype for enactment of MW_2's role-identity was, again, jointly achieved. In most of the instances where MW_2 talked over or cut off MS_2, MS_2 subsided rather than persisted, thereby jointly constructing with MW_2 that a TRP had not occurred and/or that he had no right to the floor. The only instance to the contrary is when MS_2 talked over MW_2 at Line 15, and completed his utterance to ask a direct question—a question that MW_2 disregarded and MS_2 did not manage to repeat.

In contrast, the turn taking in Interaction 1 conforms much more closely to $PROTO_{sub}$ and $PROTO_{sup}$; there was no competition for the floor to speak (except at Lines 15–16, discussed below), and thus no reversal of privileges regarding who controls access. Other instances of simultaneous speech did occur, but they occurred just prior to the grammatical end of the other's utterance and responded to its sense, and both produced them about equally: MW_1 started turns just prior to the ends of FS_1's utterances five times (Lines 12, 23, 28, 34 and 48), and FS_1 started turns just prior to the ends of MW_1's utterances four times (Lines 21, 24, 38, and 40). At two other points, MW_1 uttered acknowledgment tokens of FS_1's remarks while she was speaking (Lines 41 and 44).

Only at Lines 15 and 16 did MW_1 and FS_1 seem to not coordinate turns at speaking, where MW_1 appeared to be in the process of informing FS_1 about what he perceived as discrepancies between the client's referral to their office and documents in the file, indicating that hers was a conversion case. FS_1 took a turn at speaking to concur that this was a conversion case, whereas MW_1 resumed speaking to continue giving reasons why it seemed like a conversion case. Despite the extended talk over, and the fact that it was the subordinate who spoke contrary to the ordinary rules of turn taking and especially to the asymmetry of the role-identities of supervisor and subordinate, neither speaker interfered with what the other's turn contributed nor did they speak at cross-purposes.

Rhetorical Aspects of the Enactment of Role-Identities in Interaction 2.   The previous analysis shows that MS_2, to a degree, and MW_2, much more so, each fashioned turns at talk in a way that constrained participation in the interaction to favor enactment of their respective role-identities in ways approximating the prototypes, or diverging minimally from them. Insofar as their turns at talk were functionally means to that end, and moreover were adjusted (whether knowingly or unknowingly) to compensate for problems in enacting their role-identities that each created for the other in the interaction, the enactment of their role-identities was interactive and rhetorical.

Because of MW_2's responsibility for cases under his jurisdiction, which is included in $PROTO_{sub}$, it would risk diverging from $PROTO_{sub}$ if MW_2 acquiesced to his supervisor's mistaken opposition to what MW_2 wanted to do about the error he found. But for MW_2 to persist in seeking approval for something MS_2 initially opposed would also risk diverging from $PROTO_{sub}$ by possibly being insubordinate. Thus, the interaction put into conflict two components of $PROTO_{sub}$: that of exercising responsibility for one's professional jurisdiction versus respecting one's supervisor's authority.

The way MW_2 fashioned his turns at speaking sidestepped this temporary conflict between components of $PROTO_{sub}$ as follows. By providing MS_2 with an informational narrative about the basis of the error he had found, instead of rebutting MS_2's apparent understanding of the matter, MW_2 persisted in seeking approval to have the error corrected without displaying any disrespect for his supervisor's authority. This was also achieved by controlling access to the floor and not responding to MS_2's questions, thus preventing it from becoming relevant to take issue with MS_2's understanding (otherwise, to respect MS_2's authority, MW_2 would have to participate in his discourse about a fair hearing and risk having the interaction proceed from there on a different course from the one MW_2 evidently wanted). Finally, MW_2 displayed respect for his supervisor's authority, yet did give up responsibility for his professional jurisdiction, by asking for permission to have the error corrected once he had overcome MS_2's resistance to giving it.

Reciprocally, given his subordinate's evident unwillingness to accept MS_2's initial judgment on the matter, components of $PROTO_{sup}$ came into conflict. MS_2 could either exert leadership (by preempting further discussion and announcing a final decision about what MW_2 should do) or respect MW_2's professional jurisdiction, and thus facilitate the exercise of his responsibilities (by hearing out the reasons that MW_2 thinks something needs to be done about the error). MS_2 functionally reconciled these by being responsive to each in sequence. First, he showed respect for his subordinate's professional jurisdiction through much of the interaction by responding to MW_2's overview of the case as being information giving and not rebuttal, (i.e., by hearing him out and asking questions about the case). Second, after MS_2 changed his understanding of the case and agreed with MW_2's understanding, he then exerted leadership by producing a directive (albeit a hollow one) instead of the permission MW_2 sought to take the case back to Horowitz. For MS_2 to produce a directive rather than give permission in this instance asserts authority, whereas giving the permission MW_2 sought would be to openly follow MW_2's lead.

Interaction 3: Subordinate Discounts Supervisor

The situation in this interaction was somewhat more complicated than in the previous ones. The central figures are the female supervisor of a work area, FS_3, and a "patrolman," P (P refers to himself as a patrolman with the power to make arrests, but it is unclear whether he was a city policeman assigned to this agency or a security person employed by the agency).

Technically, FS$_3$ was not P's supervisor, but she was the authority to whom he was responding by virtue of her title, and he was nominally at her service. P had come or been called to the area after two clients had each become belligerent in their dealings with caseworkers under FS$_3$'s supervision and with FS$_3$ herself (these persons were referred to as *clients*, but actually were persons accompanying clients, a spouse and a mother, respectively, who were applying for medical benefits). Most of the interaction was between FS$_3$ and P, although there was some involvement by the two clients in succession. FS$_3$ seemed to want P to restore order, although she only formulated what she specifically wanted P to do once, regarding only one of the clients. A higher ranking male supervisor or administrator, MA$_3$, who had jurisdiction over FS$_3$, was present throughout as a silent observer until he took charge at the end.

The two clients' problems are as follows. First, a male client, mc, who had come with his pregnant wife, mcw, to obtain medical benefits for her wanted reconsideration of what had been arranged in their interview, apparently because the first benefits check would be mailed rather than issued right away, and possibly also because the benefits bypassed him as husband and caregiver. In the other case, a female client, fc, who was helping her mother, fcm, submit a claim for medical benefits became belligerent during interviews, first with a caseworker and then with FS$_3$, about the bureaucratic impasse raised by a line of questioning that placed fcm's eligibility in doubt (fcm's legal residence was out of state, and fcm's husband, although hospitalized and allegedly withholding support, was a state resident with income and property).

T3. Welfare (151:55–153:50).   Four agency staff and two pairs of clients are standing in front of an interview area. The staff are FS$_3$, the female supervisor of the area; P, a male patrolman; MA$_3$, FS$_3$'s male supervisor; and FCW, a female caseworker, who only watches. The clients are mc and his pregnant wife, mcw; and fc and her mother, fcm. The eight people are positioned as shown in the diagram below.

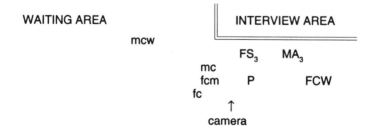

```
 1.  P:    ((to mc)) ... your pro:blem is ⌐(bein'ah) ⌐ taken
 2.  mc:                                 └(I'll tell) ┘
 3.  P:    care of by the other lady that went upstai:rs.
 4.  mc:   Yeah but I wanna know ⌐what's ⌐the problem=
 5.  FS₃:                        └ no–   │(0.2)
 6.  P:                                 └Right?
 7.  mc:    =⌐with me: why I can't get ⌐=
 8.  FS₃:    └excuse me– one minute– ┘
 9.  mc:   ⌐(          ) on Medicare to my wife⌐
10.  FS₃:  =│lemme just speak here,   (0.3) │=
11.  P:    └You' gonna    have   to   wait  ┘
12.  FS₃:   ⌐lemme just speak– (0.3)
13.  P:    =└till that lady comes down.=
14.  FS₃:  =his wife's case is being accepted through the
15.        ↓mail (0.1) and he should leave the ↓center. (0.2)
16.        He'll be getting a check in the ↓mai:l. (0.3) So,
17.        as far as I'm concerned this ⌐case ⌐is over with.=
18.  P:                                 └right┘
19.  P:    =Well, anyway, th– the worker's been talkin' to 'im
20.        ⌐(she's/is)   upstairs and (        )⌐
21.  FS₃:  └well, the worker walked away –     ┘ no, the
22.        worker is not seeing him anymore.
23.  mc:   No:, >she didn't walk away for no reason< because I
24.        ⌐was qui::et.
25.  P:    └she went upstairs and ⌐she's  coming⌐ back down.
26.  mc:                          └I was ↑qui:et. ┘
27.  FS₃:  I know what my work– where my wor⌐ker went. ⌐
28.  P:                                      └We:ll  (.)┘ listen.
29.  FS₃:  My worker is not going to see him ⌐anymore.  ⌐
30.  P:    ((to mc))                         └Whyn't you┘
31.        talk to– ((to FS)) who's your direc– who's you::,
32.        your supervisor down here.
33.  mcw:  She told us to go ho:me.
34.  mc:   >She told us ⌐to go home and I<  ⌐
35.  P:                 └Who's your super– ┘
```

```
36.  mc:    ⌐ >don't ⌐ (know about my wife, she's) <⌐
           =|         |                            |
37.  P:     ⌐ who's   |  your supervisor down here.|  =
           =|         |                            |
38.  FS₃:   ⌐ wait-   ⌐  wait.        (0.5)         ⌐

39.  mc:    ⌐ >(gonna give birth at any moment now)<⌐
           =|                                       | =
40.  FS₃:   ⌐  wait a minute (0.5) wait a minute (0.2) ⌐

41.  mc:    ⌐ >(even medically I don't) (      )<⌐
           =|                                    | =
42.  FS₃:   ⌐ wait a minute.    (0.8)      wait- ⌐

43.                ⌐ Lemme just talk-⌐
                 =|                  |
44.  P:   ((to mc)) ⌐ Look. You. Look.⌐

45.        ((P walks to mc camera–left across FS))

46.  P:    ⌐ go over the:re, ((hand on mc's shoulder to turn him))
47.  mc:   ⌐ (          )

48.  P:    go over there and siddown and ⌐ be cool::. A'right?
49.  mc:   ((walking off camera–left))    ⌐ (I'm tellin' you)(   )

50.        ((P turns and starts back camera–right across FS))
51.  FS₃:  ((to P)) ↓Look – I am the supervisor and I know
52.        where my worker ↓went. ((P returning crosses
53.        FS₃ and continues walking to off camera.))
54.  FS₃:  The worker ↑to:ld the client to leave the a:rea.
55.        (0.2)
56.  FS₃:  ((to MA₃ about P)) He's ↑walking a↑way.
57.        (1.0)
58.  FS₃:  ((to P off camera)) The worker asked the client
59.        to leave the area. The determination on the case
60.        was ma:de, they will get a check in the mail. Now
61.        he is carrying on and disrupti:ng (.) and I'd like
62.        him removed ⌐ (from- )
63.  P:               ⌐ Let's take care of this problem
64.        you're dealing with ⌐ now.
65.  FS₃:                      ⌐ Well, which problem do you
66.        want to take care of first?
67.  P:    The one you're having right ↑now.
68.  FS₃:  ⌐ I'm having two prob ⌐ lems right now.=
69.  fc:   ⌐ she won't (      )  ⌐
70.  FS₃:   ⌐ It's quite o:bvious:.
          =|
71.  fc:    ⌐ >What she wants to do, ⌐ she wants to cop out<⌐
                                     |                      | =
72.  P:                             ⌐  Which one are you    ⌐
```

73.   =gonna de::al with now?

74. FS₃: Awright, you wanna deal with this per– peo⌐ple

75. P: └↑ME?

76.   (1.0)

77.   ⌐ You   askin'   ↓me?⌐

78. fc: └>She wants to cop out.┘=⌐She's ashamed to walk away.<⌐

79. FS₃: =└She's disrupting the area┘=

80. FS₃: =⌐ and my other workers cannot <u>work</u> ⌐

81. fc: └ I'm not disru<u>p</u>ting anythi:ng ┘=

82. FS₃: = and there's a whole s::– ⌐commo⌐tion around here.

83. P: └ Let's ┘

84. P: Let's take care of the problem you're dealing with=

85.   =⌐now

86. FS₃: └<u>Which</u> problem is that. ↑These people?

87. P: Whichever one you're tak⌐ing next.

88. FS₃: └ OK, these people will be

89.   interviewed anytime they want to lower their

90.   voices and conduct the inter⌐view in a   <u>low</u> ⌐

91. fc: └>(Well when I lower)<┘=

92. FS₃: =⌐voice

93. fc: └>(my voice) She('ll) <u>still</u> insist on walkin' away,<

94.   >she's just usin' this as a copout. She's gonna<

95.   >tell my mother to go on 'n break in a mailbox and<

96.   >take some checks that don't even belong to< ↓her:,

97.   >that belong to my< ↓father.

98. fcm: ⌐(   ) ⌐

99. fc: └>She's gonna say┘ she want< =

100.   ((mc walks up and rejoins group))

101.   =>the hou:se,< ⌐okay::.

102. MA₃: └Good,

103. fc: >My mother don't <u>ow</u>n the house, how can ↑she<

104.   >(give her) the ↓house?<

105. mc: ⌐(   )

106. MA₃: └(c'n you) keep quiet now we c'n–┘ ah::

107.   ((to mc)) Are you fin⌐ished now?

108. P: ((to mc)) Listen, listen,

109.   go over here and siddown and wait for your, for

110.		your welfare worker ⌐ to come down. ⌐ A'right?
111.	mc:	└ I'll keep quiet. ┘
112.	mc:	°I'll keep quiet.°
113.	FS₃:	Wait–
114.	P:	A'right. D'yuh, d'yuh have a supervisor?
115.	MA₃:	Yuh. I'm the super ⌐↓visor.
116.	P:	└Awright. well, whyn't you
117.		deal wi– cuz I'm a patrolman here. That's– (0.2)
118.		the only (thin' I do), if there's an arrest to be
119.		↑ma:de, (0.2) I'm ↓here. ⌐Otherwise, (0.2) ⌐
120.	FS₃:	└ ( ) wait– ┘
121.	P:	social work is social ⌐ work.
122.	FS₃:	└ 'scuse me, (Mr. Bell). (0.2)
123.		Sarge– uh, whatever you're ⌐called
124.	MA₃:	((to P)) └ Awright, c'n he:, c'n
125.		he sit he:re till five o'clo:ck, and five o'clock
126.		you put them ↓out.=
127.	FS₃:	=wait–

In contrast to Interactions 1 and 2, there are marked coordination problems in Interaction 3 between FS₃ and P, and thus in the enactment of their respective role-identities. There seem to be two principal reasons for this. First, although FS₃'s turns at talk were often fashioned to exert her authority, they also made it relevant for P or the clients to respond in ways that disregard or show disrespect for her authority, as they in fact did. Such responses are treatment of FS₃ that diverge from PROTO$_{sup}$, and thereby are also conduct that diverges from what was incumbent on P and the clients in enacting their own role-identities. These reciprocal divergences from prototypes for enacting their role-identities on everyone's part create unpredictability, and therefore coordination problems.

The second reason for marked coordination problems in this interaction is not so much the equivocal relationship between FS₃ and P by virtue of their role-identities—in this case, although FS₃ was not P's supervisor, she was the authority to whom P was responding, and he was nominally at her service—but the equivocality of a patrolman's role-identity. A patrolman's rights and responsibilities are situational and variable, depending on what would be required to enforce order. This licenses a patrolman to self-define in each situation what his rights and responsibilities are, whether he is a subordinate or has authority, including the option to exercise authority over other nominally higher ranking persons (at least nonpolice staff) if circumstances require it.

In Interaction 3, P self-defined what his rights and responsibilities were, and thus what his official relationship was to FS_3, but problems arose because he unilaterally changed that self-definition twice. Initially (Lines 1–37) P's orientation was as ombudsman for mc, apparently to quiet mc by providing him with advice and counsel, largely ignoring FS_3 and treating her as mc's adversary. Subsequently (Lines 44–87), P shifted ground, orienting to mc as disorderly and to FS_3 as supervisor, seeming to ask her for direction. Finally (Lines 114–121), P moved to have MA_3 take responsibility for the situation, and to disengage himself from the interaction explicitly on these grounds: The kind of problems that FS_3 had been presenting to him were ones that MA_3 was responsible for by virtue of his role-identity, and P was not by virtue of his.

These unilateral changes in the way P was enacting his role-identity put the burden on FS_3 to be cognizant of them, and to reorient to the way P was enacting his role-identity to coordinate the enactment of her own role-identity with his. Failing to reorient would foster the coordination problems that did in fact occur. Although there is no a priori basis for considering any of P's self-definitions of his rights and responsibilities as divergent from the prototype for enacting the role-identity of patrolman, shifting unilaterally within a single interaction from one to the other would be.

Relevance Relations.   One prominent feature of the relevance relations involved in Interaction 3 is that FS_3 produced acts that make relevant either tangential or disruptive responses to her. The majority of FS_3's statements to P were descriptions of the current situation as it involved each pair of clients (regarding mc, Lines 14–17, 21–22, 29, and 51–62; regarding fc, lines 79–80 & 82, and 88–90 & 92). These descriptions seem to be relevant to (what she considered) disorderly client conduct, and to the presence of someone responsible for enforcing order, so that the "meaning in context" of her descriptions is a directive (indirectly expressed) to P to end the disorder (Fitch & Sanders, 1994). Although producing directives is consonant with the prototype for enactment of FS_3's role-identity, to have done so indirectly in this setting arguably diverged from $PROTO_{sup}$ by failing to exert leadership. Such indirection fails to exert leadership because it can have two undesirable side effects: It can make relevant an effort to "repair" the described situation or dispute the description, rather than comply with the directive (Sanders, 1991); and it leaves ambiguous and deniable that the hearer has been called on to do anything in particular (Fitch & Sanders, 1994), particularly if, as seems to be the case here, there were no standardized remedial action for P to take when FS_3 described the problematic aspects of the situation.

Because the indirection of FS_3's directives makes them ambiguous and deniable, and the information they comprise is disputable, what they make relevant other than compliance (which did not take place) is inaction (which was P's response) and rebuttal/belligerence (which was the clients' response)—precisely the reverse of the prototypical treatment of someone enacting the role-identity of supervisor. Thus, in the initial segment, when P oriented to the interaction as an ombudsman at mc's service, he disregarded FS_3's directive to enforce mc's departure, which was indirectly expressed in FS_3's story about mc's situation (Lines 14–17), and relevantly attended to its content instead. He did this first by renewing his initial suggestion that mc wait for the caseworker he had seen to request redress of the situation FS_3 described (Lines 19–20 and 25); then after FS_3 declared (twice) that "her" caseworker would not see mc anymore, P sought a supervisor over FS_3's head to whom mc could appeal (Lines 28 & 30–32 & 35 & 37). Correspondingly, by using descriptions of clients' situations as indirect directives, FS_3 made it relevant for both mc (Lines 23–24) and especially fc (Lines 69, 71, 78, 81, and 91 & 93–97 & 99 & 101 & 103–104) to dispute the correctness or completeness of FS_3's descriptions. This effectively treated FS_3 not as authority, but as a peer adversary of theirs, and treated P as the adjudicating authority.

Presupposition and Speech Acts.   Over the course of the interaction, P produced speech acts with inconsistent presuppositions about his rights and responsibilities, and reciprocally those of FS_3. FS_3 almost concurrently shifted what she presupposed about her authority in relation to P's, but in the opposite direction.

In the first segment (Lines 1–37), both FS_3 and P produced directives— hers indirect and his direct—and thus each presupposed having authority, but in conflict with what the other's acts presupposed. FS_3 indirectly directed P to remove mc from the center (Lines 14–15: "his wife's case is being accepted through the ↓mail (0.1) and he should leave the ↓center"). Contrary to FS_3's presupposition of authority to produce this directive, P ignored it. Instead, P produced several directives addressed to mc contrary to FS_3's (Lines 11 & 13: "You' gonna have to wait till that lady comes down"; Lines 28 & 30–31: "We:ll listen. Whyn't you talk to–"; Lines 44 & 46 & 48: "Look. You. Look. Go over the:re, go over there and siddown and be cool::. A'right?"). To produce these directives presupposes authority to do so—not just authority regarding mc's comportment, as might be consonant with the prototype for enactment of his role-identity as patrolman, but authority superior to FS_3's as to whether and how mc should seek redress for his grievance, which is wholly outside the jurisdiction of P's role-identity as he later defined it (Lines 118–119 &121: "if there's an arrest to be ↑ma:de, I'm here. Otherwise, social work is social work"). Instead P's directives about how mc should seek redress for his grievances presuppose an authority that supersedes FS_3's, and this was made explicit when he sought to find out to whom mc could appeal over her head.

P later upgraded the authority that his acts presupposed he had regarding mc to an authority that explicitly superseded FS$_3$'s when he addressed a directive to her—moreover, a directive that cut off and thus countered her only explicit directive to him:

61. FS$_3$:   he is <u>carry</u>ing on and disrupti:ng (.) and I'd like
62.   him removed ⌈(from–)
63. P: ⌊Let's take care of this problem
64.   you're dealing with now.

FS$_3$'s response affirmed, and thus made exist, the greater authority presupposed by P's directive: She asked P to clarify which problem he wanted to deal with (Lines 65–66). For P to provide an answer to this as he did (Line 67) again presupposed, and thus affirmed, that he had greater authority than FS$_3$.

65. FS$_3$:   Well, which problem do you want to take care of
66.   first?
67. P: The one you're having right ↑n<u>ow</u>.

However, P then shifted ground in what his utterances presupposed about the authority he had relative to FS$_3$ (Lines 72–73), presupposing instead that he was subordinate to FS$_3$. For her part, FS$_3$ did not shift ground correspondingly; rather, her acts continued to presuppose that P had greater authority. Thus, P asked FS$_3$ which problem *she* would deal with now (reversing from prior turns who between them should set the agenda). But FS$_3$ disregarded (overlooked?) this shift, and asked P her previous question about what problem *he* wanted to deal with (Line 74). Instead of answering this as he had before, and endorsing what it presupposed about his authority, P's phrasing and inflections display incredulity at the presupposition of FS$_3$'s question that it was up to him to select which problem to deal with (Lines 75 & 77):

72. P: Which one are you gonna de::al with
73.   now?
74. FS$_3$:   Awright, you wanna deal with this per– peo ⌈ple
75. P: ⌊↑ME?
76.   (1.0)
77.   You askin' ↓<u>me</u>?

A few turns after this, P partially reversed himself again in what his utterances presupposed about his authority versus FS$_3$'s—again issuing a directive to FS$_3$, but now directing her to "take charge" (Line 84). When she asked which matter he was directing her to present to him (Line 86), thus continuing to presuppose his greater authority, he again declined to exert his authority and referred the question back to her (Line 87).

84. P: Let's take care of the problem you're dealing with=
85.   =⌐now
86. FS$_3$: └Which problem is that. ↑These people?
87. P: Whichever one you're taking next.

Presupposition and Turn Taking.   Interaction 3 involves a group, which can make allocation of turns at speaking especially problematic (Edelsky, 1981). In terms of the enactments of role-identities, it is thus consonant with the divergences from prototypes of FS$_3$'s and P's enactments of their role-identities, coupled with their coordination problems, that it was P rather than FS$_3$ who took and was given the presumption of being "current speaker" or "person in charge," with the right to control who speaks next. FS$_3$ made an extended demand for a turn at speaking at two separate points that P spoke over (Lines 5 & 8 & 10 & 12, and 38 & 40 & 42–43); in a third such instance, FS$_3$'s bid for the floor was disregarded by MA$_3$ as well as P (Lines 120 & 122–123 & 127). In addition, in several turns (Lines 19–20, 28 & 30–31, 63–64, and 110–111), P continued directing mc to wait for "the lady who went upstairs," despite FS$_3$'s having said mc's case was settled (Lines 14–17) and "the lady" would not see him anymore (Lines 22 and 29), which effectively discounted that FS$_3$ had had turns at speaking at all. It is a recurrent feature of the interaction that FS$_3$ generally was given access to the floor only when other speakers did not preempt it. This diverges from PROTO$_{sup}$—that she exert leadership—and from the prototypes for enacting the role-identities of other participants on whom it was incumbent to respect her authority.

To some extent, it is what the content of FS$_3$'s indirect directives made relevant that confused the issue of who had access to the floor and who allocated turns. By making it relevant for clients to rebut her descriptions, with their rebuttals addressed to P, FS$_3$ tacitly gave the clients a claim to the floor. She also placed P in a mediator's position between the clients and FS$_3$, which gave him some responsibility for controlling turns at speaking.

Rhetorical Aspects of the Enactment of Role-Identities in Interaction 3.   The previous analysis indicates that, even more than MS$_2$ and MW$_2$ in Interaction 2, FS$_3$ and P each produced turns at talk that interfered with the other's, as well as their own, enactments of their respective role-identities. However, in contrast to MS$_2$ and MW$_2$, neither FS$_3$ nor P produced turns at talk sufficient to constrain the course of the interaction to overcome the rhetorical problems each created. This was because, unlike MW$_2$, P did not orient to the enactment of his role-identity as being dependent, in part, on FS_3's enactment of hers. This is arguably the basis for the coordination problems between P and FS_3 in enactments of their role-identities—problems that also allowed the clients to take an increasingly vocal part in the interaction (Lines 93–105) to the further detriment of the enactments of role-identities on everyone's part.

In FS_3's case, obstacles to enacting the role-identity of supervisor approximate to $PROTO_{sup}$ were created by others' acts, which functionally subverted FS_3's authority, as well as her passive acceptance of those acts (the denial to her of privileged access to the floor, rebuttal of her statements by clients, and P's lead in organizing the business at hand in Lines 62–92). Regardless of what motivated this treatment of FS_3, FS_3 "allowed" it by the way she fashioned her own turns at speaking—specifically, by the indirectness of her directives, which made it relevant (or failed to make it irrelevant) for P and the clients to produce those acts.

The only way in which FS_3's turns at speaking were fashioned responsively to the rhetorical problems she faced in enacting her role-identity was their inclusion of explicit and implicit claims to her authority through a number of self-references. She made explicit reference to her role-identity in her first turn at speaking after P had begun asking who her supervisor was (Line 51: "↓Look – I am the supervisor"). Beyond that, FS_3 produced several self-references that presupposed she was the person in charge (Line 17: "as far as I'm concerned this case is over with"; Line 27: "I know what my work—where my worker went"; Line 29: "My worker is not going to s<u>ee</u> him anymore"; Line 52: "I know where my worker ↓went"; Line 61: "he is <u>carry</u>ing on and disrupti:ng (.) and I'd like him removed (from–)"; Line 68: "I'm having <u>two</u> problems right now"; and line 80: "my other workers cannot <u>work</u>"). Although these assertions of the authority attendant on her role-identity could be viewed as FS_3's bids for P to treat her accordingly, they do not constrain the course of the interaction as to what would and would not be relevant regarding the way others treated her.

In contrast, P did fashion turns at speaking in ways that could constrain the course of the interaction, but he did so inconsistently. By shifting ground in the ways he oriented to his own and FS_3's authority, P was inconsistent about what course the interaction could take, and what parts he and FS_3 would play in that. However, the analysis here indicates that there was a consistency in the rhetorical aspect of P's turns at speaking, having to do with preferences for the course of the interaction that did not include a concern with FS_3's enactment of her role-identity as supervisor. P evidently favored (a) helping mc achieve redress, or at least an airing of his grievances; and (b) restoring order within his professional jurisdiction as a patrolman. The way the interaction with FS_3 and the clients progressed put into conflict these dual preferences for what the interaction included and how it concluded; it was possibly to overcome this conflict that P shifted his orientation toward FS_3's authority and then sought MA_3's intervention.

P's preference for the interaction to include redress of mc's grievances was rhetorically pursued in Lines 1–37 by: (a) his denying and then disregarding FS_3's turns at speaking against mc's interests, (b) his "reassuring" mc—contra FS_3's assertions—that he could present his grievance when the caseworker came back from "upstairs," and (c) his queries about whom mc could see "above" FS_3. Constraining the interaction to include at least an airing of mc's grievance would also quiet mc, and thus favor P's preference that the interaction conclude with a restoration of order. However, the interaction took a different course because neither FS_3 nor mc cooperated. FS_3 persistently countered P's reassurances that mc's grievance could be pursued, and mc, in turn, became more vocal and less orderly.

It is at that juncture that P shifted ground in his orientation to both mc and FS_3. He directed mc to withdraw to the waiting area, and then directed FS_3 to present to him the problem she was having "now." But this shift still favored P's preference for helping mc and for restoring order in the following way: It suspended mc's disorderliness without disqualifying his grievance or ejecting him, and it initiated diversion of FS_3's attention from mc's grievance to fc's disorderliness. This change in the business at hand was not achieved easily. It was when FS_3 restated her description of mc's situation, and produced her only explicit directive for P to eject him (Lines 51–54 & 58–62), that P interrupted with the directive that they should attend to the problem she was having "now." Instead of complying, FS_3 repeatedly asked what matter P wanted her to address, and he repeatedly directed her to take up the problem she was having now (Lines 67, 72–73, and 84–85), until finally he rephrased this as the problem she would take "next" (Line 87). FS_3 then introduced the situation involving fc. However, the introduction of fc's situation as the business at hand created even more disorder—through fc's extended rebuttal to P of FS_3's description (contra P's preference that the course of the interaction end with the restoration of orderliness), and then mc's return to the scene (contra P's preference for having mc's grievance aired). When MA_3 began to intervene, P responded by sending mc back to the waiting area to wait for the caseworker, and then explicitly asking for MA_3's intervention, and stating his subordinate part and his deference to MA_3's authority.

114. P: A'right. D'yuh, d'yuh have a supervisor?
115. MA_3: Yuh. I'm the super ⌈↓visor.
116. P: ⌊Awright. well, whyn't you

117.   deal wi– cuz I'm a pa<u>trol</u>man here. That's– (0.2)
118.   the only (thin' I do), if there's an ar<u>rest</u> to be
119.   ↑<u>ma</u>:de, (0.2) I'm ↓here. ┌Otherwise, (0.2)┐
120.   FS₃: └ (   ) wait– ┘
121.   P: <u>so</u>cial work is <u>so</u>cial work.

TWO CONCLUSIONS

On Interactional and Rhetorical Aspects of Enacting Role-Identities

Goffman's (e.g., 1959, 1967) analysis of social life centers on individuals. He explained individual conduct not as "expressive extensions of the character of the performer," but as "an integral part of a projection [of a definition of the situation] that is fostered and sustained by the intimate co-operation of more than one participant" (1959, pp. 77–78). In this view, performers enact their role-identities by following a script: As in theaters, each performer is independently responsible for enacting his or her part according to the script; the play comes off if each person fulfills that responsibility. This implies that, if there is trouble bringing off the play, it must either be due to the failure of one or more performers to provide the needed cooperation, or inadequacies in the script. Troubles arising from failures of cooperation or defects in the script are not treated by Goffman as matters that performers of good will can remedy, at least not during the performance in which the trouble arose. Accordingly, Goffman's analysis suggests that the outcome of such troubles will be social breakdown.

However, based on the data examined earlier, this view of individual performances and their interconnection is too simple, adequate to explain only the course of Interaction 1. Interaction 2 indicates that troubles in bringing off the play can arise even when the script is sound and the performers are cooperative. More important, both Interactions 2 and 3 reveal that, when troubles in bringing off the play arise, performers are not helpless to prevent them. Instead, they can and do fashion their turns at speaking in ways that have the potential to constrain the course of the interaction to overcome those troubles. This potential for performers to be rhetorical—to adapt the way they act their parts in situ to the way others are playing theirs in order to bring off the play—entails that performers are not independent, but interdependent—that the way they act their parts depends on the way others act theirs.

Modifying Goffman's analysis (i.e., conceiving performers to be rhetorical) accommodates a significant topic he left underanalyzed in his early work: the social definition of a person's character. Goffman (1967) pro-

posed that a person's character is not visible to others in routine circumstances, or even to the person him or herself, when what the person says
and does is called for in the script. Goffman argued that character is
manifest only in what one says and does in unscripted and risky situations
(i.e., nonroutine situations where there are no certain means to ends and
something of consequence rests on the outcome). The analysis above of
Interactions 2 and 3, as well as anecdotes and illustrations in Goffman's
(1967) chapter, "Where the Action Is," indicate that such situations can
occur in what would otherwise be the routine enactment of one's role-
identity. The only question is whether such situations are exceptions.
Contrary to Goffman's assumptions, they may well be commonplace (e.g.,
in light of the folklore among college students, medical patients, lawyers'
clients, retail customers, restaurant patrons, etc. of having to accommodate
the enactment of their role-identity to wide variations in enactments of the
reciprocal role-identity by professors, doctors and nurses, lawyers, retail
clerks, waiters/waitresses, etc.). Hence, there is good reason (in Goffman's
own work, as well as the previous data) to modify his analysis to recognize
the potential for performers to be rhetorical, and for their performances to
therefore be seen as interdependent.

Such a modification brings an analytic concern to the forefront: what
expressive resources are available to performers to overcome troubles in
bringing off the play in progress without interrupting it? The analysis of
Interactions 2 and 3 reveals that relevance relations and presuppositions
are such expressive resources. Both are means of giving communicative
acts meanings in context, which constrain the course of the interaction
without interfering with the production of communicative acts needed to
accomplish the business at hand.

From this analytic starting point, the disparate, somewhat paradoxical
facts about the enactment of role-identities can be accommodated (to the
effect that role-identities both do and do not structure individuals' conduct
and treatment), which have confounded the research literature on social
roles, role-definitions, role-enactment, and so on. On the one hand, what a
person's role-identity is makes a difference to the way he or she acts and is
treated within an institutional frame, based on the institutional definition
of the role-identity in terms of its rights and responsibilities. On the other
hand, institutional definitions of role-identities take the form of prototypes
for their enactment, such that a variety of conduct and treatment by others
among persons with the same role-identity may equally approximate the
prototype, although not just any conduct and treatment will do so. Thus,
the enactment of role-identities is theoretically compatible with persons
adjusting their conduct to take account of special demands on them posed
by the matter at hand, or because of other interactional purposes than the
enactment of a person's role-identity, or because of individual differences

in prior experience and communicative competence. Accordingly, a further basis for variations in persons' enactments of their role-identities is having the rhetorical purpose of overcoming obstacles to enacting their role-identity that are created by the conduct or treatment of role-reciprocal others.

Therefore, whether a person's enactment of a role-identity approximates or diverges from the prototype depends on what others, especially those with reciprocal role-identities, contribute to the interaction; and also on the communicative competence of each person to fashion turns at speaking rhetorically so as to constrain the course of the interaction to favor enactment of their own role-identities if interactional obstacles to doing so arise.

On the Consequentiality of Communicative Acts

The foregoing indicates a way in which communicative acts are consequential, which differs from the usual sense. In the usual sense in which communicative acts are regarded as consequential—what I call the *weak sense*—they serve to facilitate the social arrangements among people as follows. Communicative acts are viewed as an efficient, practical source of information about persons' qualities and qualities of the relationships between them that exist prior to and apart from the occurrence of such acts. Such information is conveyed both directly (through the content of the acts) and indirectly (through what can be inferred or attributed about a person or relationship from the acts that an individual produces). The social arrangements between people are said to depend on persons' extrinsic qualities, and what the qualities of the relationship between them are. Therefore, communicative acts that provide information about such qualities are said to play an important, but not an essential and certainly not a formative, part in the creation of social arrangements among people. Relevant information might be provided by other, possibly less efficient means, such as observation of the other, information from third parties, or archival research (Berger & Calabrese, 1975; Duck, 1985, 1993; Sperber & Wilson, 1986).

However, in the case of the enactment of role-identities, communicative acts do more than convey information, and therefore are consequential in a different sense—what I call the *strong sense*. Based on the analysis of Interactions 1–3, the enactment of role-identities depends on aspects of communicative acts that lie below the surface: the relevance relations between them and their presuppositions. The difference those aspects of communicative acts make in the enactment of role-identities is not just facilitative, but can only be made by those means (and perhaps other such tacit aspects of communicative acts). Moreover, the enactment of role-identities, especially in problematic instances as in Interactions 2 and 3, is a central (if not the only) means by which the personal qualities of individuals are indicated (inferred, attributed), and likewise the qualities of their relationship with each other. Because the way role-identities are enacted is an interactional, not an individual, product, the personal and relational qualities that are indicated in that way cannot be considered to exist prior to or apart from such interactions. In that case, communicative acts must play an essential and formative part in people's social arrangements that are based on the (jointly constructed) personal qualities of the people involved and the qualities of the relationships among them.

Although I have stated these two views of the consequentiality of communicative acts as if they are contraries, it is not productive to seek a basis for choosing between them. For one thing, these two views are not necessarily contraries, although they involve conflicting claims. The two correspond with the two sides of the bidirectional relationship noted earlier between the qualities of persons and relationships and the enactment of role-identities. A second reason for not trying to affirm one view and deny the other is that there is no empirical basis for doing so. For example, consistent with the weak sense of consequentiality, caseworkers interview clients in a social-services center to obtain information. In turn, they provide information to clients as if the information involved preexists and is extrinsic to the interview process. However, there are arguments to the contrary about the interview process. In keeping with the strong sense of consequentiality, interviews are represented as interactions in which persons jointly enact role-identities, and the qualities of persons and relationships are thereby jointly constructed (e.g., Aronnson, 1991; Käserman, 1991; Moerman, 1993). Now consider that, even if there were an empirical basis for claiming that communicative acts are consequential in either the weak sense or the strong sense in all interviews to date, we would have no basis, in principle, for explaining why this should be so, and therefore no assurance that acts would not be consequential in the other sense in the next interview that occurs.

Finally, it is more productive to regard these views of consequentiality as exclusive, but not contrary, because each gives rise to topics of research and theory that deserve attention. Specifically, to produce adequately functional communicative acts in the weak sense of consequentiality depends on a different competence than is needed to produce adequately functional acts in the strong sense of consequentiality. Each of these competences seems relevant in different interactions, and each is a valid topic of research and theory.

In the weak sense of consequentiality, communicative acts are consequential because of the information they provide—both through what the act tells (its content and/or implicature) and what it does socially (its illocutionary force)—so the key is to fashion communicative acts to make them maximally unambiguous. This makes it incumbent on individuals to have the competence—linguistic competence, and also the social knowledge on which Searle (1969, 1980) argued speech acts, and language meanings generally, rest—to produce linguistic forms that convey the intended information with due fidelity, accuracy, and completeness. These same expressive resources, combined with the personal quality of a disposition to be self-monitoring (Snyder, 1974, 1979), would also apply to producing linguistic forms that provide intended information indirectly (or no unintended information) through the inferences or attributions others make.

The consequentiality of communicative acts in the strong sense depends on additional competences—communicative ones, rather than linguistic and social ones. As I have defined *communicative competence*, and in accord with the analysis of Interactions 1–3, to enact one's role-identity requires one to produce communicative acts that simultaneously are responsive to others' acts, uphold one's responsibilities in the business at hand, and allow treatment by others that upholds one's rights or disallow treatment that denies one's rights. To fashion communicative acts during an unfolding interaction that are consequential in the strong sense is thus a form of problem solving.

Communicative acts produced in cooperative situations with concrete tasks, addressed to familiar and/or few persons, are more likely to meet the needs of the business at hand without unintended side effects, as long as participants provide needed information and obligatory acts. This is in direct contrast to communicative acts that are produced in competitive or conflictual situations handling abstract or complex tasks among unfamiliar or many others. The latter depend on the communicative, rather than the linguistic and social, competence of participants. The three interactions analyzed earlier illustrate this. From Interaction 1 to Interaction 3, the business at hand becomes more complex (the different social issues and arrangements at stake go up in number hyperbolically), the relationship between the supervisor and subordinate becomes less standardized, and what develops as the interaction proceeds becomes more likely to be something other than what any party expected or desired. In Interaction 1, the matter seems sufficiently standardized that the principal burden on MW_1 and FS_1 is to provide each other with information, and to do so with maximum clarity and minimum ambiguity and vagueness. But as we progress to Interaction 2 and then Interaction 3, the adequacy of the solutions to the problem of fashioning communicative acts seems to diminish, and to diminish in corresponding and reciprocal ways between the supervisors and subordinates involved.

When situational factors combine to make the chances of miscalculation and misfire higher as turns at speaking are fashioned, and without at least one participant acting rhetorically to remediate the way the interaction is unfolding, there is a potential for the interaction to "run out from under" the needs and wants of all concerned, and to take a course contrary to what any participant prefers (Cronen, Pearce, & Snavely, 1979; also see Sanders, 1992, on a progression of communicative acts on an international scale that "ran out from under" the participants). MW_2 functionally undertook such remediation when he "forced" MS_2 to receive instruction about the matter at hand, yet in a way that was not overtly insubordinate, thus avoiding what he apparently regarded as a dysfunctional possible outcome of their interaction. In contrast, neither FS_3 nor P succeeded in achieving such remediation, nor apparently even attempted it. Perhaps for that reason, MA_3 was compelled to intervene. Regardless of whether the participants did not realize they could or should remediate their interaction, or did not have the competence to do so, the course that Interaction 3 followed—in contrast with Interaction 2—is rooted in the differing communicative competences of the participants.

Thus, the basis for the consequentiality of communicative acts in the strong sense is the communicative competence of participants in social interaction—their competence to monitor the progress of an interaction and fashion their turns to effect remedial steps if it heads in the wrong direction. The social arrangements among people end up as they do because of they way they fashioned their communicative acts within the give-and-take of interaction. The social arrangements worked out in this way cannot exist apart from the communicative acts of the people in-volved, nor can they be formed in any other way.

REFERENCES

Aronnson, K. (1991). Facework and control in multi-party talk: A paediatric case study. In I. Marková & K. Foppa (Eds.), *Asymmetries in dialogue* (pp. 49–74). Hempstead, England: Harvester Wheatsheaf.

Atlas, J. D., & Levinson, S. C. (1981). It-clefts, informativeness, and logical form: Radical pragmatics (rev. ed.). In P. Cole (Ed.), *Radical pragmatics* (pp. 1–61). New York: Academic Press.

Bach, K., & Harnish, R. M. (1979). *Linguistic communication and speech acts.* Cambridge, MA: MIT Press.

Berger, C. R., & Calabrese, R. J. (1975). Some explorations in initial interaction and beyond: Toward a developmental theory of interpersonal communication. *Human Communication Research, 1,* 99–112.

Clayman, S. E., & Whalen, J. (1988–1989). When the medium becomes the message: The case of the Rather–Bush encounter. *Research on Language and Social Interaction, 22,* 241–272.

Cronen, V. E., Pearce, W. B., & Snavely, L. (1979). A theory of rule structure and types of episodes, and a study of perceived enmeshment in undesired repetitive patterns (URPs). In B. Ruben (Ed.), *Communication yearbook III* (pp. 225–240). New Brunswick, NJ: Transaction Press.

Duck, S. (1985). Social and personal relationships. In M. L. Knapp & G. R. Miller (Eds.), *Handbook of interpersonal communication* (pp. 655–686). Beverly Hills, CA: Sage.

Duck, S. (Ed.). (1993). *Individuals in relationships.* Newbury Park, CA: Sage.

Edelsky, C. (1981). Who's got the floor? *Language in Society, 10,* 383–421.

Edmondson, W. (1981). *Spoken discourse: A model for analysis.* London: Longman.

Fillmore, C. J. (1971). Verbs of judging: An exercise in semantic description. In C. J. Fillmore & D. T. Langendoen (Eds.), *Studies in linguistic semantics* (pp. 273–296). New York: Holt, Rinehart & Winston.

Fisher, B. A., & Ellis, D. G. (1990). *Small group decision making: Communication and the group process.* New York: McGraw-Hill.

Fitch, K. L., & Sanders, R. E. (1994). Culture, communication, and preferences for directness in expression of directives. *Communication Theory, 4,* 219–245.

Goffman, E. (1959). *The presentation of self in everyday life.* Garden City, NY: Doubleday.

Goffman, E. (1967). *Interaction ritual: Essays on face-to-face behavior.* New York: Anchor Books.

Greatbatch, D. (1988). A turn taking system for British news interviews. *Language in Society, 17,* 401–430.

Green, G. M., & Morgan, J. L. (1981). Pragmatics, grammar, and discourse. In P. Cole (Ed.), *Radical pragmatics* (pp. 167–181). New York: Academic Press.

Grice, H. P. (1975). Logic and conversation. In P. Cole & J. L. Morgan (Eds.), *Syntax and semantics 3: Speech acts* (pp. 41–58). New York: Academic Press.

Heritage, J. (1990–1991). Intention, meaning, and strategy: Observations on constraints on interaction analysis. *Research on Language and Social Interaction, 24,* 311–332.

Hymes, D. (1964). Formal discussion. *Monographs of the Society for Research in Child Development, 29* (1, Serial no. 92).

Hymes, D. (1974). *Foundations in sociolinguistics: An ethnographic approach.* Philadelphia: University of Pennsylvania Press.

Kartunnen, L., & Peters, S. (1979). Conventional implicature. In C.-K. Oh & D. A. Dinneen (Eds.), *Syntax and semantics 11: Presupposition* (pp. 1–56). New York: Academic Press.

Käserman, M.-L. (1991). Obstruction and dominance: Uncooperative moves and their effect on the course of conversation. In I. Marková & K. Foppa (Eds.), *Asymmetries in dialogue* (pp. 101–123). Hempstead, England: Harvester Wheatsheaf.

Kempson, R. (1975). *Presupposition and the delimitation of semantics.* Cambridge, England: Cambridge University Press.

Lakoff, G. (1987). *Women, fire, and dangerous things: What categories reveal about the mind.* Chicago: University of Chicago Press.

Levinson, S. C. (1983). *Pragmatics.* Cambridge, England: Cambridge University Press.

Levinson, S. C. (1992). Activity types and language. In P. Drew & J. Heritage (Eds.), *Talk at work* (pp. 66–100). New York: Cambridge University Press.

Lewis, D. (1979). Scorekeeping in a language game. *Journal of Philosophical Logic, 8,* 339–359.

Moerman, M. (1993). Ariadne's thread and Indra's net: Reflections on ethnography, ethnicity, identity, culture, and interaction. *Research on Language and Social Interaction, 26,* 85–98.

Philipsen, G. (1975). Speaking "like a man" in Teamsterville: Cultural patterns of role-enactment in an urban neighborhood. *Quarterly Journal of Speech, 62,* 13–22.

Reichman, R. (1985). *Getting computers to talk like you and me: Discourse content, focus, and semantics (an ATN model).* Cambridge, MA: MIT Press.

Rosch, E. (1978). Principles of categorization. In E. Rosch & B. B. Lloyd (Eds.), *Cognition and categorization* (pp. 27–48). Hillsdale, NJ: Lawrence Erlbaum Associates.

Rosch, E. (1981). Prototype classification and logical classification: The two systems. In E. Scholnick (Ed.), *New trends in cognitive representation: Challenges to Piaget's theory* (pp. 73–86). Hillsdale, NJ: Lawrence Erlbaum Associates.

Sacks, H., Schegloff, E. A., & Jefferson, G. (1974). A simplest systematics for the organization of turn-taking for conversation. *Language, 50,* 696–735.

Sanders, R. E. (1983). Tools for cohering discourse and their strategic utilization: Markers of structural connections and meaning relations. In R. T. Craig & K. Tracy (Eds.), *Conversational coherence: Form, structure, and strategy* (pp. 67–80). Beverly Hills, CA: Sage.

Sanders, R. E. (1987). *Cognitive foundations of calculated speech: Controlling understandings in conversation and persuasion.* Albany: SUNY Press.

Sanders, R. E. (1989). Message effects via induced changes in the social meaning of a response. In J. J. Bradac (Ed.), *Message effects in communication science* (pp. 165–194). Newbury Park, CA: Sage.

Sanders, R. E. (1990–1991). In reply to Vaida and incidentally to Heritage as well. *Research on Language and Social Interaction, 24,* 395–404.

Sanders, R. E. (1991). The two-way relationship between talk in social interaction and actors' goals and plans. In K. Tracy (Ed.), *Understanding face-to-face interaction: Issues linking goals and discourse* (pp. 167–188). Hillsdale, NJ: Lawrence Erlbaum Associates.

Sanders, R. E. (1992). The role of mass communication processes in producing upheavals in the Soviet Union, Eastern Europe, and China. In S. S. King & D. P. Cushman (Eds.), *Political communication: Engineering visions of order in the socialist world* (pp. 143–162). Albany: SUNY Press.

Schank, R. C., & Abelson, R. P. (1977). *Scripts, plans, goals, and understanding: An inquiry into human knowledge structures.* Hillsdale, NJ: Lawrence Erlbaum Associates.

Schegloff, E. A. (1988–1989). From interview to confrontation: Observations of the Bush/Rather encounter. *Research on Language and Social Interaction, 22,* 215–240.

Searle, J. R. (1969). *Speech acts: An essay in the philosophy of Language.* Cambridge, England: Cambridge University Press.

Searle, J. R. (1976). A classification of illocutionary acts. *Language in Society, 5,* 1–23.

Searle, J. R. (1980). The background of meaning. In J. R. Searle, F. Kiefer, & M. Bierwisch (Eds.), *Speech act theory and pragmatics* (pp. 221–232). Dordrecht, Netherlands: Reidel.

Snyder, M. (1974). Self-monitoring of expressive behavior. *Journal of Personality and Social Psychology, 30,* 526–537.

Snyder, M. (1979). Self-monitoring processes. In L. Berkowitz (Ed.), *Advances in experimental social psychology* (Vol. 12, pp. 85–128). New York: Academic Press.

Sperber, D., & Wilson, D. (1986). *Relevance: Communication and cognition.* Oxford, England: Basil Blackwell.

Spitzberg, B. H. & Cupach, W. R. (1984). *Interpersonal communication competence.* Beverly Hills, CA: Sage.

Verhoeven, J. C. (1993). An interview with Erving Goffman, 1980. *Research on Language and Social Interaction, 26,* 317–348.

Wilson, D. (1975). *Presuppositions and non-truth-conditional semantics.* New York: Academic Press.

Wiseman, F. (1975). *Welfare.* Cambridge, MA: Zipporah Films.

3

Conversation Analysis: "Okay" as a Clue for Understanding Consequentiality

Wayne A. Beach
San Diego State University

Participants in interaction routinely make available their orientations to, and thus understandings of, the moment-by-moment contingencies of unfolding actions. Conversation analysis (CA) is centrally concerned with excavating the constituent and organizing features of these collaborative efforts. How do specific kinds of actions get brought off as demonstrably relevant by and for participants? What is the distinctive, methodical, and achieved character of any given spate of interaction? On what resources do participants rely in contributing to and providing solutions for immediate interactional circumstances?

These questions begin to address how participants delicately tailor their talk-in-interaction in ways that influence the recognizable evolution of practical courses of action. By attempting to describe and explain the precise ways that participants' actions make a practical difference, impacting the continuous and negotiated character of everyday conversation, the empirical focus of CA rests with providing evidence that reveals (among other features) the inherent consequentiality of communication:

> For the target of its inquiries stands where talk amounts to action, where action projects *consequences* in a structure and texture of interaction which the talk is itself progressively embodying and realizing, and where the particulars of the talk inform what actions are being done and what sort of social scene is being constituted. . . . How does the fact that the talk is being conducted in some setting . . . issue in any *consequences* for the shape, form, trajectory, content, or character of the interaction that the parties conduct? And *what is the mechanism by which the context-so-understood has determinate*

121

consequences for the talk? (Schegloff, 1991, pp. 46,53; italics on first two *conse-quences* added; other italics original)

This chapter begins with a basic and brief overview of CA as an empirical enterprise, focusing especially on the ways in which the import of consequentiality is self-evident within such a research focus. Relationships among data collection and analysis, participants' orientations and sequential organization, and issues of "talk and social structure" (cf. Boden & Zimmerman, 1991) are summarized. Attention is then given—in some detail and as a means of empirically illustrating otherwise conceptual claims—to how "Okay" usages in casual conversations are recruited by participants to achieve particular kinds of actions: The usages are not employed as isolated tokens or discourse particles, but as positionally active and consequential for unfolding talk. Examinations of a variety of interactional environments begin to reveal how participants' "Okays" are responsive to prior talk, but also prefigure movements toward next-positioned matters as a pivotal resource impacting the shape and trajectory of conversation.

CONVERSATION ANALYSIS
AND CONSEQUENTIALITY

First, CA employs research methods fashioned after the social phenomenon being examined: the independent and natural existence of social order. A basic tenet of CA is the recognition that social order—evident within the detailed and contingent activities of societal members—exists independently of social-scientific inquiry. Irrespective of the possibility of being examined and in some way analytically dissected for purposes of research, interactants simply go about their daily business performing routine and often mundane tasks. Thus, CA gives priority to gaining access to social activities comprising a wide variety of natural settings. However, to examine such activities in "real-time" detail (i.e. on their own merits as interesting phenomena), there is a systematic reliance on carefully produced transcriptions of audio and video recordings. Recordings and transcriptions allow for repeated hearings, viewings, and inspections of "actual and determinate" (Schegloff, 1986) interactional environments:

> It was not from any large interest in language or from some theoretical formulation of what should be studied that I started with tape-recorded conversations, but simply because I could get my hands on it and I could study it again and again, and also, consequentially, because others could look at what I had studied and make of it what they could, if, for example, they wanted to be able to disagree with me. (Sacks, 1984, p. 26)

Although neither recordings nor transcriptions are conversations in and of themselves (Beach, 1990c; Zimmerman, 1988), they nevertheless preserve and embody the integrity and distinctiveness of many conversational activities. Moreover, as selected fragments of transcriptions are made available for readers' critical inspections, attention can be drawn to specific details and practical consequences of unfolding actions rather than glossed or presumed versions of what might or could have happened (i.e., idealized, intuited, and/or recollected data; cf. Atkinson & Heritage, 1984; Heritage, 1984).

Second, analysis of conversational involvements reveals the omnipresence of patterned orientations to "context." To introduce and articulate fundamental grounds for CA as an empirical social science, Heritage (1984; but also see Lee, 1987; Zimmerman & Boden, 1991) posited three central and working assumptions: "1) interaction is structurally organized; 2) contributions to interaction are contextually oriented; 3) these two properties inhere in the details of interaction so that no order of detail can be dismissed, *a priori*, as disorderly, accidental, or irrelevant" (p. 241).

Situated examination of social interaction's details is prerequisite to addressing whether and how actions emerge rapidly and spontaneously, and are delicately organized as interactional achievements. However messy and disordered naturally occurring conversations might appear, at least initially, considerable evidence exists that supports a central tenet of social interaction studies: that there is "order at all points," much of which awaits discovery by analysts, but all of which was produced in the first instance as meaningful, and thus in meaningful ways by and for interactants.[1]

Moreover, just as participants reside within and inevitably orient to the *scenic* world—composed of seeable, hearable, behaviorally recognizable actions, activities, and objects—so does CA avoid "mentalistic" or "psychologistic" explanations of patterns of action. As I noted elsewhere (Beach, 1989, 1990c), such a position does not deny the existence of a wide range of personality variables and cognitive-processing phenomena (e.g., motives, values, attitudes, beliefs, thoughts, feelings, interpretations, perceptions, memory, emotions, etc.). Rather, it focuses on the methods and practices (i.e., interactional resources) through which such phenomena may or may not visibly enter into, (i.e., be determined to be relevant and consequential in shaping and being shaped by) streams of ongoing action. Nor does CA prematurely dismiss the relevance and impact of relation-

---

[1]Goodwin (1990) traced a neglect of talk-in-interaction through the history of anthropological, sociological, linguistic, and communication research. By ignoring the embedded details of interactional conduct, the diverse range of social actions achieved through talk-in-interaction are systematically excluded. Such a position is, of course, a rejection of Chomsky's (1965) well-known, but misdirected, assessment that talk, per se, is altogether too messy, flawed, and degenerate for studies of phenomena such as *competence*.

ship "history" or "background understandings" on everyday talk-in-inter-action, or more generally knowledge about the evolving world and its past, present, and future events and possibilities. On the contrary, in the precise ways that participants use and rely on such resources in the course of organizing interaction, so may analysts attend to these actions as rel-evant to what participants treat as meaningful, and thus consequential for what and how understandings about everyday life get cogenerated (cf. Beach, 1994).

As originally described by Sacks, Schegloff, and Jefferson (1974) and further elaborated by Schegloff (1987b, 1991), context is not understood as external to or otherwise exorcized from interaction (see also Beach, 1991c; Mandelbaum, 1991). On the contrary, context is continually and intrinsi-cally re-achieved as participants display their understandings of specific moments of conversational involvement. Each emergent action is both *context-shaping* in the way it is tailored to prior and immediate circum-stances, and *context-renewing* by means of its contribution to and thus impact on next-positioned actions. For example, and to simplify, Schegloff (1991) made reference to CA's concern with "structures of single actions and of series and sequences of them" (p. 47). From this it becomes clear that even a minimal understanding of context begins with a compilation of the following: what participants' actions are responsive to, or how they emerged in the first instance; the detailed resources employed, or what actions participants are "up to" or achieving; and, consequently, where the interaction proceeds as what was once "next speaker," now "current speaker," orients in some meaningful way to prior turn-at-talk by engag-ing in some relevant next action.

It is in this basic sense that consequentiality of communication becomes important—first for participants of interaction, and secondly for analysts of conversational organization: not as some removed, telescopic conceptualization or component of social order, but as evident in how participants differentially and embeddedly reveal and document, each for the other, "what is going on" within a given spate of talk and in consider-ation of its attending relevancies (cf. Beach, 1990c, 1991b; Jefferson, 1981; Wootton, 1988).

CA has invested considerable effort in evidencing the bedrock details underlying the very possibility of an interactionally produced social order (but see also Goffman, 1983). Toward these ends, a set of interrelated and universal features of conversational organization have been put forth. As already noted, whenever participants design and place their utterances within a series of actions, a speaker's current turn projects the relevance of a next, such that the range of possible activities accomplished by the second speaker reflect an understanding of, as well as an orientation to, the emergent character of interaction. In and through the adjacent ordering (cf.

Heritage, 1984; Sacks et al., 1974) of first and second actions, utterances are seen to be "sequentially implicative" (cf. Schegloff & Sacks, 1973) in the exact ways that speakers systematically organize the occasions in which they are involved. Therefore, during a series of turns-in-interaction, speakers design their talk to the occasion of its use and with particular recipients in mind. Just as speakers rely on recipients to display whatever impact(s) their utterances might have in the course of their delivery, so do recipients overwhelmingly design their talk in "conditionally relevant" ways: Not just any response will normally suffice because some prior speaker projected the relevance of some range of appropriate and next actions. Of course, because talk has been found to be "sensitive to recipients' design," *how* some next turn-at-talk is tailored to some prior action or set of actions becomes the "grist" for analysts' "mills." This is especially so when conversation is understood more or less as spontaneously combustible: "locally occasioned and managed" in ways that any given participant's actions reshape and renew the "context"—as a set of methodically and systematically organized, yet constantly changing and updated, series of actions (cf. Jefferson, 1978).

In summary, the next turn-at-talk may be the foundational building block of human understanding. It is here that next speakers contribute to an already unfolding interactional environment, producing a wide variety of actions (e.g., agreeing/affiliating, disagreeing/disaffiliating, attending–disattending, accepting, rejecting, closing, opening, reconciling, mitigating, canceling, deleting, avoiding) and a considerably more diverse set of possibilities (in both kind and degree). Each possibility evidences little more or less than how participants display and detect one another's orientations to the occasion at hand. Exactly what gets achieved is undeniably the upshot of how speakers fashion, shape, and make available to one another their understandings of the local environment of which they are an integral part.

A third and final set of issues arises from a melding of the dual focus on interaction as "structurally organized and contextually oriented": "These two properties inhere in the details of interaction so that no order of detail can be dismissed, *a priori*, as disorderly, accidental, or irrelevant" (Heritage, 1984, p. 241). As already noted, when turning directly to interactional materials to discover how participants meaningfully organize conversation, there is an unwillingness to (a) rely on intuited or idealized data; and (b) posit, *a priori*, that interaction is driven by individuals' motives, needs, or other mentalistic phenomena (as was the case, e.g., with Garfinkel's original critique and extension of Parson's treatments of "moral norms," "need dispositions," and "personality"; cf. Heritage, 1984, chap. 2–5). Similarly, data-driven analyses tend not to be usefully informed by *a priori* theoretical musings or propositions. On the contrary, empirical observations repeatedly make clear how "theory construction," per se, is overwhelmingly premature. Due to its proclivity toward underspecification, claims and warrants about the detailed workings of interactional activities are routinely glossed by a priori theoretical propositions and, consequently, incapable of revealing recurrent practices and patterns of everyday talk.

Therefore, there is a decided "off-stage" role of theory in CA that includes a set of long-standing debates and empirical studies (see, e.g., Alexander, Giesen, Munch, & Smelser, 1987; Beach & Lindstrom, 1992; Boden & Zimmerman, 1991; Drew & Heritage, 1992; Hopper, 1989a; Mehan, 1991; Roger & Bull, 1989; Schegloff, 1987b, 1991). These studies collectively address issues such as framing "culture and/or institution" as some externalized causal agents predetermining actions and their consequences versus situating "culture and/or institution" as ongoing, methodically produced, locally occasioned, inherently accountable, altogether practical achievements. These traditional "macro–micro" debates (e.g., involving matters of power, status, role, gender, class, bureaucracy, etc.) will undoubtedly continue to receive considerable attention. However, such debates are not limited to CA and alternative social-science inquiries. There are long-standing and key debates between ethnomethodologists and conversation analysts as well, particularly "with the central role accorded to talk-in-interaction in the investigation of situated action" (Zimmerman & Boden, 1991, p.7). Thus, the debates more generally focus on issues of "larger contexts" and, relatedly, matters such as the role of extrasituational knowledge, what counts as a verifiable claim, and criteria for identifying "members' phenomena."

Although these matters are interesting and relevant, they are not addressed directly in this chapter. Rather, having laid general grounds for understanding the relationship between CA and the consequentiality of communication, I now turn to a specific operationalization of these concerns by focusing on how participants rely on "Okay" in ways impacting the unfolding character of interactions.

SITUATING UNDERSTANDINGS OF "OKAYS" IN CONVERSATION

The present analysis focuses on how participants rely on "Okay" in recognizably nontrivial, transitionally relevant, altogether pivotal ways in conversation. Basic and empirically defensible grounds for such transitional usages, and their differential consequences for ordinary talk, are elaborated. As part of a larger project on "Okay" usages (Beach, 1991b), it is not coincidental that such an undertaking commences by drawing attention to these fundamentally projective qualities. Yet such a focus does not discount how "Okays" are also specifically and unequivocally designed, by and for participants, in ways that are responsive to prior turn(s). By attending to backward and forward features of "Okay" usages, understandings can be generated regarding actions involving (as becomes evident) a host of shift-implicative moments in conversation.

Similar to what Jefferson (1981) aptly described (e.g., "Yeah") as *speaker* shift-implicative actions possessing a "topically dual-faceted character," making "topical movement transparently relevant," the following questions arise: How might "Okay" come to be understood as "on topic," yet doing something more (Jefferson, 1981: 36)? What work is involved when speakers rely on "Okay" responsively, but also transitionally, and thus en route to continuation?[2]

Before turning directly to inspections of data whose features allow for such questions to be answered, an overview of the following three primary issues seems in order. First, all "Okay" usages (employed in considerably diverse ways, and in equally varied sequential environments) can be understood as locally occasioned resources available to participants for achieving specific and relevant tasks. Apparently and contingently, participants use and rely on "Okay" as partial solutions to ongoing interactional problems. The precise nature of these problems, and how participants rely on "Okay" as one means to resolve them, are reflections of what participants initially treat as meaningful in the course of achieving interaction.

Repeated examinations of a large collection of recorded and transcribed instances of naturally occurring interactions reveal certain predominant, and at times striking, interactional moments wherein "Okay" appears indispensable for participants. One elementary set of moments—addressed herein and recurrently available for analysts' and, eventually, readers' inspections—may be summarized as follows: "Okay" is employed *pivotally*, in the midst of precise moments of *transition*, by recipients and current speakers alike, across a variety of speech exchange systems (both casual and institutional); and not just in any sequential environment, but where what is "at stake" involves movements from prior to next-positioned matter(s). Such tasks routinely evidence a universal and therefore basic

---

[2]At the outset, it is worth noting that concerns with "topically progressive" talk, as addressed in Jefferson (1981) as well as Sacks (1987), are directed less toward what is "talked about" and more toward the organizing work that "talk does" (cf. Schegloff, 1990). This distinction is important in minimizing ambiguities and thus problems emerging when *topic* is treated as more or less synonymous with *order*, compared with what participants treat as orderly "in the first instance."

feature of involvement in interaction, roughly stated: In the course of organizing conversational activities, speakers and recipients are persistent in the insertion of, and thus movement toward, elaborated and/or new orientations to ongoing talk. These movements are generally en route to activity shifts (and, although much less frequently via "Okay" in casual talk, speakership). Participants can be shown to rely on "Okay," and thus design their talk to be responsive to prior talk, yet they also shape next-positioned activities in specific ways. Such "Okay" usages are uniquely and variously consequential for unfolding interaction.

Toward these ends, priority is given to features generalizing across diverse speakers, settings, and activities by focusing on recurring, free-standing, and "Okay + [fuller turn]" occurrences: universal in scope, yet—without exception—sensitive to the contingencies of any given moment of conversational involvement.

Second, extant theoretical concerns with "discourse markers" (e.g., see Fraser, 1990; Levinson, 1983; Redeker, 1990; Schiffrin, 1987) have neither necessarily nor systematically addressed fundamentally transitional, and thus projective, qualities of "Okay" usages. Conceptual definitions of *markers*—as categorical members of classes (i.e., discourse particles, conjuctions, connectives, interjections) that signal or reveal "pragmatic relations" (Redeker, 1990; Schiffrin, 1987) as essential components for discerning sentence meaning and language grammar (Fraser, 1990), and/ or as "sequentially dependent elements which bracket units of talk," syntactically and sententially (Schiffrin, 1987, p. 31)—have not emerged from decidedly user-shaped streams or contingencies of language use. Thus, what recipients and current speakers might be orienting to via "Okay" (i.e., are occupied with and thus treat as significant in particular turn-taking environments) remains unexplicated (cf. Beach, 1990c, 1991a, 1991b; Jefferson, 1981; Wootton, 1988).

Third, a related and substantive basis exists for examining the interactional organization of particular "acknowledgment tokens," including their consequences for particular types of activities in conversation, and on which this and subsequent inquiries into "Okay" usages are demonstrably reliant (cf. Heritage, 1984, 1990; Jefferson, 1981; Schegloff, 1982). Devoid of these detailed examinations of tokens such as "Mm," "Mm-hmm," "Uh-huh," "Ah-hah," "Yeah," or "Oh" (and related other tokens, produced at times with upward intonation and, on all occasions, in precise orientation to the interactional task at hand), it may be easy to conclude that these otherwise minor features are not only disorderly and quite random, but perhaps inconsequential to unfolding talk in the first instance. But the opposite has convincingly been shown to be the case for a broad range of activities, including: initiating, extending, and terminating topics; displaying recipiency to ongoing tellings; preparing the way for movement from passive recipiency to more active speakership; and displaying receipt, possible surprise, and/or a change of state in information following prior delivery of some news via "Oh."

In terms of "Okay," the initial work by Schegloff and Sacks (1973) on preclosings in telephone calls identified key ways in which "Okay" is sequentially active: Recurrently, "Okay" emerges as a device initiating movement toward closure and/or as passing turns en route to terminating phone calls (see Segments 16–19 herein). These are the usages most commonly cited (e.g., Button, 1987, 1990; Levinson, 1983; Schiffrin, 1987) as representations of the ways participants use "Okays," noticeably and positionally, in conversation. Similarly, Schegloff's (e.g., 1968, 1979, 1986) work on telephone openings also contributes to a sequential understanding of how "Okay" marks movements to initial topic(s), and/or the business of the call (see Segments 11–15, as well as Hopper, 1991).

Although "Okay" usages have been given limited attention beyond the work on phone call openings and closings by Schegloff and Sacks, such work has occurred (cf. Condon, 1986; Merritt, 1984). Most recently, Beach (1990a) gave attention to how a "facilitator" of a focus-group meeting relied on "Okay" to initiate and manage such actions as closing preceding topics and moving on to next topics, including usages as a preclosing device employed to close down a given interactant while eliciting comments from a next (facilitator-selected) speaker. Somewhat related research on "Okay" in service encounters (cf. Merritt, 1980), as well as in recordings of interaction tasks given to families for making decisions about "vacation" (Condon, 1986), also exists. Identifiable contributions of these efforts—such as offering preliminary observations of "Okay" as a "bridge, a linking device between two stages or phases of the [service] encounter" (Merritt, 1980, p. 144), or by treating "Okay" (Goffman, 1974, 1981) as a "bracketing or framing" device that "appears as decision points at which participants choose among alternatives" (Condon, 1986, p. 75)—nevertheless reveal a tendency toward underspecification: The interactional work giving rise to "Okay" usages, participants' orientations to them, and their consequences for subsequent talk remain largely unaccounted for in the literature.

The scope of this investigation extends beyond those previously mentioned by attempting to establish transitional "Okay" usages occurring in more diverse interactional environments. Consequently, it provides a basis on which subsequent work might build, while also pointing to the need for fuller explications of the kinds of interactional tasks speakers use "Okay" for, in varieties of casual and institutional speech-exchange systems. Moreover, analyses of this type seem particularly well suited to developments in linguistic pragmatics. For example, in concluding his discussion of potential contributions of "conversation analysis" to pragmatics, Levinson (1983) observed:

> Finally, aspects of overall conversational organization also interact with linguistic structure, most noticeably in the linguistic formulae typical of openings and closings . . . but also in the use of particles like *Well* and *Okay* in pre-closings *and the like*. In the present state of our knowledge, remarks of this sort can only be suggestive of the many, largely unexplored, ways in which conversational organization interacts with sentence and utterance structure. (p. 366; first two italics original, last italics added)

Another question thus arises: Upon consideration of casual "Okay" usages, what are these "largely unexplored ways" (i.e., "and the like")?

The analysis presented here proceeds in a step-by-step manner that gradually establishes "Okay" as responsive, yet displaying state of readiness for movements to next-positioned matters. First, to understand how "Okay" is employed transitionally, it may be useful to locate noncontinuative usages with a brief overview of "Okay" as a free-standing receipt marker employed by both recipients and current speakers. Second, ways in which "Okay" has been found to work in phone opening and preclosing environments are sketched. These instances begin to reveal, through prior empirical findings, basic transitional features of "Okay." Third, it is argued that participants rely on "Okay" as a means of simultaneously attending to prior turns while also setting up next-positioned matters (topics, activities). Fourth, on this basis, a case can then be made for "Okay" as a projection device for turn and, at times, speaker transition (i.e., a *conversion technique* for extending prior and/or establishing new priorities for subsequent talk). Although "Okay" may appear as free standing, and next speakers may treat "Okay" as noncontinuative and/or closure relevant, they may nevertheless be shown to project subsequent and fuller turns (i.e., "Okay + [the work of additional turn components]"). Finally, having established a variety of "Okay" usages as transitionally relevant to ensuing talk, and having laid grounds for its examination, implications for future research are briefly sketched.

"Okay" as a Free-Standing Receipt Marker

Recipients may rely on "Okay" as a shorthand display that marks: (a) acknowledgment and/or understanding (e.g., confirmation) of, and/or (b) affiliation/alignment (e.g., agreement) with what prior speaker's utterance was taken to be projecting. In these ways "Okay" can and often does stand alone, adjacently placed and specifically designed to demonstrate recipients' orientations to the topic and activities at hand. Thus, in Segment 1,

(1) #3; (M. Goodwin, 1980, p. 676)

Sha: Your mother wants you!
→ Flo: Okay

Flo's "Okay" does not signal that she will necessarily and immediately abide by her mother's wishes; rather, it signals adequate receipt of Sha's informing (see Appendix for description of transcription conventions). In drawing attention to John's "Okay" in Segment 2,

(2) Auto Discussion: (C. Goodwin, 1987, p. 211)

Don: I'll go get some more water ((Leaves with
pitcher))
→ John: Okay.

Goodwin (1987) noted how Don's announcement of a departure simply "gets an answer in next turn from recipient" (p. 211). John's "Okay," however, is neither an answer to a question, nor does it indicate that Don has any trouble with the announcement. Such is also the case in Segment 3,

(3) SDCL: CallGdps:11[3]

G: Let's le– (I'll) let ya <u>talk</u> to him for
a minute
→ D: Okay

as D (Grandson) affiliates with his grandmother's announcement by displaying a willingness to talk with "him" (grandfather). In a similar fashion, recipients in the next two instances—from transcriptions of call-waiting

---

[3]An explanation of this data source is as follows: *SDCL* is an acronym for San Diego Conversation Library; *CallGdps* is short for an audio-recorded and transcribed phone call entitled "Calling the Grandparents"; *11* marks the page number of the transcript from which the following interactional segment was drawn. Similarly, in the following data (Segment 4), *UTCL* is an acronym for University of Texas Conversation Library, *Family Phone* is the title given to this particular recorded and transcribed conversation, and *2* is the transcript page number. Each data segment throughout is similarly abbreviated, in many cases citing specific authors and references (including dates and page numbers) from which data were collected on "Okays." In these cases, specific definitions of data source abbreviations may be obtained from individual authors. Clearly, however, idiosyncrasies do exist in labeling and abbreviating data sources.

recordings (cf. Hopper, 1989a, 1989b, 1990)—essentially grant prior speakers' requests to "Hang on":

(4) UTCL: Family Phone:2

Subscriber: Hang on I got a call on the other line.
→   Partner: Kay

(5) UTCL: D10

A: Hang on one second okay?[4]
→ B: Okay.

Finally, in Segment 6 A's request to borrow B's car is eventually granted with "Okay":

(6) Sacks:4/1/72:16

A: Can I borrow your car?
B: When?
A: This afternoon.
→ B: Okay.

In this segment, "Okay" is placed as an answer to the initial question by B as recipient—one following an insertion sequence interjected between the first and second parts of the Q–A adjacency pair (cf. Goodwin & Goodwin, 1989).

Third-Turn Receipts by Current Speaker.   Free-standing "Okays" are also employed by current speakers who initiate such activities as questions. Having received an affirmative, acceptable, and/or clarifying answer from recipient, current speakers move next to mark recognition and/or approval in third slot via "Okay":

(7) FN#6: (Davidson, 1984, p. 127)

A: You wan' me bring you anything?
            (0.4)
B: No: no: nothing.
→ A: AW:kay.

---

[4]As evident in Segment 5, "Okay?" may be tag positioned with upward intonation/ contour, and received with "Okay" in next turn. These specific usages lie beyond the scope of this analysis; they possess a different phenomenal status, occurring frequently, and are variously ordered in their own right. Examination of a collection of these usages recurrently reveals them to be devices for soliciting and ensuring agreement and/or alignment from next speaker (see e.g. Segment 21).

Davidson (1984) treated A's "<u>AW</u>:kay." as a "rejection finalizer": "Okay is an instance of a class of objects that display that the inviter or offerer is going along with the rejection and is not (for the time being) going to produce any subsequent versions" (p. 127).

Alternative versions of third-turn receipts (cf. Heritage & Greatbatch, 1991; McHoul, 1978, 1985; Mehan, 1978, 1979; Schegloff et al., 1977; Tsui, 1991) appear in Segments 8 and 9. These "Okays" are employed not as responses to recipients' acceptance–rejection (or mitigated version) of an invitation/offer, but as affirmations of the correctness of an understanding check in Segment 8,

> (8) HG:II:15–16: (Button & Casey, 1984, p. 168)
>
>   N: You'll come abou:t (.) eight. Right?=
>
>   H: =Yea::h,=
>
> →   N: =Okay

and simple information query in Segment 9:

> (9) SDCL: DrksCls:9
>
>   D: Who are you <u>go</u>nna stay with
>
>   F: <u>Pa</u>tsy
>
> →   D: O:kay

However, third-turn receipts marked with "Okay" occur in a wider variety of environments than those involving questions (and the work questions do—i.e., inviting, offering, checking understandings, clarifying, seeking information, etc.). One such segment appears next, where A provides information as grounds for minimizing S's concerns, which S then (having been informed) treats as "Okay":

> (10) SDCL: SptsTrip:6
>
>   S: There's– there's gotta be a bigger refrigerator
>   than the little one or you're gonna be:
>   (.)
>
>   A: Well it's:: it's you know (0.5) it's like the si–
>   half the size of a regular refrigerator
>
> →   S: Okay

Segments 1–10 repeatedly illustrate how "Okays," although accomplishing different kinds of actions, are adjacently placed (in second or third position), free-standing responses by recipients and current speakers alike.

Each usage examined thus far is *noncontinuative*, or what Davidson (1984) suggested is essentially a withholding by the producer to offer a "subsequent version" (p. 127). Yet these segments, and others similar to them, do not collectively warrant a "claim of exclusivity" in the free-standing status of "Okay" placements—by recipients or current speakers. Quite the contrary may be the case.[5] As evident in the following discussion, "Okay" has been shown to possess fundamental "projective" qualities.

"Okay" in Phone Call Openings and Preclosing Environments

One useful means to understand how "Okay" exceeds singularized or free-standing usage is by turning to beginnings and endings of phone calls. Relying on the considerable research conducted on these interactional events (cf. Button, 1987, 1990; Hopper, 1989b, 1991; Schegloff, 1968, 1979, 1980; Schegloff & Sacks, 1973), "Okay" has been found to have relevance for next-positioned matters.

Phone Call Openings. Consider, first, a canonical phone opening in which initial queries and responses involve "Okay":

---

[5]The distinction between free-standing "Okay's" in Segments 1–10, and subsequent descriptions of "Okay's + [continuation]," is not offered as a "black–white" proposition. Numerous instances have been collected involving "Okay + [*minimalized* turn construction unit]" (e.g., assessing, thanking, address terms, etc.), which often occur in preclosing environments, at times in apparently "redundant" fashion (e.g., "Okay all right", "Okay good"). In the following segments, for example, each "Okay" prefaces a minimalized continuation prior to the Caller "moving out of" the closing Crandall appears to be initiating (cf. Button, 1987, 1990):

> (Schegloff & Sacks, 1973, p. 321)

> | Caller: | You don'know w–uh what that would be, how much it costs. |
> |---|---|
> | Crandall: | I would think probably, about twenty five dollars |
> | Caller: | Oh boy, hehh hhh! |
> | → | Okay, thank you |
> | → Crandall: | Okay dear. |
> | Caller: | OH BY THE WAY ((continues)) |

And here Mary offers a slightly upgraded response:

> (A/M)

> | Alan: | W'l b–] bring a change a'clothes yih c'n use the ba:th r'm d'change, |
> |---|---|
> | | [|
> | → Mary: | Okhhay ghhood, |

(11)   #263; (Schegloff, 1986, p. 115)

((five lines deleted))

    C: How are you?
→   R: Okay:.
    C: Good.=
→   R: =How about you.

It is seen here that "Okay" is, essentially, both responsive to C's query and preliminary to R's reciprocal "How about you." In Segment 12, Irene's "Okay" is used in like manner in the same turn, receipted by Marilyn with an "Okay + [initial (though unexplicated) topical direction]," which Irene specifies next:

(12)   #268; (Schegloff, 1986, p. 135)

    Marilyn: Oh HI. = How're you do:in.
→   Irene: Heh okay. = How about you.
→   Marilyn: Okay, pretty goo:d. I've been busy:
                   bu(h)t, .hh   other
                          [
    Irene: Are you tea:ching?,

But in Segment 13, notice what occurs when no reciprocal "How are you" gets produced:

(13)   #250a; (Schegloff, 1986, p. 139)

    Marlene: Hi. this is Marlene:
    Bonnie: Hi,
    Marlene: How are you,
    Bonnie: I'm fi:ne,
→   Marlene: Okay. .hh D'you have Marina's
                    telephone number?

In the place of "How are you," Marlene moves directly to the business of the call with "Okay + [inbreath + question]." As Schegloff (1986) observed:

No such reciprocal is produced directly after the sequence-closing assessment ["I'm fi:ne"], nor in the inbreath which follows, which can be heard as *preparatory to further talk* by caller. Caller does not wait for the reciprocal; instead, she uses this position, otherwise the place for a return howareyou, to begin what appears to be the reason for the call. (p. 139, italics added)

In short, Marlene uses this position to initiate, if not something altogether new, at least something extended or noticeably different from the prior canonical greeting. Here Marlene's "Okay" is recruited to receipt and bring to a close activities comprising the phone opening, which Bonnie's "I'm fi:ne," initiates, giving rise to the inbreath (".hh") marking transition to a request for Marina's telephone number.

Just as variations from canonical greetings are not uncommon (cf. Hopper, 1989a, 1991), so is it that "Okay" is not infrequently in the "midst of," yet also "preliminary to," what comes next. In Segment 14, T's "Oka(h)y" is in third-turn position, marking receipt of A's prior response:

(14)   UTCL: J10.1

> A: Allan
> T: Hi: this is Tuppel.
> A: Hi
> T: You r(h)eady for today's go rou:nd?
> A: Sure h
→ T: Oka(h)y hih hih .hhhh well– I just had a call from
>   Joe and he says ((continues))

As a pivotal resource, notice also that T's "Oka(h)y" is immediately followed by "hih hih .hhhh well–"—essentially two laugh tokens, an inbreath, and a topic initial "well–"—which, not unlike Segment 13, intervenes following T's attempt to close the phone opening and as a preface to both initiating a new topic and offering a first reporting.

A similar case can be observed in Segment 15, but on this occasion a switching of speakers occurs within an embedded phone opening:

(15)   SDCL: MaligII:13

> M: Yeah (.) Wu:ll he's (.) he's umm
>   (2.0)
>   ((father is talking in the background))
> M: wait a minu:te (.) ↑ hold on ↑ hold on
>   (4.0)
> D: GOOD MORNING
> S: HI (.) how ya doin'
→ D: O:ka:y (.) ↑ Hey > waddaya wanna do about your
>   car < (.) iz there any chance you wanna try an
>   jump start it?=

S: =I'm gonna trade it (.) for'n eighty: eight
       BMW seven thirty-fi:ve=

D: Ri::ght .hhh=

D's "O:ka:y" receipts and brings the embedded phone opening to a close, and as an alternative to constructing a reciprocal "how are you/how ya doin'," transitions by relying on an attention-gaining "↑ Hey" to set up subsequent queries about jump starting the car.

Pre-Closings. Just as "Okay" can be understood as marking closure and giving rise to a shift in orientation toward initial topic(s) in phone call openings (e.g., via queries and reportings), so has "Okay" been evidenced as one routine component in "terminal exchanges" (e.g., along with "Well") and, more generally, topic closure. Schegloff and Sacks (1973) were fundamentally concerned with establishing a warrant for such claims (see also Button, 1987, 1990), as apparent in participants' orientations, that collaboratively refrain from continuing by working toward subsequent (and often relatively immediate) closure. As with Segment 16,

(16)   Schegloff & Sacks (1973, p. 304)

      A: O.K.
      B: O.K.
      A: Bye Bye
      B: Bye

a warrant toward closure becomes available. Or as Schegloff and Sacks (1973) plainly stated:

> Its effectiveness can be seen in the feature noted above, that if the floor offering is declined, if the "O.K." is answered by another, then together these two utterances can constitute not a possible, but an actual first exchange of the closing section. The pre-closing ceases to be "pre-" if accepted, for the acceptance establishes the warrant for undertaking a closing of the conversation at some "here." (p. 305)

In these ways, it turns out that a rather massive number of phone calls "begin to end" with markings such as "Okay," some that "may be said to announce it," as in "I gotta go," or,

(17)   Schegloff & Sacks (1973, p. 307)

      A: Okay, I letcha go back tuh watch yer Daktari

Many others rely on "Okay" and/or (at times) its functional equivalent in phone pre-closings (e.g., "All right") to offer recognizable attempts at closure:

(18)   Schegloff & Sacks (1973, p. 314)

→   B: <u>Al</u>righty. Well <u>I'll</u> give you a call before **we**
             decide to come down. O.K.?
     C: O.K.
     B: <u>Al</u>righty
     C: O.K.
     B: We'll see you then
     C: O.K.
     B: <u>Bye</u> bye
     C: Bye.

(19)   SDCL:Drkscls:21

→   D: Ahkay um (0.2) how <u>b</u>out if I give you a call
             like around <u>sev</u>en <u>th</u>irty
     C: A<u>kay</u>
     D: And we'll <u>fig</u>ure out <u>ex</u>a:ctly whenum (0.2) you
             want to > come get me or whatever <
     C: O<u>kay</u>
     D: At seven <u>thi</u>rty I'll <u>pro</u>bably have <u>ea</u>ten and
             be <u>sho</u>w:ered and <u>st</u>uff
     C: <u>So</u>unds good?
     D: Okay a I'll talk to you then
     C: <u>Al</u>right b ye
                          [   ]
     D: Bye

As becomes evident as this analysis unfolds, phone call openings and closings are by no means the only environments within which participants rely on "Okay" to close down and transition toward next activities or topics. In addressing how participants work to "get off/exit" varying kinds of troubling topics in conversation, Jefferson (1984) observed that a "recurrent device for moving out of a troubles-telling is *entry into closings*" (p. 191). In these kinds of contingencies, "acknowledgment tokens . . . can be accomplice to topical shift. A recurrent phenomenon is the production of a token just prior to a shift. . ." (p. 216):

(20)   Rahman:B:1:(11):6

    A: Never mind it'll <u>all</u> come right in the end,

→   J: Yeh. Okay <u>yo</u>u go and get your clean trousers on

Following a series of attempts by G to attribute wrongdoing and hold S accountable for her health by promising to make an appointment with a doctor (cf. Beach, 1991a) in Segment 21,

(21)   SDCL:G/S:16

    G: ↑ O:ne > step at a time < <u>S</u>issy
           (0.5) we'll go the <u>o</u>ne <u>ti:</u>me (0.7)
           that ch'u (0.4) promise me
            that <u>I'll</u> make the appointment   (   )
           [   ]
→   S: ↑<u>OKA:::Y</u>   Alright   (.)   <u>OKAY</u>
           <u>I'll GO</u> n– le(t)'s just <u>drop</u> <u>it</u> for t'night
→   okay? (.) I <u>don't</u> wanta talk about it anymore.
                (1.5)
    S: .hh <u>hhhh</u> I'm exhausted I havta work tomorrow
           are you still gonna go <u>walk</u> with me tomorrow:
           ((continues))

S relies on "<u>OKA:::Y</u>/Alright" in overlap, and as repeated emphasis in a "recycled turn beginning" position (cf. Schegloff, 1987c), to both affirm the promise G is requesting *and* "to start the conversation afresh; thus the name "conversation restart" (Jefferson, 1984, p. 193).

Addressing the Dual Character of "Okay"

From even an initial sketch of phone call openings, closings, and moving-out-of-troubling topics, it becomes apparent that participants rely on "Okay" in a dual fashion: to facilitate closing down some prior action(s), and, by so doing, to make possible the projection of and thus movement toward accomplishing some forthcoming and relevant activities. However, the dual character of "Okay" usages is apparent across a considerably more diverse set of interactional, and thus locally occasioned, environments than previously identified. Although routine and often taken for granted, such moments add to the richness and texture of everyday life affairs. Understanding the situated character of such moments, including what is "at stake" for the participants, is tantamount to grasping how and when "Okays" are recruited for accomplishing specific kinds of actions.

Consider the embedded "Okay" usages in Segments 22 and 23—two instances that are not atypical yet nevertheless deserve some close inspection. For example, in Segment 22, a canonical and even classic three-part "perspective display sequence" (cf. Maynard, 1989) takes place:

(22)   SDCL:HsReunion:8

    J: ↑ Was he heavier than <u>me</u>!

    A: No– (0.2) <u>yea</u> he's a lot <u>he</u>avier than you.

→   J: ↓ Okay then he's not even <u>cl</u>:ose. He said

           I'm thinner I'm skinn(i)er dude

Here, J first queries and solicits an assessment from A regarding a matter worthy of some caution: the comparison of J's weight with that of a high school classmate observed at a recent class reunion. Although A initially comes off as providing a disaffiliative reply or opinion, A quickly self-repairs and confirms what J next reports as, essentially, being in agreement with some other source ("He said"). In so doing, J relies on the third-turn "Okay" receipt in a way treating A's answer as sufficiently completed. The way is now made clear for J's subsequently achieved report. Clearly, a position is constructed by J confirming A's opinion via a next-positioned assessment (cf. Jefferson, 1981; Pomerantz, 1984) about being "thinner/ skinn(i)er dude," yet in an upgraded fashion. By taking A's utterance into account in this manner, J relies and builds on prior opinion in ways reinforcing (perhaps even exploiting) an issue J initially queried and invited discussion about: that a particular high school classmate was, in no uncertain terms, "heavier than <u>me</u>!."

In Segment 23, C (as recipient) initially comes off as agreeing with M's prior assessment and proposed solution regarding packing "the van":

(23)   SDCL:Bandchat:2

    M: There's no way thet it'll fit

           .hhh I know it won't fit in the va::n

              (.)

    M: It's gonna need an open spot

           (.) and we'll just put like a quilt?

           > in the back so it doesn't <

           .hhh scratch it up

1→   C: Okay (.)   that's fine
                  [   ]
      M: Ya know   scratch your
            °rim truck°
            [   ]
2→   C: M y :   trust me > the bed of my
            truck is so:: scratched and so: dented
            it's not gonna matter <

C's "Okay" in Line 1→ is not an isolated attempt to display sufficiency toward M's prior turn, but is employed in unison with "that's fine" as one form of sequence-closing assessment—one collaborative means of marking a no-problem orientation to what M displayed concerns about (e.g., scratching). Yet as M overlaps to reiterate and further specify °rim truck° as a focal point of concern, so does C in Line 2→ make explicit what "Okay (.) that's fine" left unstated: that "it's not gonna matter," and need not be attended to further. It is in this environment that C's "trust me" is best understood as a third attempt by C (i.e., "Okay → that's fine → trust me") to close down M's prior matters, eventuating in what is now seen as C's elaborated offering of reassurance about scratching the truck. But what might be said about where C may have been headed (i.e. some next-positioned matter C may have been en route to had the offering of additional reassurance not been occasioned)? Due to the contributions put forth by C in responding to the *interactionally generated* character of M's overlapped talk, and thus the additional and unanticipated efforts required by C to add closure and reassurance to this particular issue at hand, what C may have been *moving toward* following the "Okay" usage remains unclear (as fuller inspection of the longer transcript reveals). These sorts of contingencies, involving "Okay" usages in turn-transitional environments, inevitably shape the trajectory of speech exchange, and are addressed more fully in subsequent sections of this chapter.

It is curious, then, that although "Okay" usages of the sort apparent in Segments 22 and 23 are usefully understood as recruited components for treating some prior talk as sufficient and/or working toward achieving some closure or termination of the talk-in-progress (e.g., scratching the truck), additional actions are also transpiring. These instances and more begin to reveal how "Okay" can be deployed in turn-initial position by recipients (Segment 23) and current speakers (Segment 22), as responsive to prior turn and preparatory in movements to what is frequently offered as relevant for ensuing talk (even though, as with Segment 23, such movements are not always forthcoming). Each "Okay" appears to simultaneously resolve the problem of attending to what was projected in prior turn (e.g., acknowledging/affirming), and paving the way for next-positioned matters (e.g., reassuring, assessing). By means of contrast, and in reference to "Yeah," Jefferson (1981) suggested that:

> The token is observably, albeit minimally, "on topic"; observably, albeit minimally, attending to the rights and obligations entailed by the fact of talk-in-progress with participants distributed as "speaker" and "recipient." It is, albeit minimally, "responding to" prior talk and not—not quite yet, introducing something new. (p. 36)

Moreover, because recipients' assessments have frequently been shown to precede topical shift (Jefferson, 1981), C's final turn in Segment 23—an "offering of reassurance about 'scratching' the truck"—again assesses the situation at hand following the insufficiency of "Okay (.) that's fine" to put such matters to rest.

Concurrent Operations: Backward- and Forward-Looking Features.   When one considers the dual character of "Okay" usages, "Okay" is decidedly more than recipients' displayed attentiveness to topics or activities having already transpired; it is also essential and preliminary to what Heritage (1984), in analyzing the work of "Oh" as a "change-of-state" token, described as "additional components that achieve other tasks made relevant by the sequence in progress" (p. 302). Such insertions and movements are repeatedly achieved by first attending to (however minimally and in transitory fashion) what was taken to be projected in prior speaker's turn. Just as Heritage substantiated how "Oh" strongly indicates that its producer has been informed as a result of the immediately prior news, announcement, informing, and so on, so might "Okay" be understood as indicating that its producer agrees with, affirms, and/or understands what was projected prior—and perhaps even treats that talk as significant.[6] *But having so accomplished these objectives via "Okay," the way is now open to what is deemed relevant through additional turn components.*

Hence, a wide variety of "Okay" usages are designed by participants to be neither backward nor forward in character, but are conjugal in the ways

---

[6]There is a wider variety of relationships among "Oh" and "Okay" than described here—most notably the ways in which interactants receive particular types of prior turns with "Oh okay" (and versions thereof). Although an extended collection of segments, including "Oh + Okay," is undergoing analysis, a case for such specialized markings (e.g., "change-of-state + confirmation/ affirmation/agreement, etc.) is not made herein. however, Heritage (1990) examined other types of "Oh-prefaces" as turn-initial responses having consequence for a variety of activities (e.g., treating prior inquiries and/or questions as inappropriate).

they are wedded to ongoing activities. Such dual-character usages are not vacillating displays of decisioning, as if speakers are noticeably weighing or otherwise struggling with prior–next comparisons and their relevance to ongoing talk.[7] Rather, it is the lack of ambiguity made apparent in such "Okay" usages that readily, and altogether contingently and momentarily signals a *state of readiness* for moving to next-positioned matters. In this sense, "Okay" might best be likened neither to a firearm's bullet nor the marksman's placement of the finger on the trigger mechanism, but to the work involved in the careful "squeezing" of the trigger immediately prior to the firing and release of the bullet (complete with trajectory/aim).

At times, these dual functions are explicitly marked with two "Okays" by same speaker in consecutive turns: one for prior and one marking orientation to next. In Segment 24,

(24)   SDCL:Drkscls:14

D: Would you want to go with me?

C: ↑No not really

---

[7]Yet at times there appear to be particular usages of "Okay" that convey "special meaning." These include segments such as the following, where G's "Q:::ka::y?" treats S's prior response as something like "overresponding" or "coming on too strong," and the like—perhaps as one means to "feign" surprise, deference, or even contempt—with the position taken by S:

SDCL:CapPun:11

G: But do you think there's h:ope at ↑ a:ll
        for a– any of these people that (ha)ve
        been cha:ir:ed or: (0.4)   (lo:od) o:r.
        sho:t er–
                (0.7)
S: ° ↑ What do you <u>mean</u> hope.° get (th)em
        off the planet don't rele:ase (th)em
        an(d) have (th)em kill other people
                (1.2)
→   G: Q::: k a::y?
            [   ]
S: (I)f they can't ha.– (I)f ↑ they
            can't handle reality (.) the:n:. get the
            fuck out °ya know° ↑ get outta tow:n
                (1.2)
→   G: > Right but < d– does that still give us
            the right to:– to– ↑ ta kill (th)em
                (1.5)

Even on this occasion, however, G's "Q:::ka::y?" eventually leads to a fuller turn, as evident in G's next "> Right but <".

```
          D:      .hhh Why not
          C:      'Cuz I don't like Taco Bell
1→        D:      'Kay
                       (0.4)
2→        D:      Umkay you might feel like eating
          C:      Um
2→        D:      You feel like ta:co's anywhere
                       (1.0)
```

and specifically Line 1→, D relies on "'Kay" to acknowledge C's justification for an invitation refusal, and does not immediately pursue another
option. Yet when C also withholds speaking in the following (0.4) (transition relevant) pause, D's second "Umkay" prefigures a redo (and more
general) invitation (cf. Davidson, 1984; Drew, 1984) to eat tacos somewhere
else. In Segment 25, C and D are similarly engaged in discussing upcoming
activities, but the focus has now shifted to postdinner entertainment:

    (25)   SDCL:Drkscls:15

```
          C:      I guess the ba:nd starts at ni:ne
          D:      Oh really
          C:      Ya from what Jill told me
1→        D:      Okay when's Jill gonna go
          C:      Same time (0.2) we're gonna meet her there
2→        D:      Okay um (0.5) so you wa:nt to take your car
          C:      We can take your car if you wa:nt
          D:      .hhh hhh ↑ I meant you want– you wanna
                  have your car there so you can le:ave
          C    :         Yeah I think that'd be a better idea
3→        D:      Okay
                       (0.5)
4→        D:      Okay .hhhh well what– what time is it now
                  °I don't have my watch on°
          C:      Six o'clock
```

It is apparent that D's first two "Okays" are employed to acknowledge and
treat prior information as sufficient: C's citing Jill as a source that the band
starts at nine; that Jill will leave at the same time and meet them there. The
"Okays" in Lines 1→ and 2→ also function to preface and segment addi-

tional information queries in separate turns.[8] In Line 3→, D then receipts C's agreement to the clarification offered. With prior misunderstanding about the car now remedied, and following a (0.5) transition-relevant pause (similar to Segment 24), D's next "O<u>kay</u>" shifts attention to "what time is it now."

In Segment 24, Line 2→ and Segment 25, Lines 1→, 2→, and 4→ "Okay" signals varying degrees of on-topic/activity shift (as is discussed in more detail in subsequent sections). It is worth noting, however, that such "Okays" are not necessarily disruptive or competing with the ongoing development of these topics and activities. Although they display a general (albeit momentary or transitory) state of readiness for moving to next matters, they do not typically appear to be set up via other kinds of tokens. This is in contrast to Jefferson's (1981, 1993) illustrations of how "Mm-hmm → Uh-huh → Yeah" may (but not always; cf. Beach & Lindstrom, 1992; Drummond & Hopper, 1991) mark progressive movements from "passive recipiency" to "speaker readiness" in preparedness to shift topic and/or speakership. Although "Okay" may clearly function in activity shift-implicative ways, tokens such as "Um-hmm" or "Uh-huh" have not, in the materials examined herein, appeared as prerequisite to "Okay" placement.

More accurately, a straightforward bid for speakership seldom accounts for what "Okays" seem to be closing down and working toward (i.e., next-positioned matters) in casual interactions.[9] It is apparently uncommon for such "Okays" to be employed by speakers (in free-standing fashion) as *only* a means to signal "passive recipiency" (e.g., by working to retain the rights and privileges of current speaker/story*teller*; cf. Beach, 1991c; Beach & Lindstrom, 1992; Mandelbaum, 1989). However, some instances have been located (e.g., see Segments 18 and 19) where "Okays" are placed so as to facilitate current speaker's actions (e.g., closing a phone call). In fact, what frequently *appear* to be free-standing "Okays" are routinely not designed to display "passive recipiency," so as to retain the rights and privileges of whatever action(s) current speaker might be en-

---

[8]"Okay"-prefaced queries such as these, although not addressed in this present analysis, have been found to be predominant in two particular sequential environments: (a) during *planning* activities in "casual" talk; and (b) throughout a variety of "institutional" activities, where those "institutionally responsible" for an occasion's focus and purpose (e.g., doctors, lawyers, counselors/therapists, 911 or cancer hotline call receivers/dispatchers) deal with contingencies in the midst of what Sorjonen and Heritage (1991) and Heritage and Sorjonen (1994) referred to as "agenda-based nextness" (see Beach, 1993).

[9]In contrast, ongoing examinations of "institutional" interactions suggest that those responsible for an occasion's focus and purpose routinely rely on "Okays" not only in bidding for speakership, but also in shifting to markedly different topics or activities.

gaged in. Instead, such "Okay" usages can be identified as both closure-relevant and momentary, "on hold" prefigurings of movements toward next matters.

I turn now to an elaborated discussion of issues surrounding turn-transitional relevancies of "Okay" usages, many of which occur in environments where "next speakership" is at question, often involving overlaps and their resolution.

Next-Speaker Treatments of "Okay" in Turn-Transitional Environments

As apparent in the analysis thus far, and of particular relevance to the ensuing discussion, are ways in which "Okay" usages not only work to initiate closure for some prior actions, *but in so doing make possible and thus project continuation toward some next matters*. For this and related reasons, Schegloff and Sacks (1973) put forth "Okays" as only:

> Possible pre-closings because of this specific alternative they provide for. . . . Clearly, utterances such as "O.K.," "We-ell," etc. (where those forms are the whole of the utterance) occur in conversation in capacities other than that of "pre-closing." It is only on some occasions of use that these utterances are treated as pre-closings, as we have been using that term. . . . It should be noted that the use of a possible pre-closing of the form "O.K.," or "we-ell" can set up "proceeding to close" as the central possibility, and the use of unmentioned mentionables by co-participants as specific alternatives. That is to say, the alternatives made relevant by an utterance of that form are not symmetrical. Closing is the central possibility, further talk is alternative to it; the reverse is not the case (an asymmetry hopefully captured by the term "possible pre-closing"; "possible topic re-opener" would not do). Unless the alternative is invoked, the central possibility is to be realized. (pp. 310, 312)

In attempting to open up the possibility of moving from phone openings, of initiating phone call closings, as well as across varied other conversational activities, speakers routinely rely on "Okay" to facilitate such closures and make possible the transition to some next matters by prefacing or prefiguring a fuller turn. In orientation to such actions, however, and in the ways coparticipants treat "Okay" as a closure relevant, alternative attempts may nevertheless be made by next speaker to complete, elaborate on, and, at times, even sequentially delete the closure and movement "Okay" was taken to be projecting. Coparticipants routinely design their actions in precise orientation to, almost in anticipation of, and even as replacements for forthcoming and fuller turns of "Okay" producers. One useful example is provided by Jefferson (1986), who drew attention to the occurrence of overlaps at possible transition or completion points:

(26) SBL:3:3:R:5 (Jefferson, 1986, p. 155)

→ Milly: O:kay <u>that's</u> <u>all</u> ah wan'duh kn<u>ow</u>
             I th<u>ou</u>ght it w z mu <u>c h</u>
             [   ]   ]   ]
     Keith: Y a h w ' l   ]   ]   ]
            w e   w e   <u>don'</u> know how much is
       ↑ <u>In</u>: ↓ come h°<u>e</u>re though,

As Jefferson noted: "Again, here are a couple of cases where I take it that the recipient has particularly good warrant to treat an utterance as completed or transition-ready. . . . Somehow, 'Okay that's all I wanted to know' has a strong sense of finality about it. But, no, one can perfectly well go on with more" (p. 155).

In still other cases, recipients and/or current speakers may continue or even initiate a new turn, as if orientation is not given to the placement of "Okay" as closing, projecting, or transitioning. This is evident in Segment 27, where Vic's "Okay" might easily appear as free standing, at least in transcribed form:

(27) (Jefferson & Schegloff, 1975, p. 18)

     Vic: It's, the <u>a</u>ttitude of <u>p</u>eople!
              (1.0)
→   Vic: O<u>ka</u> y
              [
     Mike: Y' didn't getta holda–
                [   ]
→   Vic: d u h s o o p u h.
     (.)
     Mike: Listen   man.
                [
→   Vic: <u>Freak</u> it. He's a <u>b</u>itch he didn'pud
             in duh light own dih sekking flaw, .hh=
     Mike: =Y'couldn't gitta ho l–
                   [
→   Vic: Man <u>tell</u> im.
             (.)
     Mike: Jim wan' <u>home</u> uh what.
              [   ]
→   Vic: Y' kno:w?

But as Jefferson and Schegloff (1975) observed, Vic (as turn occupant) can be understood as having produced "a single, coherent utterance," beginning with "Okay," just as Mike (as turn claimant) worked to revise his question throughout an environment of "competitive continuous utterances." Such environments clearly reveal how the import of "Okay" usages is by no means determined by isolated "Okay" producers.

Quite the contrary is the case. For example, in Segment 28, B's freestanding "Okays" (see Lines 1→ – 3→) are clearly preparatory to "Okay + [fuller turn]" (*→). Yet what these turns eventuate into (i.e., the ways they may or not achieve some closure and/or move to some next actions) is mitigated and thus shaped by matters pursued by next speaker (see A in Segment 28):

(28)   SDCL:Study ((simplified transcript))

	A:	=I couldn't get over after that anyway
		I've got so many errands and stuff to run=
1→	B:	=Okay=
	A:	=that's perfect=
*→	B:	=Okay well just ha:ve uh:m
	A:	Are you gonna have her pick you ↑up
		or what ( )
		[ ]
	B:	We:ll see: I: don't know I think
		I'll probably just go home by myself because
**→		I have this appointment. but why don't you have
		her call me tonight. Is she gonna be home tonight?
	A:	I would hope so=
2→	B:	=Okay=
	A:	=I guess I'm gonna be leaving here at six to go
		back to school >I've got a class tonight.<=
3→	B:	=Okay=
	A:	a::nd so all I can do is– you know if I– if I
		don't talk to her before I leave I'll just leave
		her a note– message to call you tonight.=
*→	B:	Okay and do you remember how to get here? or do
		you want me to give you direc (tions)
		[ ]
	A:	S h e: gave me
		some instruction.
		((call moves to closing))

Notice that each of B's free-standing "Okays" is placed precisely at potential completion points by prior speaker A (i.e., at the end of turn-construction/syntactic thought units B treats as transition ready). In Line 1→, as is common (Jefferson & Schegloff, 1975), A's tagged "that's perfect" was clearly unanticipated by B; upon its completion, B moves to fuller turn (see Line *→, with the conjunction "Okay well. . .") to "ha:ve uh:m" do something that remains unspecified due to A's continuation and next query. After responding to A's query, it is apparent that in Line (**→), B address's and systematically raises the previously unspecified (and thus momentarily put-on-hold) matter: "have her give me a call tonight." In both Lines 2→ and 3→, B withholds [fuller turn] as A continues. This eventuates in "Okay + [two queries]" (Line *→), which apparently were matters that B did not abandon, but was keeping "on hold" and working toward all along.

From Segment 28, it becomes especially clear that speakers may be preoccupied with somewhat different concerns involving very similar matters (e.g., getting together to study). What is particularly interesting for analysts is how speakers' preoccupations are implicated within the resources invoked to coordinate specific kinds of emerging actions: How do coparticipants tailor their talk to the very circumstances they are caught up in, and thus occupied with (cf. Beach, 1993a)? In terms of what appears to be B's predicaments in Segment 28, "Okay" usages were recruited as attempts at closure, as well as momentary solutions to problems associated with achieving next-positioned matters in precise unison with next-speaker continuation. In these ways, B's actions are not best understood as standing in opposition to A's stated concerns (or vice-versa), but rather as delicately tailored to the "spontaneous combustability" of the moment. Although the "Okay" usages are important as resources for initiating closure and raising next-positioned matters, they only represent a portion of the complexities and competencies of everyday language users.

As with Segment 28, it is within these and related sequential environments that free-standing "Okays" may prefigure movements toward fuller speakership and the articulation of next matters. In addition, turn-initial "Okays" preface what is soon (and more specifically, as with the "'Kay but. . ." incompletion marker below) to be revealed as a next topical matter (e.g., catching a bus or trolley):

(29) SDCL:TwoCops:1

      M: So the bite .h the bite:r can
             probably can claim self defense
                  (1.5)
      D: Who knows
                  (1.8)

      D: But   uh
                [   ]
→   M: Okay
      D: I imagine it won't even go
            to court
              (0.8)
*→   M: 'Kay but if some– for some reason
            it does (.) then I < ca:n > the::n
                catch <u>a:::</u>   (0.6) b:us downtown
            [   ]
      D: ((clears throat))
      M: (.) or the trolley .hh do hh do you
            have any cash at all? (.) like
            enough for the trolley?

In one sense, "Okays" can be recycled to reinitiate additional tasks that, due to overlap with D's continuation, failed to emerge following M's initial "Okay." Similar cases are not uncommon:

(30)   SDCL:Drkscls:14

      D: And then <u>um</u> (0.5) and > I was just gonna wait
            for them to <u>talk</u> to you <
→   C: 'Kay=
      D: = > But I figure if I go about nine <u>Larz</u> is gonna
            go and his <u>friend</u> <u>Eric</u>'s comin– <u>Eric</u>'s <u>gonna</u> go
            with <u>Larz</u> I guess <
→   C: 'Kay
               (0.5)
*→   C: > Well I was thinking more (.) a little
            earlier than: tha:t <
      D: Like when
      C: Cuz (0.2) they start charging cover after
            <u>eight</u> <u>thirty</u>

In Segment 31, following M's preemption ("Mm: <u>ye:s</u> uh huh"), C relies on "<u>O</u>kay" both as third-turn receipt and as an initiation of "getting back on track" with the telling at hand. Notice, however, that C did not immediately continue due to the overlap of M's "I liked it" assessment:

(31)   SDCL:Bandchat:5

       C: Did you ev e r s ee tha t
                         [   ] [   ] [   ]
       M: Mm: ye:s   uh huh
→   C: O Kay
             [   ]
       M: I   liked it
              (0.2)
→   C: UH::M:
              (1.0)
*→   C: They have ha:d over five hundred orders: from
            the magazine for=tho:se uh (.) video– tapes

Overwhelmingly, then, an understanding of what "Okays" appear to be prefacing or setting up (see Line *→) is recurrently (and eventually) apparent, even within overlapping environments resulting from next-speaker collaborations:

(32)   SJ:I:6:1–2 (Schegloff, 1980, p. 137)

     Pete: Yer havin a g'rage sale,
     Hank: Yeah.hh
     Pete: Well fer cryin out loud.
     Hank: If I c'n possibly get away I'll be do:wn.
→   Pete: We:ll h   o k a y w–
                 [   ]
     Hank: If I: ey eno ugh other he:lp so I
            don'have t'stay here.
→   Pete: Oh I see, .hh h
                    [
     Hank: But u h
                      [
*→ Pete: We:ll we just tryin tuh
            contact everybody t'   see if they're=
                      [
     Hank: Yeah.
*→ Pete: =gonna show up down there

(33)   SDCL:Mavmolca:7

    A: = > It's– it's < a polish (.) ah:: nail har(d)ner
            and polish dryer=

    K: =Ugh hu(g) h:
                  [

    A: It– it does the sam e th–
                                    [   ]

    K: A n: that's
            ba:sically the same thing.=

    A: = ↑ Ugh hugh=

→   K: =Ok ay–
                [   ]

    A: Th at's right (.) its the °same   thing°
                                    [   ]

*→   K: See
            I think i– that's so: hot (.) to have
            something that you can spray on like   that.
                                    [   ]

    A: Ss:::
            ((imitating spraying))

Clearly, speakers employing "Okay" are not necessarily daunted by having "Okay" overlapped, or left as momentarily free standing or "dangling" as a result of next speaker's continuation and/or shift of activity. In fact, "Okays" (alone and/or in recycled fashion) may signal the likelihood, and even persistence, of subsequent movements to next-positioned matters.

Interjective Continuations by Current Speaker.   It is an overstatement to suggest that the free-standing placements of "Okay," and/or various versions of "Okay + [well]" (as a topic initial lexical item), necessarily guarantee forthcoming and fuller turns designed to ensure that matters of importance get addressed. Although "Okays" may clearly prefigure upcoming actions (as in Segments 28–33), they nevertheless eventuate in momentarily withheld, as well as failed attempts to gain the floor. Therefore, the opportunity to make next-positioned matters explicit is therefore, at least for the moment but often indefinitely, passed by. In these cases, participants' "Okays," and whatever trajectories they display, are "interjectively" deleted.

Two examples appear next (Segments 34 and 35), both involving current speakers' (B,Y) continuations, regardless of recipients' (D,X) attempts to move toward [fuller turn]:

(34)   SDCL:Detox:12 ((simplified transcript))

      B: I see– I see thee: a: (0.2)
                > this road < ? I take it an I
                turned arou::nd and I di'n know
                where the hell 'wz (.) so I
                did > a bunch °a fucki:n u turns°
                .hhh < I tried ta < pa .hhh (.)
                trace back and all this. > fin:ally
                I said fuck it < take Linda Vista .hh
                    (0.2)
→   D: Mmkay
      B: Cuz it felt right .hhh pt. (.) a::nd
→   D: Well how   (long-)   how long
                    [   ] [   ]
*→ B: Really   ↑Linda Vi sta at thee
                end ? (.) war (wrr) I'm sposed t'hook up
                ((continues))

(35)   UTCL:J66.4

      Y: U:m (1.0) eh– hopefully I'll be able to get
                with the printer and it'll just take you
                following up to make sure they're
                    (1.2)
      X: For what we intended them to be
              [   ]
      Y: That it's: proof rea:d   and all
                that   stuff
                    [   ]
→   X: Okay well   we
                    [
*→Y: And I'll call Beverly da– u:h
                ((continues))

Continuations of this sort are successful for two basic reasons. First, current speakers refrain from treating recipients' "Okays" as uncontestable clues that signal movement (i.e., as "bids" for extensions and shifts that must be aligned with, abided by, and/or deferred to). Second, recipients producing "Okay + [movement toward fuller turn]" withhold fuller pursuit toward a given matter (again, at least until a later moment in the interaction, and perhaps indefinitely).

Throughout Segments 26–35, "Okay" is preliminary to additional turn-construction components; the result is an extended turn type. As originally exemplified in Sacks et al. (1974), and more recently made apparent in Schegloff (1987a), extended turns evidence some kind of achievement. Yet when these achievements are overlapped or otherwise deleted as noncontinuative, immediately following an "Okay," some form of structural constraint exists on the minimization of turn size. Such constraints indicate that, although "Okay" may be employed as an initiation of closure, such usages are preliminary to fuller turns achieving alternative actions (e.g., making a phone call, giving directions, catching a bus, making plans, continuing a telling, etc.). Yet, as noted previously, coparticipants may nevertheless treat "Okay" as free standing/noncontinuative. Thus, they may proceed accordingly, completing prior or initiating new turn components, at times effectively deleting the closing–opening work speakers' "Okay" usages were designed to accomplish. These junctures are similar to the kinds of interactional work evident at "transition spaces" described by Jefferson (1986), as well as what Button (1987) coined "opportunity spaces," as speakers move out of phone closings by expanding prior or initiating new topic(s) (see also Lerner, 1987, 1989).

SUMMARY AND IMPLICATIONS

Examinations of a rather diverse set of interactions suggest that "Okays" can be employed by recipients and current speakers alike to achieve a wide variety of actions. Although all talk-in-interaction is meaningfully constructed, and thus temporally situated only in reference to some prior–next environment, "Okay" usages do not appear randomly, but are recruited by coparticipants to achieve particular kinds of actions at specific moments of involvement. It has been shown that "Okays" routinely and differentially appear as: (a) free-standing/noncontinuative response tokens, used and relied on by participants to display numerous orientations to what was taken to be meaningful in prior talk; (b) predominant resources for initiating closure of some prior talk and action; and (c) projection devices revealing recurrent transitional movements across a variety of "Okay" placements. Even when recipients or current speakers may (in next turn) treat prior "Okay" usages as noncontinuative, and/or move to sequentially delete the actions "Okay" was taken to be projecting (i.e., "Okay + [fuller turn]"), what participants appear to be prefacing or setting up via "Okay" is recurrently and (eventually) apparent, unless, of course, speakers subsequently refrain from moving to next-positioned matters that prior "Okay" was relied on to set up.

From the empirical analysis of "Okay" usages offered in this chapter, it becomes possible to gain a partial understanding of how talk amounts to action, how actions are inevitably consequential in shaping interactional environments, and how talk too easily assumed to be "messy and chaotic" is, in the first instance, meaningful for participants and, in just these ways, quite delicately organized. Such displays of organization are not inherent, a priori features of "Okay" per se, but consequences of how "Okays" are consistently employed by coparticipants as momentary solutions to certain kinds of interactionally generated problems. For conversation analysts, the ongoing task is to reveal the methodical ways that everyday language users create and resolve ordinary problems, not to disembody people from their commonsensical predicaments. By relying on recordings and transcriptions of naturally occurring (not contrived or idealized) conversations, analysts report, describe, and construct explanations for data so as to invite readers' critical inspections of scenic and collaborative activities. Gaining access to the meaningful nature of participants' actions emerges from direct observations of real-time interactions, and is not necessarily facilitated by a priori theoretical starting points: explanations rooted in reflections, musings, readings, and/or indirect observations of communicative behavior. Moreover, the activities of social life are shown to be best understood not by invoking causally determined and structured a priori forces (e.g., personality variables, culture, sociodemographic background; cf. Beach & Lindstrom, 1992), but as participants' locally occasioned, consistently updated, and practically achieved orientations to context.

This is not to say that conversation analysis treats as irrelevant, or otherwise loses sight of, actual concerns with history or tradition. On the contrary, in the precise ways that participants must rely on, invoke, and adapt to degrees and types of knowledge (cf. C. Goodwin, 1984, 1987; M. Goodwin, 1990; Sacks, 1975, 1985), and as embedded within recurring modes of action (e.g., stories, teases, accusations, excuses, nicknames), evidencing and earmarking particular kinds of meaning for those relationally involved, history and tradition are distinct forms of practical achievement. Treating such phenomena as occasioned and consistently updated here-and-now actions, rather than entities somehow removed due to matters of past origin and nature, draws attention to how interaction transcends temporal boundaries in the course of its construction.

Having illustrated and established basic and sequential features of "Okay" in casual interactions, and several kinds of contingencies that participants get caught up in during the course of organizing social activities, attention can now be more fully drawn to a related set of concerns we might formulate as "Okays and their *consequences*": What is it that participants are moving *toward*, that is, what specific *actions* do "Okays" precede by both recipients (e.g, topically extended and "mitigated" continuations, queries, and the work they achieve) and current speakers (e.g., story continuations and planning activities)? Examining ways in which "Okays" are consequential for prior and unfolding actions does not, of course, dismiss the importance of understanding how participants use and treat "Okays" themselves as meaningful. Toward these ends (and as mentioned only in passing throughout this chapter), ongoing investigations rest with such usages as upward-intoned and tag-positioned "Okays?", specially and phonologically marked versions (e.g., "Q:::ka::y?", ↑ Q::ka:y."), conjugal employments (e.g., "Oh okay"), and "Okays-in-a-series" (e.g., in *doing* getting off troubling topics). Finally, as a means to track and pursue understandings of cross-situational usages of "Okay" in the accomplishment of task-and setting-specific activities, attention is also being given to universal and particular contrasts among participants' "Okay" usages within "casual" and "institutional" (e.g., legal, medical, classroom, therapy/counseling) occasions.

APPENDIX

The transcription–notation system employed for data segments is an adaptation of Gail Jefferson's work (see Atkinson & Heritage, 1984; Beach, 1989). The symbols may be described as follows:

:	*Colon(s):*	Extended or stretched sound, syllable, or word.
OKay	*Underlining/Italics:*	Vocalic emphasis.
(.)	*Micropause:*	Brief pause of less than (0.2).
(1.2)	*Timed Pause:*	Intervals occur within and between same or different speaker's utterance.
(( ))	*Double Parentheses:*	Scenic details.
( )	*Single Parentheses:*	Transcriptionist doubt.
.	*Period:*	Falling vocal pitch.
?	*Question Mark:*	Rising vocal pitch.

↑ ↓	*Arrows*:	Marked rising and falling shifts in intonation.
° °	*Degree Signs*:	A passage of talk noticeably softer than surrounding talk.
=	*Equal Sign*:	Latching of contiguous utterances, with no interval or overlap.
[ ]	*Brackets*:	Speech overlap.
[[	*Double Brackets*:	Simultaneous speech orientations to prior turn.
!	*Exclamation Point*:	Animated speech tone.
–	*Hyphen*:	Halting, abrupt cut off of sound or word.
> <	*Less Than/*	Portions of an utterance delivered at a pace
	Greater Than Signs:	noticeably quicker than surrounding talk.

ACKNOWLEDGMENTS

This revised chapter appeared originally as "Transitional Regularities for 'Casual' "Okay" Usages," *Journal of Pragmatics, 19* (1993): 325–352. Appreciation is given to Elsevier Science Publishers B.V., Amsterdam, the Netherlands for permission to reprint portions of this article in the present volume.

REFERENCES

Alexander, J., Giesen, B., Munch, R., & Smelser, N. J. (Eds.). (1987). *The micro–macro link.* Berkeley: University of California Press.

Atkinson, J. M., & Heritage, J. (Eds.). (1984). *Structures of social action: Studies in conversation analysis.* Cambridge, England: Cambridge University Press.

Beach, W. A. (Ed.). (1989). Sequential organization of conversational activities [Special issue]. *Western Journal of Speech Communication, 53,* 85–246.

Beach, W. A. (1990a). Language as and in technology: Facilitating topic organization in a Videotex focus group meeting. In M. J. Medhurst, A. Gonzalez, & T. R. Peterson (Eds.), *Communication and the culture of technology* (pp. 197–220). Pullman: Washington State University Press.

Beach, W. A. (1990b). On (not) observing behavior interactionally. *Western Journal of Speech Communication, 54,* 603–612.

Beach, W. A. (1990c). Orienting to the phenomenon. In J. A. Anderson (Ed.), *Communication yearbook 13* (pp. 216–244). Newbury Park, CA: Sage.

Beach, W. A. (1991a). Avoiding ownership for alleged wrongdoings. *Research on Language and Social Interaction, 24,* 1–36.

Beach, W. A. (1991b). *"Okay" as projection device for fuller turn: Displaying "state of readiness" for movements toward next-positioned matters.* Unpublished manuscript.

Beach, W. A. (1991c). Searching for universal features of conversation. *Research on Language and Social Interaction, 24,* 351–368.

Beach, W. A. (1993a). The delicacy of preoccupation. *Text and Performance Quarterly, 13,* 299–312.

Beach, W. A. (1993b). Transitional regularities for "casual" "okay" usages. *Journal of Pragmatics, 19,* 325–352.

Beach, W. A. (1994). Relevance and consequentiality. *Western Journal of Communication, 58,* 51–57.

Beach, W. A., & Lindstrom, A. L. (1992). Conversational universals and comparative theory: Turning to Swedish and American acknowledgment tokens-in-interaction. *Communication Theory, 2,* 24–49.

Boden, D., & Zimmerman, D. H. (Eds.). (1991). *Talk and social structure.* Cambridge, England: Polity Press.

Button, G. (1987). Moving out of closings. In G. Button & J. R. E. Lee (Eds.), *Talk and social organization* (pp. 101–151). Clevedon, England: Multilingual Matters.

Button, G. (1990). On varieties of closings. In G. Psathas (Ed.), *Interaction competence* (pp. 93–148). Lanham, MD: University Press of America.

Button, G., & Casey, N. (1984). Generating topic: The use of topic initial elicitors. In J. M. Atkinson & J. Heritage (Eds.), *Structures of social action: Studies in conversation analysis* (pp. 167–190). Cambridge, England: Cambridge University Press.

Chomsky, N. (1965). *Aspects of the theory of syntax.* Cambridge, MA: MIT Press.

Condon, S. L. (1986). The discourse functions of OK. *Semiotica, 60,* 73–101.

Davidson, J. (1984). Subsequent versions of invitations, offers, requests, and proposals dealing with potential or actual rejection. In J. M. Atkinson & J. Heritage (Eds.), *Structures of social action: Studies in conversation analysis* (pp. 102–128). Cambridge, England: Cambridge University Press.

Drew, P. (1984). Speakers' reportings in invitation sequences. In J. M. Atkinson & J. Heritage (Eds.), *Structures of social action: Studies in conversation analysis* (pp. 129–151). Cambridge, England: Cambridge University Press.

Drew, P., & Heritage, J. (Eds.). (1992). *Talk at work.* Cambridge, England: Cambridge University Press.

Drummond, K., & Hopper, R. (1991). *Back channels revisited: Acknowledgment tokens and speakership incipiency.* Chicago, IL: Speech Communication Association.

Fraser, B. (1990). An approach to discourse markers. *Journal of Pragmatics, 14,* 383–395.

Goffman, E. (1974). *Frame analysis.* New York: Harper & Row.

Goffman, E. (1981). *Forms of talk.* Philadelphia: University of Pennsylvania Press.

Goffman, E. (1983). The interaction order. *American Sociological Review, 48,* 1–17.

Goodwin, C. (1984). Notes on story structure and the organization of participation. In J. M. Atkinson & J. Heritage (Eds.), *Structures of social action: Studies in conversation analysis* (pp. 225–246). Cambridge, England: Cambridge University Press.

Goodwin, C. (1987). Forgetfulness as an interactive resource. *Social Psychology Quarterly, 50,* 115–130.

Goodwin, C., & Goodwin, M. H. (1989). Interstitial argument. In A. Grimshaw (Ed.), *Conflict talk* (pp. 85–117). Cambridge, England: Cambridge University Press.

Goodwin, M. H. (1980). He-said-she-said: Cultural practices for the construction of a gossip activity. *American Ethnologist, 7,* 674–695.

Goodwin, M. H. (1990). *He-said-she-said.* Bloomington: Indiana University Press.

Goodwin, M. H., & Goodwin, C. (1987). *Stories as participation structures.* Unpublished manuscript.

Heritage, J. (1984). A change-of-state token and aspects of its sequential placement. In J. M. Atkinson & J. Heritage (Eds.), *Structures of social action: Studies in conversation analysis* (pp. 299–345). Cambridge, England: Cambridge University Press.

Heritage, J. (1990, July). *Oh-prefaced responses to inquiry.* Paper presented at the International Pragmatics Conference, Barcelona, Spain.

Heritage, J., & Greatbatch, D. (1991). On the institutional character of institutional talk: The case of news interviews. In D. Boden & D. Zimmerman (Eds.), *Talk and social structure: Studies in ethnomethodology and conversation analysis* (pp. 93–137). Cambridge, England: Polity Press.

Heritage, J., & Sorjonen, M. L. (1994). Constituting and maintaining activities across sequences: *And*-prefacing as a feature of question design. *Language in Society, 23,* 1–29.

Hopper, R. (1989a). Conversation analysis and social psychology as descriptions of interpersonal communication. In D. Roger & P. Bull (Eds.), *Conversation* (pp. 48–65). Clevedon, England: Multilingual Matters.

Hopper, R. (1989b). Speech in telephone openings: Emergent interaction v. routines. *Western Journal of Speech Communication, 53,* 178–194.

Hopper, R. (1990). Sequential ambiguity in telephone openings: "What are you doin." *Communication Monographs, 56,* 240–252.

Hopper, R. (1991). *Telephone conversation.* Bloomington: Indiana University Press.

Jefferson, G. (1978). Sequential aspects of storytelling in conversation. In J. Schenkein (Ed.), *Studies in the organization of conversational interaction* (pp. 219–248). New York: Academic Press.

Jefferson, G. (1981). *Caveat speaker: A preliminary exploration of shift implicative recipiency in the articulation of topic* (Final Report). The Netherlands, Social Science Research Council.

Jefferson, G. (1984). On stepwise transition from talk about a trouble to inappropriately positioned next matters. In J. M. Atkinson & J. Heritage (Eds.), *Structures of social action: Studies in conversation analysis* (pp. 191–222). Cambridge, England: Cambridge University Press.

Jefferson, G. (1986). Notes on "latency" in overlap onset. *Human Studies, 9,* 153–184.

Jefferson, G. (1993). Caveat speaker: Preliminary notes on recipient topic-shift implicature. *Research on Language and Social Interaction, 26,* 1–30.

Jefferson, G., & Schegloff, E. (1975). Sketch: *Some orderly aspects of overlap in natural conversation.* American Anthropological Association.

Lee, J. R. E. (1987). Prologue: Talking organization. In G. Button & J. R. E. Lee (Eds.), *Talk and social organization* (pp. 19–53). Clevedon, England: Multilingual Matters.

Lerner, G. H. (1987). *Collaborative turn sequences: Sentence construction and social action.* Unpublished doctoral dissertation, University of California, Irvine, CA.

Lerner, G. H. (1989). Notes on overlap management in conversation: The case of delayed completion. *Western Journal of Speech Communication, 53,* 167–177.

Levinson, S. C. (1983). *Pragmatics.* Cambridge, England: Cambridge University Press.

Mandelbaum, J. (1989). Interpersonal dimensions of conversational storytelling. *Western Journal of Speech Communication, 53,* 114–126.

Mandelbaum, J. (1991). Beyond mundane reasoning: Conversation analysis and context. *Research on Language and Social Interaction, 24,* 333–350.

Maynard, D. W. (1989). Perspective-display sequences in conversation. *Western Journal of Speech Communication, 53,* 91–113.

McHoul, A. (1978). The organization of turns at formal talk in the classroom. *Language in Society, 7,* 182–213.

McHoul, A. (1985). Two aspects of classroom interaction, turn-taking, and correction: A research report. *Australian Journal of Human Communication Disorders, 13,* 53–64.

McHoul, A. (1990). The organization of repair in classroom talk. *Language in Society, 19,* 349–377.

Mehan, H. (1978). Structuring school structure. *Harvard Educational Review, 45,* 311–338.

Mehan, H. (1979). *Learning lessons: Social organization in the classroom.* Cambridge, MA: Harvard University Press.

Mehan, H. (1991). The school's work of sorting students. In D. Boden & D. H. Zimmerman (Eds.), *Talk and social structure* (pp. 71–90). Cambridge, England: Polity Press.

Merritt, M. (1980). On the use of "O.K." in service encounters. In J. Baugh & J. Scherzer (Eds.), *Language in use* (pp. 139–147). Englewood Cliffs, NJ: Prentice-Hall.

Pomerantz, A. (1984). Agreeing and disagreeing with assessments: Some features of preferred/dispreferred turn shapes. In J. M. Atkinson & J. Heritage (Eds.), *Structures of social action: Studies in conversation analysis* (pp. 57–101). Cambridge, England: Cambridge University Press.

Redeker, G. (1990). Ideational and pragmatic markers of discourse structure. *Journal of Pragmatics, 14,* 367–381.

Roger, D., & Bull, P. (1989). *Conversation.* Clevedon, England: Multilingual Matters.

Sacks, H. (1975). Everyone has to lie. In M. Sanches & B. Blount (Eds.), *Sociocultural dimensions of language use* (pp. 57–80). New York: Academic Press.

Sacks, H. (1984). Notes on methodology. In J. M. Atkinson & J. Heritage (Eds.), *Structures of social action: Studies in conversation analysis* (pp. 21–27). Cambridge, England: Cambridge University Press.

Sacks, H. (1985). The inference-making machine. In T. van Dijk (Ed.), *Handbook of discourse analysis: Vol. 3. Discourse and dialogue* (pp. 13–23). London: Academic Press.

Sacks, H. (1987). On the preferences for agreement and contiguity in sequences in conversation. In G. Button & J. R. E. Lee (Eds.), *Talk and social organization* (pp. 54–69). Clevedon, England: Multilingual Matters.

Sacks, H., Schegloff, E. A., & Jefferson, G. (1974). A simplest systematics for the organization of turn-taking for conversation. *Language, 50,* 696–735.

Schegloff, E. A. (1968). Sequencing in conversational openings. *American Anthropologist, 70,* 1075–1095.

Schegloff, E. A. (1979). Identification and recognition in telephone conversation openings. In G. Psathas (Ed.), *Everyday language: Studies in ethnomethodology* (pp. 23 –78). New York: Irvington.

Schegloff, E. A. (1980). Preliminaries to preliminaries: "Can I ask you a question?" *Sociological Inquiry, 50,* 104–152.

Schegloff, E. A. (1982). Discourse as an interactional achievement: Some uses of "uh huh" and other things that come between sentences. In D. Tannen (Ed.), *Analyzing discourse: Text and talk—Georgetown University roundtable on languages and linguistics* (pp. 71 –93). Washington, DC: Georgetown University Press.

Schegloff, E. A. (1986). The routine as achievement. *Human Studies, 9,* 111–152.

Schegloff, E. A. (1987a). Analyzing single episodes of interaction: An exercise in conversation analysis. *Social Psychology Quarterly, 50,* 101–114.

Schegloff, E. A. (1987b). Between micro and macro: Contexts and other connections. In J. Alexander, B. Giesen, R. Munch, & N. J. Smelser (Eds.), *The micro–macro link* (pp. 207–234). Berkeley: University of California Press.

Schegloff, E. A. (1987c). Recycled turn beginnings: A precise repair mechanism in conversation's turn-taking organization. In G. Button & J. R. E. Lee (Eds.), *Talk and social organization* (pp. 70–85). Avon, England: Multilingual Matters.

Schegloff, E. A. (1990). On the organization of sequences as a source of "coherence" in talk-in-interaction. In B. Dorval (Ed.), *Conversational organization and its development* (pp. 51–77). Norwood, NJ: Ablex.

Schegloff, E. A. (1991). Reflections on talk and social structure. In D. Boden & D. H. Zimmerman (Eds.), *Talk and social structure* (pp. 44 –70). Cambridge, England: Polity Press.

Schegloff, E. A., & Sacks, H. (1973). Opening up closings. *Semiotica, 7,* 289–327.

Schiffrin, D. (1987). *Discourse markers.* Cambridge, England: Cambridge University Press.

Sorjonen, M. L., & Heritage, J. (1991). And—prefacing as a feature of question design. In L. Laitinen, P. Nuolijüavvi, & M. Saari (Eds.), *Asennonvaihtoja [Changes in footing]: Essays in honor of Auli Hakulinen* (pp. 68–84). Helsinki: Vastapaino.

Tsui, A. B. M. (1991). Sequencing rules and coherence in discourse. *Journal of Pragmatics, 15,* 111–129.

Wootton, A. J. (1988). Remarks on the methodology of conversation analysis. In D. Roger & P. Bull (Eds.), *Conversation* (pp. 238–258). Clevedon, England: Multilingual Matters.

Zimmerman, D. H. (1988). On conversation: The conversation analytic perspective. In J. A. Anderson (Ed.), *Communication yearbook 11* (pp. 406–432). Newbury Park, CA: Sage.

Zimmerman, D. H., & Boden, D. (1991). Structure-in-action: An introduction. In D. Boden & D. H. Zimmerman (Eds.), *Talk and social structure* (pp. 3–21). Cambridge, England: Polity Press.

4

Social Communication Theory: Communication Structures and Performed Invocations, a Revision of Scheflen's Notion of Programs

Wendy Leeds-Hurwitz
University of Wisconsin–Parkside

Stuart J. Sigman
State University of New York, Albany

with
Sheila J. Sullivan
Canisius College

The vision of human action embraced by social communication theory (Leeds-Hurwitz, 1989; Sigman, 1987) is one in which ongoing behavioral productions are structured by, and therefore held accountable to, a repertoire of historically given paradigmatic and syntagmatic constraints. However, behavioral productions are not limited by, nor identical to, these a priori constraints. Social communication theory's essential problem is accounting for ongoing communication as simultaneously the adherence to a priori programs (Scheflen, 1968) and the performance of a unique event. The fact that productions are not completely limited by prior expectations, idealizations, and grammars, and are not identical to such community guidelines for behavior, is why we are able to argue for the consequentiality of the communication process.

In this chapter, we sketch a relationship between persons' ongoing performance of behavior and the sociocultural structures supporting such performance. This relationship between process and structure, or performance and competence, is the location for communication consequentiality (Gumperz, 1984; Hymes, 1971). Communicators enter segmented moments of sociocultural life with expectations, assumptions, and regulations governing what may (not), must (not), and will (not) likely transpire. But the correlations among these expectations, assumptions, and regulations, and what actually transpires, are generally not exact.

This chapter represents both an application and a reconsideration of a theory with which we have been associated for several years (Leeds-Hurwitz, 1989; Sigman, 1987), and which derives from the interdisciplinary efforts of several scholars to forge a sociocultural theory of communication (Bateson, 1972; Birdwhistell, 1970; Goffman, 1967; Hymes, 1974b). Appropriately, just as the chapter is concerned with how communicators make use of prior sociocultural resources for behavior in both predictable and novel ways, and thus live the essential consequentiality of communication, so the chapter invokes and revises our social communication theory antecedents.

To write of the consequential character of communication is to suggest that, although all human action can be seen against a background of a priori resources, the communication process embodies a dialectic between these general (i.e., transsituational) constraints and communicators' local (i.e., in-the-moment) production of behavior. The communication process is consequential in that it permits, indeed requires, participants to attend to and take account of the actualities of "behavior as performed" by self and others. This behavior as performed is only partially and incompletely governed by a priori grammars, scripts, schemata, and so on. The chapter argues for an analysis of three tensions that comprise and permit the consequentiality of communication: (a) the tension between the lived and the ideal, (b) the tension between a current episode and comparable (past and future) ones, and (c) the tension between the separate lived moments within a single event. The momentary resolution of one, two, or all three tensions is provided for by the communication process (its consequentiality), not simply by the a priori resources.

With regard to the first tension, there are programs (Scheflen, 1968) that define—in some a priori sense—what communicators can and should do in particular situations. Specifically, actors are said to be bound by a priori programs (i.e., idealized scripts) for their communication episodes, which are, at least theoretically, to be faithfully enacted. According to early theorizing by Birdwhistell (1970) and Scheflen, programs are not simply cognitive resources for behavior, but social determinants of it.[1] In this sense, there is a coercive power to programs; they *must* be performed.

Our current thinking suggests that the performance of programs gives rise to its own dynamic and is neither fully predicted by nor adherent to the a priori programs. Thus, the communication process is consequential because communicators are capable of more than blind-faith reenactment of a priori structure, and because their conduct may serve to modify or, in some other way, make creative use of a priori structure. Programs are constantly subject to change according to what actually transpires in each

---

[1] Ray Birdwhistell must be acknowledged for originating many of the central ideas of this approach to social interaction, although in this case his influence has been personal (as teacher and co-worker of many of the relevant authors), rather than through his publications, which do not address programs explicitly. In particular, Scheflen often noted Birdwhistell's major role in the development of his ideas.

real-time event. In this sense, structure is not a given, but rather continuously under production (cf. Giddens, 1984); communicators do not follow programs rigidly, but rather use past structures as a resource for their current needs and circumstances. This is comparable to Rawlins' (1992) "dialectical conception [which] maintains that any social formation is revealed through and constituted by the endless interweaving of idealistic and realistic factors" (p. 14).

The second tension that communicators face concerns the relationship between behavior within the current episode and behavior from remembered previous and projected future episodes. Social communication theory contends that communicators, as members of sociocultural collectivities, enter bounded episodes with knowledge of history that can be drawn on and "taken for granted" (Schutz, 1967), and anticipations of a future toward which behavior can be directed. History and tradition represent a moral resource for communicators; they may choose to draw on it as a stored value, but may also feel compelled at particular moments to do so. The actual moment-by-moment production of behavior represents the communicators' individual and collective temporary resolution of pressures derived from history and tradition (e.g., to produce consistency and noncontradiction between two or more episodes or identities displayed in these episodes). The consequentiality of communication lies in the temporary nature of such resolution, each moment of which is ongoing and subject to subsequent revisiting, reconsideration, and revision.

The third tension concerns the multiple acts and their connections, which comprise a single communication event. The tension derives from the necessity for each participant to coordinate the multiple behavioral resources, ideologies, and goals with those of others present—more specifically, to fit behavioral contributions into the ongoing flow in a coherent and relevant manner. This third tension is thus produced and resolved by the communicators' ongoing construction of the episode. The focus here is more explicitly on the coordination between individuals in the present communication moment, rather than between past, present, and future (as in the second tension), or between the ideal and the actual (as in the first tension). (See Sanders, chap. 2, this volume; Beach, chap. 3, this volume; as well as our own data for illustrations of this tension and its resolution.)

We propose a revision of Scheflen's notion of *programs* to take into account these and related ideas. Although actors can indeed be seen to live and act within knowledge of antecedent behavioral structures, their conduct cannot strictly be considered the end result of sociocultural programs. Social communication theory recognizes that communication episodes simultaneously function as instantiations of a priori behavioral resources and productions of novel and ephemeral events. Moreover, the theory recognizes that, in addition to linguistic and sociolinguistic competence (cf. Hymes, 1974), there is a separate skill that communicators evidence as they perform behavior derived from the sociocultural resources in ways fitting each actual moment and in coordination with other persons' behavior. This latter skill permits communicators to employ behavioral resources in sequentially relevant slots, and to influence the ongoing course of interaction through the creation of slots entailing varying degrees of sequential relevance. As such, social communication theory has the potential to make a substantial contribution to discussion regarding the connection between structure and process in communication. However, it must be admitted that, to some degree, social communication theory has been hampered by its structural heritage—a problem we specifically address throughout the remaining discussion.

This chapter proposes that the notion of *programs* be supplemented by that of *performance* because the consequentiality of communication means that communicators perform (produce) a real-time event, rather than merely allow some a priori program to unfold. Actors have a repertoire of communication programs, as well as a set of skills for performing pieces of programs on an ongoing basis in coordination with whatever else is happening. Programs can be thought of as a sociocultural resource, whereas performances can be thought of properly as a communication resource (and product)—as that which permits (and results from) the "doing" of communication or of behaving meaningfully.

This chapter is divided into five sections: (a) examination of the original concept of programs and its influence on social communication theorizing; (b) discussion of several more process-oriented concepts designed as correctives to the original structural thinking; (c) presentation of a case study drawn from ethnographic fieldwork illuminating the difference between a focus on programs and a focus on performances; (d) discussion of a vocabulary for examining *behaving* as an ongoing performance or activity, rather than *behavior* as a static or structured entity; and (e) consideration of how this discussion contributes to our understanding of communication as consequential.

PROGRAMS IN SOCIAL COMMUNICATION THEORIZING

The theoretical conception of *programs*, described most directly by Scheflen (1964, 1965, 1979), draws heavily on the larger research tradition broadly labeled social communication theory. Alternatively named the *structural approach* (Duncan, 1969; Kendon, 1982, 1990; Leeds-Hurwitz, 1987), this tradition takes the analysis of interaction structure as its central goal rather than antecedents or consequents of behavior. Methodologically, interaction is recorded and analyzed after it has occurred, thus permitting the repeated viewing of the behavior under analysis (ideally, of multiple renderings of the target episode or behavior). However, we contend that this method has led to a reification of structure and weak consideration of process. If a particular stretch of behavior on film or videotape is available, and comparisons with similar behaviors in related contexts are as well, then these are the obvious questions to ask: What are the component parts of this particular behavior (or episode)? What are the structural alternants of each behavior unit? The less obvious questions would be: What does it mean that this behavior, rather than another, occurred at this time? How is this behavior new and innovative, and different from prior occurrences? The former two are structural questions, and the latter two are process questions.

The critical research in establishing social communication theory was *The Natural History of an Interview* (NHI; McQuown, 1971a; see also Leeds-Hurwitz, 1987). Originally begun in 1955 at the Center for Advanced Study in the Behavioral Sciences, the project extended well into the 1960s. Generally well known for its multidisciplinary focus, combining the work of linguists, anthropologists, and psychiatrists in a study of communication, NHI was the first major study to use microanalysis as the primary method of analyzing social interaction. As a result, it was a landmark in the development of both kinesics and paralanguage, and the beginning of what has since been labeled the *structural approach* to communication. The larger study can be divided into four parts: (a) a seminar in the fall of 1955, resulting in a linguistic transcription of a psychiatric interview that had been audiotaped; (b) a seminar in the spring and summer of 1956, where analysis of filmed behavior was begun, emphasizing selection and initial transcription of critical scenes; (c) continued analysis of the filmed behavior between 1956 and 1961 (at irregular group meetings), resulting in divisions of the scenes into major segments; and (d) final detailed transcriptions of the chosen scenes between 1961 and 1968 (primarily at the home institutions of Birdwhistell, Brosin, and McQuown, working with colleagues and students).

Because the researchers involved with NHI took the transcription of the behavior they wished to analyze as their first and major goal, an emphasis on structure was incorporated into the project from its inception; later this was taken for granted and left unquestioned. In the foreword to NHI, McQuown (1971b) wrote that he expects the study to be a first step in working out "a general theory of the structure of human communicative behavior" (p. 5). Apparently, there was no explicit decision made to focus on structure in lieu of process. Indeed, because the researchers were focusing on actual behavior and not psychiatric abstractions, to some degree they considered their work to be directly about the communication process. For example, Bateson (1971) wrote: "Of all the elements and vicissitudes of formation and re-formation of relationships, perhaps the most interesting is that process whereby people establish common rules for the creation and understanding of messages"(p. 22).

The researchers viewed their work as "a starting point for further research," not as a final statement, a fact generally ignored (McQuown, 1971b, p. 3). Due to its exploratory nature, no description of the structural approach was included in the final NHI document. The most explicit comments were published separately by Scheflen (1964, 1965, 1979), as a result of his collaboration with Birdwhistell during the fourth and final stage of the NHI research, and later expanded by Scheflen's collaborator, Kendon (1982, 1990). Both Scheflen and Kendon did more than record the methods and ideas underlying the NHI group's work; they extended these in unique and original ways. It is Scheflen's theoretical construct of *programs* that is of particular relevance in this regard.

Programs was a central concept in Scheflen's writings over several years, his assumption being that all interactions follow programs. Briefly, *programs* can be defined as "patterns of behavior" that are learned and passed on through cultural transmission (Scheflen, 1979, p. 10). They are "traditional formats or templates, learned and used by each member of a culture, that *determine* behavior" (Scheflen, 1964, p. 317; italics added), alternatively described as "standard units or configurations of behavior" (Scheflen, 1965, p. 12). As generally presented, programs incorporate the following characteristics:

1. Programs provide for performance of standard, recognizable behavioral units, integrated hierarchically and structured to be performed successively in steps.
2. Programs are specific to subcultural categories according to ethnic, class, regional, and institutional traditions.
3. Programs are context specific, that is, a given situation, task, and/or social organization may evoke a given program performance.
4. Programs have variants (or "branches"), alternative units, and prescribed steps to meet common contingencies that may arise.
5. Programs offer common meanings—or function, significance, or purpose—in reference to larger systems of meaning to experienced performers.
6. Programs prescribe social organization and division of labor in the performance, therefore, there are roles and complementary, parallel, and other relations across individuals' actions.
7. Programs consist of elements and sequences that represent the values, purposes, and precepts of the larger social collectivity and cultural tradition.

8. Programs provide for commutative integration through a number of behavior channels, each of which has subdivisions crudely analogous to bands. Collectively, these possibilities organize behavior of different logical types, and into different hierarchies, levels, and orders. (Scheflen, 1968; see also Sigman, 1987).[2]

In short, programs are "'grammars' of action and context" (Scheflen, 1979, p. 14).

The study of programs leads to a focus on events, rather than individual participants within those events, and to an emphasis on what is unchanging and stable across events, rather than what is innovative and distinct (cf. Shokeid, 1992, for a similar observation about research in cultural anthropology). They imply a view of face-to-face interaction as scripted and rule governed, rather than as constructed on a moment-by-moment basis in response to particular acts in the here and now. The value of the social communication approach to these matters is that "it allows us to recognize that a group has an existing structure that determines possible activities rather than allowing us to act as if participants made up group process as they go along" (Scheflen, 1965, p. 7). This assumes that people behave in patterned ways, and that programs are the identifiable building blocks for such patterned behavior. Programs enable interaction to be maximally predictable because they sustain and organize human relationships (Birdwhistell, 1970).

The predictability of sociocultural life derives from programs, which permit participants to consider what has already occurred in a given event, as well as anticipate future possible behavior, based on their knowledge of the a priori structures: "[T]hese anticipations of what *will* happen, determine the action as much as what *has* just happened" (Scheflen, 1965, p. 14; italics in original). This is the essential value of the concept of *programs*: it provides the mechanism by which persons are believed to organize their interactions and their lives in sociocultural collectivities more broadly. Programs, or parts of programs, are presumed to be known by each participant prior to interaction participation, although the cognitive representation of such knowledge is not addressed within social communication theory. From the research vantage point, programs are abstractable by the analyst upon observing sufficient examples of the type of interaction under study. A program is appropriately outlined only after extensive analysis of multiple examples of a particular type of behavior and event.

Even in his original statements, however, Scheflen (1965) recognized

---

[2]See Scheflen (1965) for an earlier, and substantially different, discussion of the characteristics of programs. We have chosen to make the major published list the focus of our discussion here (Scheflen, 1968), but have tried to consider various comments from previous articles and unpublished papers.

that, "to abstract the program does not do justice to the dynamic complexity of an actual performance" (p. 21). An issue highlighted in later sections of this chapter is that, once persons learn programs, they may join them together in new ways, or adapt them to new circumstances. Whether persons act in accordance with or in contrast to them, programs provide a partial baseline for behavior. Thus, programs are only one part of the story; they are not a complete explanation of social interaction from a behavioral, nonpsychological standpoint. It is this issue that we consider in further detail.

PERFORMANCE PERSPECTIVES

Several correctives to structural thinking have been proposed, more or less directly addressing the issue of how structure and process, or competence and performance, are related. Hymes' (1962) ethnography of communication extends our understanding of structure and many of the elements of process, but in our estimation still maintains a largely structural orientation (Gumperz & Hymes, 1972). This is reasonable, given Hymes' formal training in structural linguistics, but it is not obvious, because he explicitly intended to move beyond that early training. Hymes' (1971) notion of *performance* was an attempt to get away from the earlier linguistic emphasis on *competence*—always an essentially structural conception (see Leeds-Hurwitz, 1984).

Hymes' work sparked a series of attacks on the too-rigid adherence to structural concepts, extending from linguistic anthropology (Bauman & Sherzer, 1974a) to folklore (Ben-Amos & Goldstein, 1975; Paredes & Bauman, 1972) to oral performance (Fine, 1984; Fine & Speer, 1977). Each of these is examined briefly because each contributes to the discussion of the interplay between structure and performance.

Linguistic anthropology was the obvious home of the field that Hymes established in 1962, although it quickly influenced other disciplines as well. Bauman and Sherzer edited their reader in 1974 as the direct result of a conference held in 1972; it was the major inheritor of the research program outlined by Hymes (1962). Although after the fact Bauman and Sherzer (1989) named *performance* "the most central organizing concept" (p. xviii) in their volume, at the time they named "the description of speech acts, events, and situations" as their central concern (1974b, p. 163). This is a good indication of the conflict between the process goals and the structural assumptions inherent in the ethnography of communication.

There is considerable similarity between Scheflen's notion of *programs* and Hymes' division of behavior into acts, events, and situations. One of Hymes' students, Irvine (1974), made this particularly clear when she included as an appendix to her chapter, a "grammar of rules for greeting" among the Wolof of Senegal. This is essentially an example of a program as outlined by Scheflen. Similarly, and in the same volume, Basso (1974) called for "a grammar of rules for code use together with a description of the types of social contexts in which particular rules (or rule subsets) are selected and deemed appropriate" (p. 428).

In both Scheflen's work and the various examples from the ethnography of communication literature, a clear statement is made that the structures under study are not fixed absolutely, but rather develop and emerge through performance. Bauman and Sherzer (1974b) wrote: "It is important to stress that the acts, events, and situations described by Irvine, Salmon, and Abrahams, and some of those described by Kirshenblatt-Gimblett, Stross, and Sherzer, are not absolutely fixed in their structure, but rather develop and emerge through performance" (p. 164). However, it is our contention that this and other statements, although appropriate and necessary, are suggestive more than completed, and, in actuality, have gone unheeded by the majority of researchers even within the ethnography of communication tradition. After the performance analysis goal has been stated, actual research into communication patterns rarely emphasizes what can be learned about the creation of structure through performance or the role of performance in the unfolding of structure. In brief, the emphasis to date has been on what might be termed *grammar*, that is, rules for action. It is our recommendation that the next step—investigating the role of performance in the employment and creation of structure (grammar)—be taken.

As Bauman and Sherzer (1989) pointed out in their most recent writing on the subject, two conceptions of performance are used in the ethnography of communication literature: the first is *performance as speaking praxis*, or "the situated use of language in the conduct and constitution of social life" (p. xviii), where everyday life is viewed as a performance; the second is *performance as artful*, a specially marked way of speaking where "the act of speaking is put on display, objectified, lifted out to a degree from its contextual surroundings, and opened up to scrutiny by an audience" (p. xix). The emphasis within early ethnography of speaking research, as documented in the Bauman and Sherzer (1974a) volume, seems to be on the latter of these two types of performance.[3] Our emphasis here, in keeping with a shift to larger concerns with communication in everyday life, is on the former.

---

[3]See, for example, Hymes' (1974b) explicit comments on the subject, where he discussed structures and uses in some detail. The meaning he gave to *performance* seems to be that of artistic performance; he discussed "the acceptance of responsibility to perform" required of performers by their audiences. The same definition was maintained by Bauman (1977; see also Bauman & Sherzer, 1974c).

The verbal art approach has been influential on oral performance within speech communication studies. Fine's (1984) research into oral performance (see also Fine & Speer, 1977), begun under the auspices of the center for research into the ethnography of communication established by Bauman and Sherzer at the University of Texas–Austin, is one example. Due, in part, to this influence, and in part to traditional emphases within oral performance studies, Fine's focus is on artful practice, rather than on everyday interaction, and on the artistic components of performance, rather than the structure–performance connection (cf. Hymes, 1975). In addition, Fine emphasized the problems of transcription of actual performance, rather than analysis of behavior.

With regard to its role in folklore studies, the idea of performance seems to have been developed jointly by folklorists and Hymes, who cited each other's works (cf. Ben-Amos & Goldstein, 1975; Hymes, 1972).[4] The new emphasis on performance within folklore served as a critique of then-existing research, which had emphasized taking individual items of verbal art, as well as other aspects of traditional behavior such as material culture and belief systems, out of context for analysis (Abrahams, 1968; Ben-Amos, 1971; Paredes & Bauman, 1972). As a result of this early work on performance, the understanding of what constitutes folklore and its appropriate study methods changed: The relationship between the performer and audience became as significant as the artistic form of expression, or genre, itself (Abrahams, 1976). Kirshenblatt-Gimblett (1975) is often cited as one of the early exemplars of this new shift of emphasis, clearly grounding a particular artistic form, a parable in this case, in its context of telling. Yet despite explicit references to a focus on storytelling performance, Kirshenblatt-Gimblett ultimately provided a structural analysis of the event (see in particular the elaborate charts on pp. 124–125, showing how the various parts of the performance are related).

The concept of *performance* has continued to be of major significance within folklore for the past several decades, with an emphasis on "close analysis of individual communicative events in natural contexts" (Mills, 1990, p. 7) generally taken for granted. Bronner (1988) named *performance* as one of the three key words around which research in folklore to date has

---

[4]In his earliest discussions of the subject, Hymes (1974b) referred to the fact that "the term 'performance' has come into prominence in recent folkloristic research" (p. 443), specifically citing a Ben-Amos conference presentation from 1967, a Roger Abrahams publication in 1968, and an Alan Lomax publication in 1968. Yet as a student in folklore classes at the University of Pennsylvania with Ben-Amos and Goldstein in the mid-1970s, one of us (Leeds-Hurwitz) is sure that Hymes was always credited with having been responsible for the new emphasis on performance (his chapter in Ben-Amos & Goldstein, 1975, was particularly influential). Clearly there was considerable mutual influence at work.

been organized. His presentation of the most recent trend, which he labeled *praxis*, addresses the issue of those parts of communication falling beyond artistic performances, although it is too soon to tell whether others will elaborate on his brief suggestions.

In brief, ethnography of communication research, in all its various guises, moved away from an analysis of language structure toward observation of multiple channels in context, stating the need for an examination of communication process. However, with observations recorded in the form of field notes, audiotapes, films, or videotapes, and analysis requiring multiple "viewings" of comparable events, what resulted was essentially structural analysis: an emphasis on the parts of the event, or the connections between various grammatical levels (act, event, situation), rather than the process by which individuals creatively make use of the structural resources. Hymes' ethnography of performance tradition extends our understanding of structure, as well as many of the elements of process, yet it is limited by a largely structural framework, and by a clear emphasis on performance as a ritualized or artful event.

Hymes is not the only major author to set a trail away from structure and toward process; several other comparable attempts also exist: ethnomethodology (Garfinkel, 1967), structuration theory (Giddens, 1984), and performance theory (Schechner, 1988; Turner, 1987). In each of these cases, however, the attempt to resolve the connection between structure and process remains incomplete, or the focus is on a particular, limited realm of performance. It is our position that each of these process traditions lacks a rich understanding of structure, inadequately accounting for the structure–process relationship.

Garfinkel's (1967) ethnomethodology eschews grammatical or rules investigations, emphasizing instead the transcontextual interpretive procedures employed by collectivity members as part of making sense of action around them. Garfinkel rejected rules as an a priori explanation of human conduct because this would require a view of persons as "judgmental dopes" wired to behave in certain ways, but unable to make determinations that would fit rules to particular circumstances. As Heritage (1984) summarized this position, "what is being eliminated or suppressed in [the normative] form of theorizing is the range of contingencies, as interpreted by the actor, which may influence the actual outcome of a chain or sequence of actions" (p. 111). Our analysis of the following case study leads us to a similar conclusion—that programs- or rules-based explanations are inadequate—but we take a more moderate position from that of ethnomethodology. We contend that descriptions of programs provide valuable sociocultural insights, but that students of communication must examine the process by which program resources find their way into performance, and not stop at a description of the programs. Therefore, unlike Garfinkel, we do not abandon the notion of *rules* in favor of inter-pretive procedures. Rather, we ask how rules are implemented by real-time actors during, and as part of, real-time performance events.

Giddens (1984) also influenced the understanding of the interplay be-tween structure and performance, which he phrased as the ways in which action (performance) and structure intersect. His solution, *structuration theory* is described as "a broad perspective upon the study of action, structure and institutions" (Giddens, 1989, p. 297). However, we are in agreement with Huspek (1993), who wrote that Giddens deemphasized structure as constraining: "[T]here is little if any provision on this account for structure to operate as a determining force.... This ... is consistent with Giddens's general treatment of agency, for to attribute a determining property to structure would be to usurp agency's privileged status within his theory" (p. 10). In contrast, our goal is to explicitly address how structural constraints enter into performance, and how the consequential character of communication recognizes, operates within, and transcends such constraints.

Finally, performance theory, as articulated by Turner (1969, 1974, 1982, 1987) and Schechner (1985, 1988), can be noted. These theorists have a series of mutually influencing books on the studies of ritual performance within anthropology and performance within the domain of theater, re-spectively. Their interests concern two particular types of performance and the connections existing between them: highly ritualized performances studied cross-culturally (Turner's interest), and theatrical performances (Schechner's interest). Essentially, as with folklore and oral performance, these authors emphasized artful, ritualized performance. In contrast, our goal in this chapter is to account for the enacted structure inherent in less organized, less deliberate performances in everyday life.

In summary, the foregoing overview of previous attempts to discuss the role of performance in the study of structure demonstrates that none of these authors adequately accounts for the way in which a particular performance represents both the implementation of an underlying struc-ture (program) and the creation of a heretofore nonexistent interaction. For the most part, these authors have other agendas, hence this is less a critique of their work than an illumination of the gap in the theoretical literature. In the following pages, we attempt to fill that gap, making suggestions for an initial understanding of the role of performance in establishing, revising, and ultimately maintaining interactional structure. We begin by present-ing details of a particular case study. By examining how communication performances simultaneously invoke and transcend sociocultural pro-grams in one particular setting, we illuminate some of the characteristic features of communication that define it as consequential.

AN ETHNOGRAPHIC CASE STUDY

Overview

Sullivan (1989) specifically examined the contributions of a priori sociocultural programs to the actual performance of a communication episode, and the relationship between a priori structure and process. The study consisted of ethnographic interviewing and observation surrounding an exclusively female social event, the "basket party"—a combined sales and socializing event involving a sales consultant, a hostess, and a dozen or so invited guests. The research was conducted in western New York state during 1987. Three basket parties were studied, with interviews conducted with participants both before and after each party, and observation and audio recording of interaction for all three parties. The preparty interviews provide evidence for a program for the basket party in the form of participants' reported expectations for the upcoming event based on participation in previous such events or comparable ones.[5] The field notes and transcriptions based on the observed–recorded interactions permit an analysis of what actually transpires at each party and a comparison of these actualities with the a priori (reported) program.

Initial Orientations to the Party

The participants oriented to the basket party in terms of several enticements and functions of the event: (a) the opportunity to visit with one's girlfriends and to make new friends, (b) the availability of a same-sex socializing context approved of by husbands and boyfriends, (c) and the occasion for seeing and purchasing the latest home merchandise.

The preparty interviews revealed that participants oriented to the basket party as a "multifunctional event" (although they did not use that expression). The repeated implication was that the women felt they needed a reason beyond pure socializing to sponsor or attend a women-only gathering. To a large degree, the sales and socializing aspects of the event were joined by the participants. In their reports to the interviewer, the participants referred to the sales aspect of the event in terms of its function to provide a needed excuse for women to gather together.

---

[5]We recognize problems of treating interview data as the basis for analyzing programs, but, as Sullivan (1989) described, a potential tautology results when the identical interactional data are used to study both structure and implementation. We also acknowledge the choice to summarize across subjects within a category to arrive at the program, rather than treat each subject's report as a separate program. Thus, we compare broad expectations with actual occurrences, not a specific individual's expectations and behavior.

Consultant: Some people do these parties as a reason to get together with their friends.

     Int: What kinds of things will go on at the basket party?

   Guest: It will be just like a regular party I guess but we need a reason to get together.

   Guest: [It] is a chance to be with other girls y'know sit and talk and y'know I like to shop so there's everything all rolled into one.

   Guest: That's probably why [women] go to [home parties] is just to get out of the house. I mean husbands don't like you to go to bars; when a woman goes to a bar it's like oh no god o they're gonna be getting into trouble and they're gonna go see male strippers and who knows you know they're gonna be picking up guys. . . . I don't know why it is but husbands don't really care [about home parties] . . . even though you're spending money . . . I don't know of any husband that really objects.

These women seemed to consider themselves socially isolated, and they thought of events such as basket parties as ways to overcome this isolation. For instance, one home-party neophyte who worked as a secretary expected several of the other guests attending a particular party to be co-workers (indeed, the pool of invitees was generally drawn from family members, neighbors, and office colleagues). She pointed to the difficulties in socializing with her co-workers at the office, but noted that a basket party made this possible: "It keeps people busy; it gets people socially together. . . . Besides I just like talking to these girls and that's just the best place to do it I guess and not at work."

This is not to deny the tangible effect held by the sales aspect of the party for the participants. Certainly, this is true for the hostess (who receives complementary baskets based on the total number of sales) and the consultant (whose livelihood is the selling of the baskets). For instance, in the context of talking about hostesses who tell their guests, "Don't feel obligated to buy," the consultant stated that she tries to discourage such sentiments: "Please don't say that to them, and I always try to say not because of me, which is a lie of course . . . but I say because . . . if you're gonna go through all this trouble I want you to benefit by it, which I truly do." Consistent with this, the guests tended to treat the sales aspect of the party as a socially expected, rather than an individually valued, feature of the event. When asked to describe typical occurrences at basket parties, at some point in their responses the participants stated: "And then they'll sell the baskets"; "And then you decide what you want to um if you wanta buy anything and what you wanta buy"; "So you buy something from them when they have a party."

What explains the social pressure to purchase? Although the possible utilitarian and symbolic (prestige) features of the baskets cannot be overlooked (Sullivan, 1989), the pressure exerted by the sets of social relationships from which invitations to hostess and/or attend a party are drawn is also key. The women who were invited to such events, those who hostessed the events, and the sales consultant all seemed to recognize that an invitation functioned implicitly as a request for "help" in constructing a satisfactory sales event. In other words, the event and the preexisting social networks tapped into for the event provided a performance pressure (i.e., to attend, to participate in the games, to purchase, etc.). The consultant acknowledged that already existing friendships explained why some women initially agreed to hold parties: "Some people initially had them because they were friends of mine and they wanted to help me out." Similarly, one former hostess felt obliged both to attend a party and make a minimal purchase for the following reasons: "I've boughten enough now that it may be [I'll] look for something little to buy this time. . . . [I'm going] cause she invited me and she booked the party off a my party so I feel kind of obligated to go."

Furthermore, the informants perceived the triple activities of hostessing, attending, and buying in terms of reciprocal obligations. The help the guests provided to the hostess (i.e., by attending and making purchases) functioned like money in the bank, which could and must be repaid in kind upon request.

In summary, informants reported a series of obligations involved in their participation in the basket party resulting from their friendship with the hostess. These general obligations interacted with their expectations for specific structural units of the event.

The A Priori Program: Reported Expectations

Interviews with the three categories of participants revealed that they held and could talk about a set of expectations for the likely and required events at the upcoming basket party. For those participants who had never attended such an event, or had attended a variant (e.g., a Tupperware® sales party), these expectations were drawn from stereotyped information about such events, others' reports about such events, and their own related experiences.

> As my mother says, "Does a basket party mean you all bring a basket?" [on the analogy of a covered-dish dinner]. I said, "No mother, I think we're supposed to buy them."

Couple of 'em [guests] wanted to know what a basket party was. I don't know if they figured weave stuff, some of 'em did, said, "We gonna weave or something?"

For those participants with first-hand knowledge of basket parties, the data were perhaps more detailed than, but equivalent to, those in the former group with little prior experience.

Both participant groups offered three activities during the interviews to account for the composition and temporal progression of the event. This is captured by the following informant report: "I think they'll have everybody come in and feel comfortable and then get to know everybody . . . look at baskets and possibly buy a few." (Informants also referred to invitational and preparatory sequences prior to the actual evening, which are not discussed here; cf. Sullivan, 1989.) On the basis of this and comparable reports, it seems that the within-party activities can be segmented into the following three phases: (a) activities expected to occur after guests have first arrived at the party ("Have everybody come in and feel comfortable"), (b) activities during the sales presentation ("Look at baskets"), and (c) activities subsequent to the presentation ("Possibly buy a few").

The three categories of participants held different, but complementary, expectations for the party's starting time. For example, when asked what time she expected to arrive at a party scheduled to begin at 7:30 p.m., the consultant stated: "I'll probably be there at 7:00. . . . I'll set up my display. . . . I wanna have it look really nice cause that's the first thing they're gonna see." In contrast, hostesses predicted staggered arrival times. For one party scheduled to begin at 7:00 p.m., the hostess stated: "People will probably get here between 7:00 and 7:30."

During the first phase of the party, it appears that socializing activities were in the forefront of the informants' expectations (e.g., greeting, making introductions, chatting, offering and receiving beverages, etc.), whereas sales activities (e.g., the presence of the consultant and her display) were in the background. According to a preparty report from one hostess, the arrival of the first guest set the following sequence in motion: "They come in, of course being greeted by the hostess, and then basically sit around and just talk with other guests that are there. Drink coffee. Talk." A guest invited to this hostess' party provided the nearly identical expected sequence during her preparty interview: "You come in, greet the hostess, everybody else. It's like a little social gathering that goes on for a while; usually there's beverages of some sort, cocktails or whatever."

Informants clearly expected that the role of the consultant and the merchandise she had brought would be highlighted during the second phase of the basket party. Some guests referred to this segment with terse descriptions (e.g., "Do the baskets," "Go through the baskets," "[Go] through all the baskets"), acknowledging the expected existence of the phase, but not elaborating on its component units. Others provided detailed versions of the activities comprising the presentation phase: "The person doing the show will stand up in front, thank us for being there, go into her spiel showing the different baskets, and she'll say if there are any questions let her know or feel free to browse with the baskets." Others in this camp specified some of the transition and subsequent behaviors on the part of the hostess and guests:

> **Guest:** Probably [the hostess will] introduce the woman who's speaking, the woman will go through her descriptions of the baskets . . . possibly go into some of the uses for the baskets.

> **Guest:** You [the guest] generally sit down and listen to what the person [the consultant] has to present.

> **Hostess:** During the presentation, they're more interested in what's going on, what the product is and then communicating a little between themselves as far as what they think if they think something jotting it down. . . . I've never been to one where there's dead silence throughout the whole thing.

Finally, it is during the postpresentation phase, according to the informants' reports, that the dual functions of the basket party (sales and socializing) are expected to reemerge and indeed converge. In their reports about postpresentation expectations, participants mentioned such activities as deciding what (or whether) to buy, ordering baskets, talking with the other guests, and enjoying dessert. As the following quotations indicate, the participants articulated a clear sequence—moving from the buying to the socializing subphases, with some intermingling of the two periods reported:

> **Consultant:** And then I invite them to look at the baskets or whatever and they do. And then they bring their little orders in and I figure them out for them, and sometimes people say, "Gee I really gotta go." Sometimes they stick around for an hour just talking and laughing.

> **Hostess:** Then they're given time to choose their particular basket. They order it and they pay for it, then they might talk for a while longer and go home.

> **Guest:** After [the presentation] it's a matter of deciding what it is you wanta buy and then generally a socialization period afterwards.

> **Guest:** After we see them [the baskets], we'll have probably some kind of desserts and we'll order our baskets.

In brief, then, informants were prepared for an event with three recognizable subphases (i.e., prepresentation socializing, the sales presentation, and postpresentation purchasing and socializing), each with its own distinct behaviors and responsible person(s).

Performing the Basket Party: Program Invocations and Emergent Behavior

Space limitations do not permit an exhaustive description of each of the three iterations of the basket parties that were observed. Instead, we analyze the observational materials here by asking about their relationship to the informants' program-based expectations. This discussion permits us to consider how it is that a priori programs come to be enacted, how such enactments can be seen as faithful instantiations of the programs when combining expected and unexpected activities, how elements neither explicitly mentioned nor contained within the informant reports nevertheless are generated as part of program implementation, and how both expected and emergent activities are integrated into the ongoing flow of communication. Overall, this analysis permits consideration of "the uncertainties, the arbitrary, the idiosyncratic, and the private, which contain much of [persons'] struggles and achievements in society" (Shokeid, 1992, p. 241). It is in the comparison of expected and performed behavior that we may locate features of communication consequentiality.

Programs as Potentials.   The observational data indicate that the program, as operationalized in this case by the participants' articulated expectations, is treated by them as a set of potential constraints on their actually enacted behavior.[6] We suggest that the program constraints are potential because it was not always the case that actual performances followed through on the stipulations of the reported program.

The constraining nature of the program can be seen in the ways participants oriented to each other's actions and to the unfolding events during a performance. Observations support the earlier informant perspective— that the sales consultant held a different status and was set apart from others at the party, even when they were all neighbors and previously acquainted with each other. For example, guests were expected to stop whatever they were doing when the "main event" was announced by the

---

[6]We treat the preparty expectations as components of the event program because they were offered by informants as regulations and prescriptions for participation in the event, rather than simply predictors of likely activity. However, our method does not permit assessment of the cognitive or social strength of the programs.

hostess and/or consultant. However, it was not simply expecting the sales presentation that led people to stop their socializing and prepare for it, which would amount to a weak interpretation of the informant data. Rather, the sales presentation was the ostensible "business at hand" and had to be performed. As the interviews revealed, there was an obligation to listen (and, to some degree, to buy).

This does not mean that transitional activity was unneeded for this moral force to be invoked, or that all persons assiduously adhered to this moral force. Indeed, the a priori expectation behind attending to the sales spiel does not, in and of itself, explain its enactment because it is necessary to analyze the actual behavioral contributions of the multiple participants as they oriented to and accomplished this force. Moreover, consistent with our contention that programs represent potential constraints, attention to the sales consultant could just as easily be withheld as granted by the basket party guests. Attention is not automatic, and requires contribution and coordination on the part of all participants.

In one observed instance, for example, guests apparently lost interest in the sales presentation, and the representative shortened it as a result. The consultant began her talk by expressing some nervousness to the group, saying, "I haven't worked in a while but I'll give it my best shot," but then offered some of the usual elements of her narrative (e.g., the history of the basket-making family, a description of the sales convention and factory she had recently visited, a recitation of the basket-making process, etc.). However, subsequent behavior—some of it part of the program, some not—seemed to be treated by the guests as indicative of the presentation's imminent conclusion:

> The activity of distributing the [wish-]lists [and pencils] seemed to be taken by the other participants as a signal to begin talking with one another. While the list distribution and talk were going on another ex-co-worker of [the hostess's], Dora, arrived. After greeting her, Caryn got her a glass of punch and Dora squeezed onto the couch between Genie and Linda, two of her co-workers. When everyone finally had a list and a pencil, and Dora and the co-workers had greeted each other, Carol tried, but seemed to have some difficulty, regaining their attention. (Sullivan, 1989, pp. 123–124)

It may be that the wish-list distribution had different meanings for the consultant and the guests, and that each group followed through in subsequent conduct on the respective meaning of that behavior. For the former, it represented a way her audience members could keep track of which items they were interested in during the course of the presentation; for the latter, it may have represented the actual sales-selection opportunity, and therefore the impending conclusion of the sales talk.

As part of this incident, a modest effort seemed to be made by the various sets of participants to overcome the problem:

> Several times, especially when the [side conversations] became very loud, Carol either turned her back to them for a number of seconds as she apparently searched for a particular basket, or stopped talking altogether and waited for the room to quiet down. . . . [T]he guests seemed to become more interested in their own conversations and less interested in the baskets. It was probably in response to this growing restlessness that Carol "promised" the guests at least three times that she was about done: "We're almost done I promise." (Sullivan, 1989, pp. 124–125)

The sales representative complained to the ethnographer afterward that the guests had been "standoffish" and "rude" to her, both prior to and during the presentation. This reaction would seem to indicate that the program held force for the sales representative, but that the process did not provide her with an avenue for making adjustments beyond the ones described previously. It is likely that she did not use harsher sanctioning because of other features of the program she was trying to enact (e.g., to be friendly and ingratiate herself with her potential customers). Thus, it was not simply a local coordination problem in the event that ensued, but the collapse of the very program (at least for the consultant) underlying the event. Interestingly, only two guests did not purchase baskets at this party, and so the event was financially, if not interactionally, successful for the consultant (see the later discussion on the "inconsequentiality" of communication).

In brief, programs can be assiduously followed, partially attended to, totally abandoned, adhered to by some participants and abandoned by others, and so on. Although background knowledge of program structure may be necessary for researchers and participants to assess particular outcomes, they must also consider what transpires within any single episode in order to account for meaning production (see the later discussion on Garfinkel's, 1967, unique adequacy requirement).

Emergent Behavior.   There are varying layers of specificity to the informants' reflections and reports on their expectations, and therefore varying layers of specificity to programs and their enactment. Analysis of the observations reveals that participants may orient to a general "standing concern" (Jacobs, Jackson, Stearns, & Hall, 1991) for the performance event, and/or they may perform a detailed and precise program-based behavioral unit. In other words, there is a difference between participants' adhering to the "sales and socializing expectations" and the "we must greet at this point in the process" aspects of the program, respectively. In the former case, participants implement a general goal or spirit for the event in whatever way they can and in whatever way they see as appropriate at the moment (cf. Hymes', 1974a, discussion of *key*), whereas in the latter case, they perform a specific behavior or routine in a sequentially appropriate slot.

This distinction between goals and structures as separable features of programs becomes salient as we examine emergent behavior. *Emergent behavior* is defined here as behavior not accounted for, or predictable from, the participants' reported programs. Such behavior might consist of deviations from the program features (e.g., lack of attention paid to the consultant in the earlier example) or the appearance of units not covered by the program altogether. But emergent behavior does not simply happen when unexpected behavior occurs. Rather, for at least some cases in the observational corpus, it appears when the performance of otherwise expected structures might prove "ungrammatical" or "undesirable," given more general and expected goals or outcomes for the event or a subsidiary phase. In other words, emergent behavior can be related to moments when the program cannot or should not be performed. Consider the following incident:

> [The sales consultant] prepared for favor-time as she usually did by writing the names of baskets on the backs of three wish-lists. Her usual strategy was to give small favors to the women who received the specially marked wish-lists. However, during the period of passing out wish-lists, pencils, catalogs, and so on, I [the ethnographer] realized that I had ended up with one of the specially-marked wish-lists. Since I did not want the other guests to suspect that there was any kind of favoritism operating, I signaled my predicament to the consultant by pointing to the back of my wish-list, and she nodded her head at me, apparently indicating that she understood. (Sullivan, 1989, p. 213)

The sales consultant altered the standard program implementation by eliminating favors altogether in this one case.

Existential performance contingencies may give rise to deletions from and/or additions to the program. It is not the contingency that gives rise to the change from the program, but rather its potential meaning or consequence. That is, as in the deletion of party favors because of possible negative repercussions at the one party, there may be some other standing concern or coherence restriction (derived from the program or even more general sociocultural rules) that would be negatively cast on the group's activity should the program be assiduously followed.

A second example provides additional insights into emergent behavior and its appearance as a momentary solution to some of the multiple, often conflicting, goals with which persons enter communication events. The creation of a smoking lounge at one party resulted from conflicts between the hostess' expectations and obligations (for satisfying her guests, providing ample socializing opportunity, enabling relationship co-members to interact, and protecting her home) and those of her smoking guests.

> She appeared to be unhappy about the idea [of allowing smoking in the house], so it was suggested that the smokers go outside to do their smoking. After Carol had completed her display, she and I went outside [to the front porch] to smoke.... [T]he area just outside the front door became the smoking section and throughout the evening, except during the presentation, two or more women could be found there smoking and talking. (Sullivan, 1989, p. 128)

Apparently because this was not a standard feature of the event program, guests had to be repeatedly informed about the decision.

Guest 1:	I'll be right back. I'm gonna go out
Guest 2:	(sing-song voice:) We know where you're goin.
Guest 3:	Look at this gosh the whole house just emptied out.
Guest 4:	Where'd they go?
Hostess:	[Outside to] smoke.
Guest 3:	That's the way to do it.
Guest 4:	Didn't you let anybody smoke in here?
Guest 3:	It didn't really deter anyone though.
Hostess:	[You can smoke but you can't] exhale.

Indeed, the establishment of a no-smoking policy for within the home, and the attendant creation of the smoking area on the front porch, did not prove totally satisfactory for the participants, and both activities were revisited in talk during the course of the evening. For example, on a few occasions when smokers were observed entering or exiting the house, comments were made disparaging the effect this movement was having on sociable interaction.

> [W]hen a group of smokers moved back into the house they were greeted with the following comment from one of the non-smoking guests: "I was gonna say we were gonna move everything outside." The hostess appeared to interpret this as a negative reaction to the emergent (unexpected) no-smoking policy, [a] sanction since her next contribution both supported the guest's comment and suggested a remedy for the situation: "Yeah I mean I was really thinking maybe I should dig up some ashtrays do you want me to?" (Sullivan, 1989, pp. 203–204)

Not everything that is unexpected or nonprogrammatic necessarily produces a disruption in the ongoing behavioral flow. Some unexpected behaviors may be integrated into this flow, perhaps because they adhere to a set of superarching goals, whereas others may not. In the first example, no mention was made of the wish lists by the consultant, despite its presumably a priori status for her. In contrast, in the second example, the hostess did account for and attempt to remedy the creation of a separate smoking area. We do not mean to imply that the consultant's response to the researcher's receipt of the marked paper was inevitable; we reason that she could have redistributed wish lists, acknowledged the embarrassment, and so on. All such behaviors, although differentially meaningful, share the background of expectations regarding wish lists, complementary gifts, and fairness, but represent different solutions to the posed dilemma.

One aspect of communication analysis must consider the moral force, not only behind the expectations (both sequential and goal oriented) brought to an event, but behind the behavior units actually performed during the event. A crucial issue to consider with regard to the relationship between programs and performances is that deviations from the former result not from unexpected occurrences per se, but rather from unexpected occurrences that provide a priority and coerciveness (e.g., in the form of an interaction frame or activity, which at that moment has to be attended to and/or completely implemented). In this regard, we can note those unexpected items that may have cropped up but were dropped relatively quickly or not explicitly noted, such as the nonappearance of the wish lists or fleeting conversational topics. Their momentary appearance was not compelling enough—did not have a "coercive feature"—to be continued, in comparison with the smoking lounge, which apparently did.

We can also consider the "secondary" influences of both planned and unplanned behavior on the episode being performed. For example, the creation of the smoking lounge appeared to prevent or delay the enactment of certain expected activity at the one party, where women stayed on the porch smoking instead of entering the house and greeting those already arrived. This occurred even when the lounge contained strangers and the house contained friends. Thus, the participants' behavior conformed to one overarching goal of making new friends, as expressed during preparty interviews, and abandoned the second goal of socializing with acquaintances, although both results seemed to be accidental, not deliberately produced.[7] However, the creation and maintenance of the smoking area did not interfere with the accomplishment of another pro-

---

[7]Implicit here is a distinction between behavior that is performed in the service of (i.e., as part of person's orientation to and implementation behavior of) an a priori program, and behavior that is coincidentally included in reports of a priori structure. We make the distinction on the basis of the apparent normative force that persons express and seemingly attend to during the performance (e.g., an explicit transition statement invoking a program element, vs. no statement that people should be mingling), but recognize the need for further research on this point.

gram element—the sales presentation. The smokers did indeed join the nonsmokers approximately 5 minutes before the presentation began, with some indication that the smokers' voluntary entrance provided the hostess with a signal for beginning the announcement sequence. The smokers remained seated and physically oriented to the sales consultant throughout the presentation, returning to the smoking lounge only after the presentation was completed. The sales presentation, as the official business at hand, served as a powerful constraint on emergent behavior such as using the smoking lounge. The participants acted as if socializing were a more flexibly structured activity (into which unexpected features could be easily integrated) than the sales presentation.

Thus, unplanned-for events may reveal the relative valence or significance attached to the various aspects of the program. For example, during one preparty interview, it was reported that a sales person failed to show up at a Tupperware® party. The informant and others present seemed to prefer it that way, because now they could socialize solidly for 3 hours. Yet at the end of the evening, they perused the catalog and left purchase orders, thus demonstrating the force of at least one part of the event. The ultimate goal, clearly stated and understood by participants, is the purchase of objects. Therefore, that goal may be respected even when a critical participant is missing.

In brief, then, not only is there a tension between the two structures (sales and socializing) of a single basket party, which is worked out during a performance, but a tension between the constituent structures and more general goals. The previous data may indicate that this tension is constantly being oriented to during interaction, producing either momentary adherence to a priori structures and goals or novel forms.

In conclusion, it seems that participants: (a) orient to the implementation of expected features unless or until they are prevented from doing so by the emergence of unexpected features that have some moral weight to them; (b) orient to the implementation of unexpected features as long as the emergent feature is providing interactional constraint and the a priori feature is not; and (c) return to the implementation of temporarily suspended expected features when the unexpected feature is no longer interactionally relevant, or when the expected feature holds a more weighty moral obligation over the participants.

Communication as Irrelevant.   There are some prior expectations that seem to demand attention no matter the actual communication performance and the contingencies of this performance. In some respects, this speaks to the inconsequentiality of communication. For example, informants reported that, no matter how poor a particular sales presentation may be, if they feel loyalty or friendship toward the hostess they will make a purchase anyway. The previous informant quotes reveal the importance of participants' prior relationships with each other for their participation in the various aspects of the event (attendance, purchasing, etc.); they enter with a set of expectations to fulfill without necessary regard for the performance. Even the one party where the sales presentation was given minimal attention by the guests resulted in sales for the consultant. The reported Tupperware® party, at which the sales talk did not occur (although purchases were still made), may also point to the inconsequentiality of some performances.

Having stated this, however, it must be acknowledged that it is potentially misleading to push for the notion of *inconsequentiality*, and to suggest that relationship considerations automatically produce certain behavioral outcomes. It is true that a weak or absent performance by the sales consultant may still occasion purchasing. However, as already noted, it is not the polished persuasive behavior of the consultant that leads to sales behavior, but the carrying out of the set of friendly obligations among the other participants. Indeed, the act of meeting and performing—even in the absence of the consultant in one case earlier and no matter the poor performance quality in another—may be necessary for the participants to fulfill the aforementioned set of friendly obligations to attend parties and make purchases. In other words, the framework of a basket party is still present and valid, and only a single element is missing or badly performed. Thus, we can say that the performance is consequential at one level of analysis (in terms of sheer existence), even if not at another (in terms of the quality of the performance or its faithful adherence to the program).

Coordinating Activity During Performance.   The availability of particular participants, their movement through space (e.g., in the form of entrances and exits), and the multiple simultaneous demands that fall on the multiple participants at any one time may determine the order in which program elements are actually performed and the degrees of expansion (i.e., energy or intensity, duration or speed) of these elements.

As noted previously, not all elements of the reported expectations were indeed enacted at any or all of the three basket parties observed. Two possible explanations for this, deriving from the program, are that the degree of moral force behind the expected element may be relatively weak, and/or that the expectation may constitute a mythology or ideal—not one that the participants expect to invoke or implement actively during performance. But these program features are mediated by participants' actual lived experiences and production of an event.

For example, an examination of two basket parties reveals that after guests arrived, engaged in greetings and introductions, and received offers of refreshments, they tended to engage in conversations with previous acquaintances, thus implementing one expectation (that they will socialize with friends and neighbors) at the expense of at least a portion of another (that new friendships will develop). During these two observed parties (excluding the one with the improvised smoking lounge), previously acquainted participants established and maintained spatially bounded areas—face formations (Kendon, 1990)—that resulted in the inclusion of acquainted participants in conversation and the exclusion of unacquainted participants. In other words, although mechanisms for establishing relationships between those previously unacquainted were used by the hostesses and some of their guests (i.e., introductions), these mechanisms apparently did not consistently function as a segue into extended conversation among the unacquainted participants. Both the continual offering of refreshments and the arrival and movement of other guests may have intruded on topic elaborations taking place between any one introduction and subsequent interaction. The constant influx of people, resulting in relatively short introductions, followed by elaborate offerings of drinks and opportunities to "catch up" with friends, may have precluded other interactional arrangements.

Thus, goals and expectations concerning engaging in conversation with all types of participants were not always implemented at junctures where they might have been expected to occur. This suggests that the expectation of talking with unacquainted participants may be a "mythology" about how these women feel they should behave during such gatherings, with minimal force behind it. This minimal force, combined with a chaotic performance atmosphere, resulted in nonimplementation. (The one notable exception to this was the party with smoking on the front porch, where the interaction space permitted or perhaps even forced conversation among unacquainted participants.)

Transitions between particular program elements may not be contained in the program; in both this case and the case where transitions are built into the program expectations, the participants may nevertheless need to produce transitions relevant to the actual moment of their production. As noted earlier, participants expected that, at some point during the party, they would all "do the baskets." It was further expected that "the person doing the show will stand up in front, thank us for being there, [and] go into her spiel." Some transition behavior was specified. For example, for the hostess, it was assumed that "probably she'll introduce the woman who's speaking"; for the guests, it was assumed that they "generally sit down and listen to what the person has to present." But in order for a transition from socializing to the sales phase to be accomplished, participants must signal that now is the time for this to occur. Moreover, all participants must contribute and coordinate their behavior for this transition to happen. Such coordination involves participants not only integrating their behavior with each other's, but also meshing their current behavioral obligations (to effectuate their piece of the transition) with their immediately preceding conduct (whether they are standing or seated, en route to getting a drink, etc.).

The following illustrates the gradual unfolding of the socializing to sales transition at one basket party:

Consult:	Is everybody here?
Hostess:	A few more ladies I think they're gonna be late I think the only person that might be missing is my neighbor.
[Untranscribed conversations]	
Hostess:	Anybody else need an ashtray? You guys all set for ashtrays?
Guest 1:	I think so.
Hostess:	Anyone like a refill before she starts?
[Untranscribed conversations]	
Hostess:	Does anybody else need something?
Guest 2:	Are you waiting for us?
Hostess:	If anybody wants refills. . . .
Consult:	Does anybody else want something to drink before I start?
Guest 3:	I have to use the bathroom first.
[Untranscribed conversations]	
Consult:	O.K. Well, I'm just waiting until everybody's all ready.
Guest 1:	Are you gonna start officially?
Guest 2:	She's starting now.
Consult:	I'm gonna start now.

To some degree, the present discussion raises questions about the cognitive structuring of the program. Is it that transitions are not part of the program, or that the cognitive task involved in reporting about expectations does not give rise to reports of transitions? It may be that, although participants recognize that transitions must be enacted, they do not specify how such transitions will or should be enacted because this is dependent on the performance moment and not the program. In this regard, there may be worthwhile distinctions to be made between two types of programs and events: those for which ritualistic transitions are not precoded (e.g., a basket party), and those for which ritualized solutions are provided (e.g., during High Mass). In the former, nonritualized situation, participants choose from a standardized repertoire of transition behaviors that are not specific to, and therefore not program features of, a particular communication episode. Moreover, they must uniquely perform those behaviors that result in a transition from their then-current activity and location to the next phase's activity and location.

In summary, as with the major periods or activities of an event, so too do the transitions between activities or periods require accomplishment. Regardless of whether the transitions are program based and tied to the target episode, or general and applicable across a variety of episodes, they demand coordination across participants and their behavior in the actual moments of their production.[8]

Performance Summary. The previous discussion reveals a number of insights concerning the relationship between a priori programs and lived performances. First, although programs represent a sociocultural resource for meaningful behaving that contains a variety of degrees of moral force, actual performances may adhere to or abandon some (or all) components of a particular program. Repair work may be initiated when a local coordination problem in the implementation of a program ensues, but the wholesale abandonment of a program by some participants may make it impossible for the other participants to coordinate their behavior with that of the former. Second, performances may realize both the standing concerns and the sequential structures embodied by the program, but at particular moments it may be necessary for the participants to abandon one in favor of the other, and to fill in underspecified features of a program behavior. Thus, the communication process produces emergent behavior that provides a moral coerciveness or constraint of its own. Third, the significance of an event may reside less in its performance quality than in the utter fact of its having been performed, ironically combining the consequential character of communication performance with its inconsequentiality. Fourth, some components of a program may have mythological status for participants, and performance activities may shape the incidental implementation of these components. Finally, transitions between recognized subprograms can be seen to derive from the program itself, from a standardized repertoire of transition devices, and—most important from the vantage point of communication consequentiality—from participants coordinating their

---

[8]Although it is not possible to totally assess the degree of requisiteness underlying the various reported activities (e.g., whether they represent pieces of an underlying program, stereotyped expectations, presumptions with little moral force, etc.), we can use the transitions to approach such an analysis. For example, different moral orientations are implied by the following invocations: "Let's do this folks and get it over with"; "Here's what's happening next"; "We have to do this or all hell will break loose." The basket party data show the high degree of constraint placed on participants resulting from the transition to the sales talk, and the low degree on the heels of the postpresentation transitions, which revealed a bundle of permissible activities (exiting, smoking, using the lavatory, eating dessert, etc.).

efforts with whatever else they are individually and jointly doing at the moment when transitions are called for.

INTERACTION TENSIONS

Programs represent generalized sociocultural resources for communicators as they confront real-life occasions for behaving. They are both idealizations of communication episodes and organized regulations (constraints) on behavior performed during and as part of these episodes. At the level of a knowledge-based resource, programs represent the competence persons are socialized into, bring to an interaction, and, in varying ways, attempt to execute. However, performances may not be judged exclusively, or even primarily, on the basis of their fidelity to the programs (competencies). This is because real-time behavioral events, as opposed to their idealizations, present communicators with coordination problems and opportunities, with multiple participants and often competing goals. Coherence with and relevance to what else is actually taking place, as opposed to what should occur, are equally powerful standards for judging performance.

Thus, communicators engage in multiple activities: (a) implementing or enacting a program, (b) attending to the actually unfolding behavioral production, (c) aligning this actual conduct with the a priori expectations in cases where the one does not integrate adequately with the other, (d) establishing coherence between sequentially unfolding behaviors (whether programmatic or emergent) both they and others produce, (e) interpreting the present conduct in light of previous episodes engaged in with those or with other coparticipants, (f) projecting and adjusting to the future consequences of current programmatic and/or emergent behavior, and (g) revising their vision of the program based on actual behavior.

In this regard, we propose that there are at least three categories of tensions that communicators experience as they set about producing sociocultural episodes (cf. Montgomery, 1992; Rawlins, 1992, for alternative approaches to communication and dialectical tensions; cf. Turner, 1974, for an anthropological perspective).[9] One set of such tensions derives from the program because, as previously described, the program represents a set of constraints, restrictions, and potentialities on communicators' conduct. As Moore (1975) wrote, "every interaction contains within it elements of the regular and elements of the indeterminate, and both are 'used' by individuals" (p. 221). We contend that there are at least three ways in which

---

[9]We refer to episodes as *sociocultural* when considering them from the vantage point of their governing programs, and we refer to them as *communicational* when considering them in terms of actual conduct.

communicators respond to, or resolve, the tensions imposed on them by program obligations:

1. *Invocation* involves communicators publicly and explicitly making use of the program (i.e., behaving in ways that call attention to the behavior as being governed, predicted, and/or organized by the program). This involves "following the pattern" in ways that signal recognition that such is indeed occurring. Announcing the transition from socializing to the sales presentation is an example of invocation.

2. *Alignment* occurs when persons find themselves unable or unwilling to adhere strictly to the program restriction. Alignment (Stokes & Hewitt, 1976) permits participants to behave in ways that cohere for the moment without threatening the integrity and applicability of the program. In this way, the program remains as a powerful a priori sociocultural force to be reckoned with on future occasions, but one that is held in abeyance at the immediate time. The consultant's efforts to speed up the sales presentation and solicit attention from the wayward audience members are examples of this.

3. *Revision* combines elements of both invocation and alignment, in the sense that attention is called to the connection between the program (more likely, some subsidiary feature) and possibly deviant behavior. However, in this case, the behavior is not fit to the program, but rather the program is fit to the behavior. With revision, a new structural possibility is announced, proposed, and made available for negotiation. This is comparable to Morris and Hopper's (1980) "legislation" device (see also Cronen, chap. 1, this volume). The in situ creation of a smoking lounge represents a revision of the socializing portion of the basket party. Revision may or may not represent a complete reformulation of the already existing program.

These mechanisms to relate programs and actual conduct are comparable to Moore's (1975) processes of *regularization*. Moore defined these as "attempts to crystallize and concretize social reality, to make it determinate and firm" (p. 234). Individuals engage in such communication practices to establish and affirm rules, customs, and institutions—in short, the sociocultural order. In so doing, a sense of stability, predictability, and ongoing history is gained from the existence of programs as well as their use.

The program–performance tension represents a tension between different layers or levels of behavioral generality or abstractness. As suggested previously, however, communicators confront not only this tension between idealized and actualized levels, but within the level of actual conduct as well. Communicators confront the additional tensions of relating

their behavioral contributions to other interaction episodes (past or projected), as well as relating their behavioral contributions to other behavior
within the current bounded episode. In the former case, the second tension, communicators relate their behavior within any given episode to
similar episodes at other times and with other people. Such "intertextuality"
(Kristeva, 1969), or cross-referencing (Birdwhistell, 1970; Scheflen, 1967),
brings past events in particular into the current one, and projects some
semantic or functional connection between current and future events.
Tensions arise from the obligation to conduct oneself consistently with
previous performances (Davies & Harré, 1991–1992; Goffman, 1959) and
with agendas established during prior episodes (Sigman, 1991).

Under such circumstances, the boundaries between episodes become
inexact and tenuous. One of the chief differences between programs and
actual conduct is that the latter may not evidence clearly demarcated
beginnings and endings, as it emerges from previous episodes and feeds
into future ones, with numerous intertwining links across space and time
(cf. Birdwhistell, 1970; Sigman, 1987). In contrast, programs inhabit an
idealized sociocultural location, where guidelines for producing and interpreting boundary markers can be rigidly maintained.

Previous encounters among participants may establish shared story
repertoires, the result being a constraint on what can subsequently be told
and how. These expectations may constrain speech at both the sentential
and discourse levels (Tannen, 1978). Finally, current experiences may
establish new structural obligations and possibilities for subsequent encounters (Sigman & Donnellon, 1988).

New behaviors—those not expected or part of the original a priori
program—may subsequently be "transported" by participants and used
for other events. A new structural element (program) may emerge from
performed behaviors. In this way, performed behaviors are consequential
both in the moment of their production and in the long term. The experience of each new event may be incorporated into subsequent programs;
thus, programs are filled with culture-general and experience-specific
repertoires.[10]

As can be seen, programs are open to manipulation and adaptation to
situational needs and contingencies. Despite the implicit suggestion that
programs govern behavior, it is also useful to see them as resources (with
entailed moral force) for action. Persons select and (re)combine portions of
programs—the consequential character of communication in operation—

---

[10]See Sullivan (1989) for a discussion of how a repertoire of standard stories is built by the
consultant, and how participants learned that a basket party was not analogous to a covered-
dish social, but more like a Tupperware® sales gathering.

that are made to work at particular moments of interaction. Each new combination is then available for future manipulation and adaptation, making for a complex and ever-growing system of programs. Moore (1975) labeled this phenomenon processes of *situational adjustment*:

> [P]eople arrange their immediate situations (and or express their feelings and conceptions) by exploiting the indeterminacies in the situation, or by generating such indeterminacies, or by reinterpreting or redefining the rules or relationships. They use whatever areas there are of inconsistency, contradiction, conflict, ambiguity, or open areas that are normatively indeterminate to achieve immediate situational ends. . . . These processes introduce or maintain the element of plasticity in social arrangements. (pp. 234–235)

Invocation, alignment, and revision are three aspects of the same process—acting in the here and now while selectively drawing on the past and rewriting the potential future. Alignment and revision are especially related to the indeterminacy of programs; it is the inability of any program to predict all contingencies that participants may encounter that gives rise to the varying degrees of adherence to or modification of programs (cf. Garfinkel, 1967). Thus, communication is consequential because it demands from participants the competence to enact programs (invocation), and to do so in ways fitting within the immediate moment (alignment and revision) of ongoing behavioral production.

This leads to the third tension, which finds communicators making adjustments in their behavior to what has just been performed, or to what is about to be performed. This tension derives from the immediate, or "local," circumstances of the interaction, and may require the greatest amount of cognitive attention and interactional skill on the part of participants. Certainly, conversation analysis would seem to support this view (see Beach, chap. 3, this volume) because it is here that the negotiation of meaning occurs on a moment-by-moment basis. Ongoing sociocultural life requires effort on the part of members because there is always the potential for things to fall apart if such effort is not forthcoming. Because culturally constituted social order is a human construction, continual and continuous action is required, as is the communicative competence to coherently act and respond in the here and now (see Sanders, chap. 2, this volume). Human constructions cannot exist without humans to maintain them, or without activity.

Attention to this action-to-action tension involves at least the following: *coherence, relevance, adjacency,* and *formulation*. These discourse devices are used by conversationists to relate their utterances to sequentially prior ones (cf. Heritage, 1984). Relatedly, Kahneman, Slovic, and Tversky (1982) referred to interpretive heuristic devices—such as *salience, availability, recency*, and *prototypicality*—as the basis for how people interpret and produce behavior.

Sullivan's (1989) original study (from which the previous case study is derived) analyzed the ways in which the participants engaged in "small talk" with each other, the manner in which greetings and introductions transpired, and how exits into and out of face formations and focused talk were handled. In no cases were such behaviors mentioned in the preparty interviews. This may be due in part to the lack of informant awareness of such microbehaviors, and due, in part, to their nonintegralness to the basket party program. They represent a set of generalized behaviors not specific to the one event or event program. Previous research supports that informants focus their remarks about scenes on motives, goals, and personalities, not constitutive behavioral units (cf. Levy Fogle, 1991; Mathiot, Boyerlein, Rhoda, Levy, & Marks, 1987). Nevertheless, such microbehavior is produced by communicators, and so it is necessary to consider how the unanticipated production of a conversational unit establishes relevant and irrelevant next slots, and how communicators may exploit this feature of communication.

In brief, sociocultural programs, the history of interaction experiences with one's coparticipants, and the actual moment-by-moment production of behavior all constrain and engender communication performances. These performances are consequential because they are not completely predicted by the a priori programs and experiences, and because the ongoing production of behavior (in adherence to and/or in modification of programs and history) establishes its own in-the-moment constraints on the participants. Thus, communication creates and resolves the experiencing of the three tensions in any particular circumstance.

SUMMARY

We contend that social communication theory's notion of *programs* needed revision (and, by extension, all ethnographic and discourse research that generates descriptions of rules and resources, in lieu of descriptions of actual conduct and performance). This revision is not of the concept of programs, but rather of the uses to which the concept is put. We have argued that participants enter communication episodes with a set of expectations for those episodes. These expectations represent a moral force binding the communicators to perform particular sequences of behavior and to reach particular goals, but they are not equivalent to real-time communication events. In this respect, Scheflen's initial articulation of programs represents an appropriate level of sociocultural analysis—that of the structural resources that regulate and are presupposed by particular moments of behaving. However, communication analysis, in recognition of the consequential nature of the communication process, with provision for varying degrees of adherence to and revision of sociocultural resources, must address the employment or implementation of programs, not merely or primarily the structure of the programs.

This position on the consequential nature of communication, and more specifically on the relationship between programs and performances, is similar to that of Fish (1980) on the meanings derived from reading:

> In [reading], which is the actualization of meaning, the deep structure plays an important role, but it is not everything; for we comprehend not in terms of the [text's] deep structure alone but in terms of a *relationship* between the unfolding, in time, of the surface structure and a continual checking of it against our projection (always in terms of surface structure) of what the deep structure will reveal itself to be; and when the final discovery has been made and *the* deep structure is perceived, all the "mistakes"—the positing, on the basis of incomplete evidence, of deep structures that failed to materialize—will not be canceled out. They have been experienced; they have existed in the mental life of the reader; they *mean*. (p. 48; italics in original)

What Fish implies is true of written texts, but not true of interactions between corporate agents (e.g., persons, organizations). Fish implies that readers are drawn along a somewhat inevitable path toward the text's meaning—that while the meaning is shaped by the path any one reader takes, nonetheless there is some particular meaning waiting at the reading's end, in part as the result of the reader's embeddedness in an interpretive community. The consequential nature of communication *as an interactional phenomenon* belies this because there is no inevitable endpoint for meaning. The meaning of behavior, and of the programs that help structure it, is always subject to negotiation and revision.[11] Indeed, unlike a written text, which is in hand and complete at the time of reading, a behavioral production is not fully known in advance (although the program potentially structuring it may be); rather, it is incomplete and unfinished, and subject to further production and interpretation. Unlike a written text, which comes to the reader without its author available to amend and clarify and dispute, human interaction is inherently multiparticipant (Birdwhistell, 1970). This leads to incompleteness because communication episodes

---

[11]Fish's (1980) later essays reject an essentialist view of texts, stating that "linguistic and textual facts, rather than being the objects of interpretation, are its products" (p. 9), and "formal units are always a function of the interpretive model one brings to bear (they are not 'in the text')" (p. 13). Nevertheless, we contend that written texts are complete in ways that face-to-face interactions are not.

throughout their occurrence are open to revision by any of the participants. It is the communication process that adheres to (or not) and fulfills
(or not) the constraints and potentials represented by programs. As suggested earlier, programs that organize communication episodes represent
possible, albeit powerful, constraints; the endpoint of meaning is not
definitive, resulting from the process of program implementation, not the
program itself.

In this regard, then, we contend that persons possess programlike
knowledge for all matter and sort of sociocultural episodes: participating
in a basket sales party, going on a date, watching television at home,
conducting an employment screening interview, and so on. These and
other communication episodes are defined and regulated by programs. In
many, and perhaps most, cases, more than one program (or component
features from multiple programs) may provide potential constraints on a
particular real-time event. Although programs represent routinized solutions to the moment-by-moment problems that communicators face, they
also represent abundant and multiple solutions, only one of which can be
brought to bear at a particular real-time moment. It is in and during
communication that a particular selection from the multiple possible programs is made, each choice being consequential for further selections.
Stated differently, although programs represent ritualized solutions, they
must nonetheless be enacted and realized during particular moments of
sociocultural life, with each specific enactment having a potential for
changing both the meaning derived from the particular event and the
organization and contents of the presupposed program. From this vantage
point, the program is not the given that Scheflen assumed, but rather an
original imposition of order constantly available for renegotiation and
subject to contingent deviation, thus providing a logic for both stability
and revision.

Although it is true that the participants in the basket party followed
through on the party program, that they did so must be examined in terms
of their performance actions and not the program itself. The participants'
actions made the program relevant—the arrival times of the guests, the
setup behavior by the hostess and sales consultant, and so on all served to
bind the participants to further implementation of the program—simultaneously drawing on (and therefore reifying and continuing) the existence
of the program, maintaining its organization and contents, and, in subtle
(and not so subtle) ways, redesigning it. Both the invocation and maintenance serve to reify the program, although such reification is always open
to further revision.

Garfinkel's (1967) unique adequacy requirement for the description of
sociocultural episodes is appropriate here. Garfinkel and Wieder (1992)
wrote of this ethnomethodological guideline that "for the analyst to recog-

nize, or identify, or follow the development of, or describe phenomena of order* in local production of coherent detail the analyst must be *vulgarly* competent in the local production and reflexively natural accountability of the phenomenon of order* he[/she] is 'studying' " (p. 182; asterisks and italics in original). To understand how meaning and order are generated in an event, and what that meaning and order are, the analyst as well as the participants must examine the moment-by-moment (local) production of that event, and not take analytic recourse in a priori conceptions of social structure and the like. The position we have adapted from social communication theory is more conservative; it suggests that the observable event is not self-sufficient, and that the programs or rules notion is not altogether adequate either. Although we recognize the consequentiality of the communication process (the local production, as it were), this consequentiality mediates and, in turn, is tempered by programmatic considerations not directly available in any single event (e.g., the sociocultural programs, previous interaction episodes). Although the communication process is consequential, it is not unboundedly so because there are transsituational tensions and constraints placed on local behavioral production. At the same time, it is in the local production of behavior in conformity with or deviation from the three tensions described earlier that consequentiality resides.

Given that the communication process is variously consequential in and to people's lives, the question arises as to the kinds of lives these are. The answer from social communication theory concerns the role of history and tradition—in the form of sociocultural programs—and the processes by which history and tradition are activated and employed in ongoing moments of behavior. Our concern is equally with the processes by which the sociocultural programs are changed, modified, and revised before being "returned" to history. Thus, social communication theory posits that communicators are simultaneously embedded in (constrained by) a sociocultural framework and empowered to behave in ways that momentarily transcend this framework. Communicators are rooted in both structure and process.

We have further suggested that members of social collectivities experience a multitude of tensions that derive from their recognition that each moment of behaving is both a "fitting into" the immediate ongoing flow and a "reference to" or calling up of history. These tensions are not oppressive or fearsome, however, because they permit behavior that is simultaneously conservative and creative. Communicators are empowered to behave with the full recognition that their actions are simultaneously historical and novel, and, in both cases, that their actions are potentially meaningful. As Bateson (1990) wrote: "Composing a life involves a continual reimagining of the future and reinterpretation of the past to give meaning to the present, remembering best those events that prefigured what followed, forgetting those that proved to have no meaning within the narrative" (pp. 29–30). A profound sense of pleasure may actually be gained by communicators when they remember past events, and a profound sense of security may be gained when a priori programs are available and able to be integrated into present events—because in this way they experience membership in a continuous social group and an identity with a recognizable trajectory. As one of us previously wrote: "Thus, relational history and previous interactional experience do not merely constitute a background, a memory box, for discourse [and interaction]; rather, they can be seen to exist in the foreground of discourse [and other] behavior, as a treasure chest of information to be periodically opened, examined, and celebrated" (Sigman, 1987, p. 33).

From this perspective, there is a social existence for members, in which patterned projections of future behaviors, episodes, and relationships are routine. Any current moment of social life can be seen as pushing participants toward new, but not altogether unfamiliar, experiences and terrain. This happens because of the consequentiality of behavior in the moment of its production, and because, in terms of programs, behavior in the moment predictably projects the shape of what is yet to come. In Ervin-Tripp's (1972) terms, each choice influences and subtly interacts with others: Any choice is made out of a selection of possibilities from which only a limited set can become real (rule of alternation). At the same time, every choice limits future choices (rule of co-occurrence). Today's reality entails and constrains tomorrow.

Implied in the previous discussion is a particular conception of the relationship between programs and action—between structure and process. It is time to resolve the connections between and among these terms. *Programs* (a) are institutionalized assumptions of how events will occur, (b) are outlines of behavior that people bring to interaction, and (c) help participants predict what will come next—what choices entail what other choices. They are abstract, exist theoretically, are never made concrete, and are rarely discussed explicitly except by analysts. *Actions* are concrete behaviors that are visible to all participants, as well as analysts. They are immediate, they occur, they have form and content, and they may be directly described by participants and observed by analysts. However, their meaning resides in both the concrete sequential occasioning of their production and in the program that specifies each behavior's likely occurrence and co-occurrence with other behavior.

Traditionally, the relationship between structure and process has been conceived of linearly, with the former underlying, guiding, and indeed producing the latter. Although we still believe that structure (programs), in some senses, forms the background for, and therefore precedes, process, the relationship is best viewed as a logical, rather than a temporal, one. Performances rely on programs, yet particular performance acts may revise programs for both that moment and the future. As Moore (1975) wrote, "the fixed in social reality really means the continuously renewed" (p. 235). It is not simply that programs produce real-time behavior because it is also real-time behavior that invokes programs, making them available for later revision and (re)use.

Ultimately, any theoretical discussion implies and leads to a set of research questions. Given the preceding discussion, and the aims of social communication theory more generally, a particular set of questions concerning the relationship between sociocultural resources (programs) and the communication process can be made explicit. These questions are not to be answered here—although some initial data from the one case study illuminate aspects of these questions—but may be used to organize future research projects influenced by social communication theory. Unlike some alternative approaches to the study of ongoing sociocultural life represented in this book, social communication theory is committed to uncovering the layers of history and tradition that are enacted on a real-time basis. The goal is not simply to illuminate the behavioral mechanisms by which face-to-face interaction is produced as consequential, but rather how these mechanisms invoke sociocultural programs on the one hand, and represent responses and adjustment bids to the unfolding multiparticipant and multigoal event on the other hand.

Given these concerns, the following questions are raised: How is a program implemented? How do participants signal which program from the repertoire is to be implemented at a given moment? How do participants combine parts of previous programs, and what restrictions, if any, are there on such recombination? How are pieces of the program eliminated, revised, re-run, and so on? How do participants signal which piece(s) of the program they and/or others will be held responsible for? How do participants signal where in the program's progression the actual performance is at any given moment?

From the revised position on social communication theory articulated here, a comfort with both observational and informant data in the study of communication, and a tendency to seek out comparative data across multiple events, naturally flow. Answers to the previous questions, and others yet to be formulated, require two orders of data: data about actual lived experience, and data about sociocultural programs, idealizations, and expectations. Both would be best served by ethnographic fieldwork across repeated events, with an emphasis on direct observation and recording of ongoing behavior, as well as on informant perspectives on observed behavior and its relationship to expectations and past experiences (cf. Arliss, 1989–1990). Detailing program features is exceedingly complex, however, because analytic choices concerning the boundaries of particular programs are difficult to make. For example, in the case study employed here, we have assumed (along with the original author) that verbalized reports about expectations imply the existence of programs that will structure subsequent behavior. But expectations may sometimes represent mere predictions, without the moral force that programs and their component rules are assumed to have. An alternative methodology, one relying almost exclusively on observations and more in keeping with Scheflen's observational stance, would attempt to derive both structure and process from the same data: "summarizing" and extrapolating across several iterations of an event to derive what is standard (which has been the traditional activity of structural researchers) on the one hand, and concentrating on the particulars within each single event to arrive at the contribution of the communication performance on the other hand (but see our concerns about this technique—based on Sanders' chapter—in chap. 8, this volume).

Although methodological variations have yet to be worked out, we strongly urge that communication scholars not simply study actual communication events to derive what is standard, rule governed, or program based. Communication scholars must uncover how the communication process is consequential in the ways in which this standard, rules set, or program is used, invoked, and lived by sociocultural members. Such a research strategy represents an understanding and appreciation of the consequentiality inherent to communication phenomena.

ACKNOWLEDGMENTS

The data for the case study presented in this chapter are drawn from Sullivan's doctoral dissertation under Sigman's direction; the performance analysis in this chapter has been written jointly by Sigman and Leeds-Hurwitz based on Sullivan's initial observation and write-up.

REFERENCES

Abrahams, R. (1968). Introductory remarks to a rhetorical theory of folklore. *Journal of American Folklore, 81*, 142–158.

Abrahams, R. (1976). The complex relations of simple forms. In D. Ben-Amos (Ed.), *Folklore genres* (pp. 193–214). Austin: University of Texas Press.

Arliss, L. (1989–1990). An integration of accounts and interaction analyses of communication in long-standing relationships. *Research on Language and Social Interaction, 23*, 41–64.

Basso, K. (1974). The ethnography of writing. In R. Bauman & J. Sherzer (Eds.), *Explorations in the ethnography of speaking* (pp. 425–432). Cambridge, England: Cambridge University Press.

Bateson. G. (1971). Communication. In N. A. McQuown (Ed.), *The natural history of an interview* (pp. 1–40). Chicago: Microfilm Collection of Manuscripts on Cultural Anthropology, Fifteenth Series, Joseph Regenstein Library.

Bateson, G. (1972). *Steps to an ecology of mind*. New York: Ballantine.

Bateson, M. C. (1990). *Composing a life*. New York: Penguin.

Bauman, R. (1977). *Verbal art as performance*. Rowley, MA: Newbury House.

Bauman, R., & Sherzer, J. (Eds.). (1974a). *Explorations in the ethnography of speaking*. Cambridge, England: Cambridge University Press.

Bauman, R., & Sherzer, J. (1974b). Introduction to part IV: Speech acts, events, and situations. In R. Bauman & J. Sherzer (Eds.), *Explorations in the ethnography of speaking* (pp. 163–166). Cambridge, England: Cambridge University Press.

Bauman, R., & Sherzer, J. (1974c). Introduction to part V: Shaping artistic structures in performance. In R. Bauman & J. Sherzer (Eds.), *Explorations in the ethnography of speaking* (pp. 311–314). Cambridge, England: Cambridge University Press.

Bauman, R., & Sherzer, J. (1989). Introduction to the second edition. In R. Bauman & J. Sherzer (Eds.), *Explorations in the ethnography of speaking* (2nd ed., pp. ix–xxvii). Cambridge, England: Cambridge University Press.

Ben-Amos, D. (1971). Toward a definition of folklore in context. *Journal of American Folklore, 84,* 3–15.

Ben-Amos, D., & Goldstein, K. (Eds.). (1975). *Folklore: Performance and communication*. The Hague: Mouton.

Birdwhistell, R. L. (1970). *Kinesics and context: Essays on body motion communication*. Philadelphia: University of Pennsylvania Press.

Bronner, S. J. (1988). Art, performance, and praxis: The rhetoric of contemporary folklore studies. *Western Folklore, 47,* 75–102.

Davies, B., & Harré, R. (1991–1992). Contradictions in lived and told narratives. *Research on Language and Social Interaction, 25,* 1–35.

Duncan, S. (1969). Nonverbal communication. *Psychological Bulletin, 72,* 118–137.

Ervin-Tripp, S. (1972). On sociolinguistic rules: Alternation and co-occurrence. In J. J. Gumperz & D. Hymes (Eds.), *Directions in sociolinguistics: The ethnography of communication* (pp. 213–250). New York: Holt, Rinehart & Winston.

Fine, E. (1984). *The folklore text: From performance to print*. Bloomington: Indiana University Press.

Fine, E., & Speer, J. (1977). A new look at performance. *Communication Monographs, 44,* 374–389.

Fish, S. (1980). *Is there a text in this class? The authority of interpretive communities*. Cambridge, MA: Harvard University Press.

Garfinkel, H. (1967). *Studies in ethnomethodology*. Englewood Cliffs, NJ: Prentice-Hall.

Garfinkel, H., & Wieder, L. H. (1992). Two incommensurable, asymmetrically alternate technologies of social analysis. In G. Watson & R. M. Seiler (Eds.), *Text in context: Contributions to ethnomethodology* (pp. 175–206). Newbury Park, CA: Sage.

Giddens, A. (1984). *The constitution of society: Outline of the theory of structuration*. Berkeley: University of California Press.

Giddens, A. (1989). A reply to my critics. In D. Held & J. B. Thompson (Eds.), *Social theory of modern societies: Anthony Giddens and his critics* (pp. 249–301). New York: Cambridge University Press.

Goffman, E. (1959). *The presentation of self in everyday life*. Garden City, NY: Doubleday.

Goffman, E. (1967). *Interaction ritual*. Chicago: Aldine.

Gumperz, J. J. (1984). Communication competence revisited. In D. Schiffrin (Ed.), *Meaning, form and use in context* (pp. 278–289). Washington, DC: Georgetown University Press.

Gumperz, J. J., & Hymes, D. (Eds.). (1972). *Directions in sociolinguistics: The ethnography of communication*. New York: Holt, Rinehart & Winston.

Heritage, J. (1984). *Garfinkel and ethnomethodology*. Cambridge, England: Polity Press.

Huspek, M. (1993). Dueling structures: The theory of resistance in discourse. *Communication Theory, 3,* 1–25.

Hymes, D. (1962). The ethnography of speaking. In T. Gladwin & W. C. Sturtevant (Eds.), *Anthropology and human behavior* (pp. 55–83). Washington, DC: Anthropological Society of Washington.

Hymes, D. (1971). Competence and performance in linguistic theory. In R. Huxley & E. Ingram (Eds.), *Language acquisition: Models and methods* (pp. 3–24). New York: Academic Press.

Hymes, D. (1972). The contribution of folklore to sociolinguistic research. In A. Paredes & R. Bauman (Eds.), *Toward new perspectives in folklore* (pp. 42–50). Austin: University of Texas Press.

Hymes, D. (1974a). *Foundations in sociolinguistics.* Philadelphia: University of Pennsylvania Press.

Hymes, D. (1974b). Ways of speaking. In R. Bauman & J. Sherzer (Eds.), *Explorations in the ethnography of speaking* (pp. 433–451). Cambridge, England: Cambridge University Press.

Hymes, D. (1975). Breakthrough into performance. In D. Ben-Amos & K. Goldstein (Eds.), *Folklore: Performance and communication* (pp. 11–74). The Hague: Mouton.

Irvine, J. T. (1974). Strategies of status manipulation in the Wolof greeting. In R. Bauman & J. Sherzer (Eds.), *Explorations in the ethnography of speaking* (pp. 167–191). Cambridge, England: Cambridge University Press.

Jacobs, S., Jackson, S., Stearns, S., & Hall, B. (1991). Digressions in argumentative discourse: Multiple goals, standing concerns, and implicature. In K. Tracy (Ed.), *Understanding face-to-face interaction: Issues linking goals and discourse* (pp. 43–61). Hillsdale, NJ: Lawrence Erlbaum Associates.

Kahneman, D., Slovic, P., & Tversky, A. (Eds.). (1982). *Judgment under uncertainty.* New York: Cambridge University Press.

Kendon, A. (1982). The organization of behavior in face-to-face interaction: Observations on the development of a methodology. In K. Scherer & P. Ekman (Eds.), *Handbook of methods in nonverbal behavior research* (pp. 440–505). Cambridge, England: Cambridge University Press.

Kendon, A. (1990). *Conducting interaction: Patterns of behavior in focused encounters.* Cambridge, England: Cambridge University Press.

Kirshenblatt-Gimblett, B. (1975). A parable in context: A social interactional analysis of storytelling performance. In D. Ben-Amos & K. Goldstein (Eds.), *Folklore: Performance and communication* (pp. 105–130). The Hague: Mouton.

Kristeva, J. (1969). *Semeiotike: Recherches pour une semanalyse.* Paris: Éditions du Seuil.

Leeds-Hurwitz, W. (1984). On the relationship of the "ethnography of speaking" to the "ethnography of communication." *Papers in Linguistics, 17,* 7–32.

Leeds-Hurwitz, W. (1987). The social history of *The natural history of an interview*: A multidisciplinary investigation of social communication. *Research on Language and Social Interaction, 20,* 1–51.

Leeds-Hurwitz, W. (1989). *Communication in everyday life: A social interpretation.* Norwood, NJ: Ablex.

Levy Fogle, J.-A. (1991). *Testing social communication theory through an analysis of participant-respondent data.* Unpublished doctoral dissertation, State University of New York at Buffalo.

Mathiot, M., with Boyerlein, P., Rhoda, F., Levy, J.-A., & Marks, P. (1987). Meaning attribution to behavior in face-to-face interaction: A hermeneutic-phenomenological approach. *Research on Language and Social Interaction, 20,* 271–375.

McQuown, N. A. (Ed.). (1971a). *The natural history of an interview.* Chicago: Microfilm Collection of Manuscripts on Cultural Anthropology, Fifteenth Series, Joseph Regenstein Library.

McQuown, N. A. (1971b). Foreword. In N. A. McQuown (Ed.), *The natural history of an interview* (pp. 1–5). Chicago: Microfilm Collection of Manuscripts on Cultural Anthropology, Fifteenth Series, Joseph Regenstein Library.

Mills, M. A. (1990). Critical theory and folklorists: Performance, interpretive authority, and gender. *Southern Folklore, 47*, 5–16.

Montgomery, B. M. (1992). Communication as the interface between couples and culture. In S. Deetz (Ed.), *Communication yearbook 15* (pp. 475–507). Newbury Park, CA: Sage.

Moore, S. F. (1975). Epilogue. In S. F. Moore & B. Myerhoff (Eds.), *Symbol and politics in communal ideology* (pp. 210–238). Ithaca, NY: Cornell University Press.

Morris, G. H., & Hopper, R. (1980). Remediation and legislation in everyday talk: How communicators achieve consensus. *Quarterly Journal of Speech, 66*, 266–274.

Paredes, A., & Bauman, R. (Eds.). (1972). *Toward new perspectives in folklore*. Austin: University of Texas Press.

Rawlins, W. K. (1992). *Friendship matters: Communication, dialectics, and the life course*. Hawthorne, NY: Aldine de Gruyter.

Schechner, R. (1985). *Between theater and anthropology*. Philadelphia: University of Pennsylvania Press.

Schechner, R. (1988). *Performance theory*. Boston: Routledge & Kegan Paul.

Scheflen, A. E. (1964). The significance of posture in communication systems. *Psychiatry, 27*, 316–331.

Scheflen, A. E. (1965, December). *Systems in human communication*. Paper presented at the meeting of the American Association for the Advancement of Science, Berkeley, CA.

Scheflen, A. E. (1967). On the structuring of human communication. *American Behavioral Scientist, 10*, 8–12.

Scheflen, A. E. (1968). Human communication: Behavioral programs and their integration in interaction. *Behavioral Science, 13*, 44–55.

Scheflen, A. E. (1979). On communication processes. In A. Wolfgang (Ed.), *Nonverbal behavior: Applications and cultural implications* (pp. 1–16). New York: Academic Press.

Schutz, A. (1967). *The phenomenology of the social world*. Evanston, IL: Northwestern University Press.

Shokeid, M. (1992). Exceptional experiences in everyday life. *Cultural Anthropology, 7*, 232–243.

Sigman, S. J. (1987). *A perspective on social communication*. Lexington, MA: Lexington.

Sigman, S. J. (1991). Handling the discontinuous aspects of continuous social relationships. *Communication Theory, 1*, 106–127.

Sigman, S. J., & Donnellon, A. (1988). Discourse rehearsal: Interaction simulating interaction. In D. Crookall & D. Saunders (Eds.), *Communication and simulation: From two fields to one theme* (pp. 69–81). London: Multilingual Matters.

Stokes, R., & Hewitt, J. P. (1976). Aligning actions. *American Sociological Review, 41*, 838–849.

Sullivan, S. J. (1989). *The basket party: An ethnography of reported expectations and enacted behaviors for accomplishing a women's sales and socializing event*. Unpublished doctoral dissertation, State University of New York at Buffalo.

Tannen, D. (1978). The effect of expectations on conversation. *Discourse Processes, 1*, 203–209.

Turner, V. (1969). *The ritual process*. Ithaca, NY: Cornell University Press.

Turner, V. (1974). *Dramas, fields and metaphors*. Ithaca, NY: Cornell University Press.

Turner, V. (1982). *From ritual to theater*. New York: PAJ Publications.

Turner, V. (1987). *The anthropology of performance*. New York: PAJ Publications.

II

REFORMULATING AND CRITIQUING THE FOUR PERSPECTIVES

5

Commentary

Vernon E. Cronen
University of Massachusetts, Amherst

How nice it is to have kindred spirits in the discipline. My first reaction to reading the other chapters in this book was one of delight, particularly as I remembered the response that Pearce and I received when we began to raise some of these issues in the mid-1970s and early 1980s. Doing rigorous qualitative casework instead of laboratory experiments, treating meaning as constituted in a conjoint process not concepts in the head or points in semantic space, and considering patterns of action rather than quantities with central tendencies all seemed sheer heresy to most in the discipline. We were often asked to "recant" or at least disappear, although not usually in such polite language.

We were not totally alone; Philipsen was already doing excellent ethnographic work, and scholars such as Nofsinger were already discovering the potential of conversation analysis, with its insistence on considering the detail of actual discourse. However, the flowering of qualitative work on situated conversation in recent years has been remarkable, and my colleagues' chapters in this volume give some idea of the richness of the "heretical" work going on now.

Surely the most fundamental matter that connects the chapters in this volume is the insistence that communication is the fundamental process through which we constitute ourselves as human agents and create human forms of life. To make this claim is the equivalent of saying that communication is a discipline, and not merely a field.

I am sure the reader is struck with the diversity of approaches that the authors take to their tasks. I "spie out the land" rather broadly, whereas others present particular studies illustrating claims of various breadth. Sanders (chap. 2, this volume) wants to make some large points about institutional and instantiated meanings; Beach (chap. 3 this volume) takes the most microcosmic approach, developing his argument for a hitherto unrecognized function of "Okay"; and Leeds-Hurwitz and Sigman, with Sullivan (chap. 4, this volume) challenge Scheflen's early ideas about the relationship between the programs actors bring to a conversation and the pattern of action the actors produce.

This diversity makes the task of writing a commentary about our combined efforts somewhat difficult. Therefore, I first review some important matters about which there is some, although not total, agreement. Next, I highlight two issues that are common to all the chapters, and I offer some comments about them. On these issues, there is important disagreement. One is overtly discussed. It concerns the relationship between context and action. The second is unstated, but implicit. This disagreement is about what a theory is supposed to do. Finally, I say a few brief words about the importance of treating communication quite comprehensively, as I have attempted to do in my own way. In the course of this discussion, I make specific reference to Coordinated Management of Meaning (CMM) theory because it is a way to organize the concepts developed in my foregoing chapter into a methodology for studying situated practices. One might think of my chapter as an updated guide to the CMM's tools.

SOME POINTS OF AGREEMENT

The authors in this book seem to converge on the idea that patterns of interaction are situated creations. For example, Sanders observes how the actions of one speaker impose constraints on the participation of others. He goes on to argue that institutional prototypes are not sufficient to understand the character of the interaction patterns created. He claims instead, as does CMM theory (Cronen, Pearce, & Xi, 1989–1990), that meaning is a situated accomplishment. Leeds-Hurwitz and Sigman, with Sullivan, argue in a similar vein that programs, or prior conceptions of an episode that actors bring to a situation, will not suffice to explain the interaction observed. Their case study shows the rich variety of patterns that may be constructed. Beach's conversation analysis (CA) perspective is persistently attentive to the details of interactional achievement. The old concept of *context* is taken to be an interactional achievement, not merely a frame within which communication occurs. In my own chapter, I stress the interactional creation of meaning, and I insist on a reflexive relationship

twofold thrust. First, *selfhood* becomes a shorthand term for the embodied abilities of particular human beings. Second, it is seen to include a particular kind of ability—that of engaging in "situated identifying" (for a discussion of this, see Cronen & Pearce, 1991–1992).

Compare the CMM metaphor to its competitors. If the abilities that persons bring to a situation are described as *prototypes* or *structures*, it is necessary to postulate criteria for assessing how closely any performance is to model. Next, it is necessary to postulate an internal "assessor" that uses the criteria and makes a decision. This mentalism is not necessary. Of course, we may learn episodes in which the matching game is played, but that is quite another matter. What is brought back in the competing metaphors is the representational view of meaning that I discuss in my chapter, and that none of the contributors seems to want to revive. In the grammatical view, no prototype or structure is represented in conversation. The substantialized utterance is informed by various aspects of the grammars that actors know. The act of substantializing abilities under the concrete conditions of conjoint action, and the responses of the other actor, act reflexively upon those abilities. This approach avoids, in principle, the problem of bringing together institutional standardizations, idiosyncratic abilities, and cultural features, and the situated responses of the other. As I argue, all utterances have idiosyncratic and social dimensions. These are not natural opposites because, for in the Wittgensteinian perspective, idiosyncrasy is socially constituted.

I want to hazard a guess as to why metaphors such as *prototype* and *structure* have had wide appeal. Dewey (1925) observed that, by his time, it had already become commonplace to suppose that the unconscious is a kind of model or reflection of the conscious. For example, Freud's notion of the *unconscious* is a sort of human play, in which sons vie with fathers for the mothers. However, our heads contain brains only—no stage on which miniature actors act, and no slots where scripts, structures, and so on are kept. Learning is a chemical change in the brain, and thinking is a continuous process of neural activity substantialized as utterance or as an individual internal review of thoughts in words and images.

In CMM theory, the grammatical abilities of human agents are organized in narrative form or bits of narrative; it is in patterns of discursive action that grammatical abilities are formed. The character of thought is related to the nature of the experience, of which thinking is a part. CMM also describes various hierarchical and looped relationships in these grammars.

CMM researchers explore the stories that persons can tell, and they organize the data as hierarchies of stories and bits of stories. However, this does not mean that we think a person's head "contains" stories. Just as there is a difference between a rule and rule formulation, as I describe, there is a difference between a useful formulation that organizes the data obtained about grammatical abilities and the claim that persons' heads contain strips of narrative. Exploring constitutive aspects of rules using CMM is simply our way to investigate the grammatical abilities of persons through the stories they tell and the relationships among those stories.

The Implicit Issue: What Kind of Theory Sought?

Why are we doing this, and what kind of theory are we trying to create? It has been my contention for some time that a communication theory should be a practical theory (Cronen, 1994). The word *theory* comes from the same root as the Greek word *theater*. The physical world, argued Aristotle, stands before us and is unchanged by our conceptions of it. This is rather like a play, in which the viewers' ideas about what they watch do not change the action. Moreover, in the study of the physical world, we are concerned with lawful relationships, not moral judgments. Aristotle distinguished the term *theoria* from *praxis*. The practical arts study concerns us because by pursuing them, we attempt to make life better. In addition, the practical arts concern the doing of people—human agents—not physical objects.

What kind of study should communication be? Clearly the logical positivists wish to be firmly rooted in the tradition of *theoria*. Theories like CMM bear a debt to what has been learned in the Western tradition of theory building. However, CMM is not a set of predictive propositions about communication. Instead, it is a way to collect and organize data, formulate interpretations of social action, and develop critique and/or intervention. The test of such a practical theory is its use for critique and intervention in particular situations. The ideas advanced in my chapter are intended to advance the refinement of practical theory. What of the other approaches described in this book? Sanders and Leeds-Hurwitz et al. seem rather close to CMM; they are trying to get their conceptual houses in order so as to better understand and analyze particular cases of human interaction, whether in mundane episodes of suburban life or in formal institutions.

The goal of Beach's orientation to CA seems to be quite different. Some CA research is directed toward an understanding of particular social phenomena, such as the social construction of old age and doctor–patient relationships. However, Beach seems more interested in establishing what the functions of "Okay" really are. Can one legitimately question this in light of the other things he says about language and meaning? If *what* an utterance means is a matter of *how* it is used in real social action, and if cultural grammars are incommensurable, then the functions of any expression will be emergent and culturally varied. I do not doubt that Beach can formulate some functions and argue that this or that function is fulfilled by an utterance in any cultural discourse. However, what would that mean? I fear it would mean nothing more than the fact that Rosaldo (1991) could classify the utterances of the Ilongot according to speech act theory. However, although she could so classify their utterances, she concluded that the result of imposing such a universal system would miss the quiddity of Ilongot discourse. The procedure would ignore the way utterances cohere to create the Ilongot form of life. I think the kinds of work being pursued by the contributors to this volume have implications for what a theory is and what kinds of questions make sense to ask. Shouldn't we be trying to answer questions of this form: What are the meanings of x in various language-using communities?

CONCLUSION

The disagreements I have with the other chapter authors in no way diminish my optimism about the ability of the discipline of communication to create powerful ways for doing socially useful work. My one disappointment, however, is the lack of scope in much of the work on situated talk.

The other contributors have chosen to put off questions about embodiment, emotion, aesthetics, moral order, and the like. I have doubts about whether a coherent conception of human talk can be formulated prior to considering nonlinguistic matters that are integral to the unity of experience. The greatest difference between my own way of working and the other ways represented in this volume lies here.

REFERENCES

Cronen, V. E. (1994). Coordinated management of meaning: Theory for the complexities and contradictions of everyday life. In J. Siegfried (Ed.), *The status of common sense in psychology* (pp. 183–207). Norwood, NJ: Ablex.

Cronen, V. E., & Pearce, W. B. (1991–1992). Grammars of identity and their implications for discursive practices in and out of academe: A comparison of Davies and Harre's views to coordinated management of meaning theory. *Research on Language and Social Interaction, 25,* 37–66.

Cronen, V. E., Pearce, W. B., & Xi, C. (1989–1990). The meaning of "meaning" in the CMM analysis of conversation: A comparison of two traditions. *Research on Language and Social Interaction, 23,* 1–40.

Dewey, J. (1925). *Experience and nature.* New York: Dover.

Pearce, W. B. (1989). *Communication and the human condition.* Carbondale: Southern Illinois University Press.

Rosaldo, M. Z. (1991). The things we do with words: Ilongot speech acts and speech act theory in philosophy. In D. Carbaugh (Ed.), *Cultural communication and intercultural contact* (pp. 373–407). Hillsdale, NJ: Lawrence Erlbaum Associates.

Tomm, K. (1985). Circular interviewing: A multifaceted clinical tool. In D. Campbell & R. Draper (Eds.), *Applications of systemic family therapy: The Milan method* (pp. 35–45). London: Grune & Stratton.

6

A Retrospective Essay on *The Consequentiality of Communication*

Robert E. Sanders
State University of New York, Albany

If a person could successfully communicate just by knowing the language (or code) others use, and having something to say—if it were not problematic to achieve coherence, understanding, and coordination—then communication would be the neutral vehicle that many think it is: a means to influence what happens between people by informing them about the external circumstances they are in, and what the demands on them and options of response are as a result. But if (as the contributors to this volume maintain) coherence, understanding, and coordination have to be worked at and are joint achievements of the people involved, then taking part in the communication process—by placing demands on people and structuring options of response—influences what happens between them, apart from the demands of the external situation. From the former perspective, communication is consequential in what I call the *weak sense* (per the concluding discussion of my chapter); from the latter perspective, communication is consequential in the *strong sense*.

The positive achievement of the chapters of this volume is that each makes a distinct case for the consequentiality of communication in the strong sense. Making this case is a needed step forward with reference to showing the limits of the dominant view of communication as consequential only in the weak sense. It is also a step forward with reference to previous views of communication as consequential in the strong sense. This view is held by proponents of symbolic interactionism and ethnomethodology, who hold that the social world people occupy only exists in and through communication: Such ideas have been tied to the metaphysical view that the social world is essentially a symbolic construction. In contrast, the chapters in this volume argue that communication is consequential in the strong sense because of empirically grounded demands that the communication process places on people.

However, I want to look beyond the volume's value in its contemporary intellectual context, and rather focus on what has to come next. The chapters of the volume either indirectly (Beach's chap. 3 and Cronen's chap. 1) or directly (Leeds-Hurwitz & Sigman's chap. 4 and my chap. 2) confront a paradox (hereafter, The Paradox) that I do not think we (nor anyone else) have satisfactorily resolved. This is not a failure on our parts, as much as it marks the early stage we are in of examining the communication process from the consequentiality perspective.

On the one side of The Paradox, it seems essential that, for people to communicate with any degree of efficiency or effectiveness, they must start out with enough in common so that each can understand what the other's utterances and behavior mean—say a shared language (or code of some kind) and shared knowledge of the social and physical worlds around them. Without that, even the simple achievement of mutual understanding—never mind the achievement of cooperation and coordination on the business at hand—would have to be worked out *de novo* each time people encounter each other in a groping, provisional, and highly labor- and time-intensive way (Sanders, 1987). Of course, it rarely happens that way, except, for example, when the natives of hitherto "lost tribes" and anthropologists come face to face.

On the other side of The Paradox, insofar as communication is consequential in the strong sense—so that coherence, understanding, and coordination have to be worked at—communication cannot wholly or directly consist of the application of a previously learned code and knowledge. Rather, to say that the process of communication makes a difference entails that it is through communication that we produce or construct what our talk and acts mean (a code) and what the physical and social circumstances are, or their qualities, in which we find ourselves (mutual knowledge).

The most straightforward resolution of The Paradox would be to conjoin its two sides, assuming that both are empirically real, as follows: Except in special, rare circumstances, people do, indeed must, rely on shared codes and shared knowledge to communicate. But these are only a starting point for the communication process, and may be transformed or displaced through that process (where such transformation or displacement is often only temporary in the moment, or restricted to just those persons together, but sometimes is permanent and even massive; see Sanders, 1992, on political upheaval in Eastern Europe and the former Soviet Union). However, saying these ideas conjoin is easier than specifying in any detail how the process works—what the principles and interrelationships are that make it possible and systematic to utilize a priori codes and knowledge without those being privileged and controlling in the communication process.

In the remainder of this chapter, I comment in more detail on each of the volume's chapters, and I conclude by explaining what I envision we should work toward but are far from attaining—the principles underlying the interplay between situated and a priori aspects of the communication process.

Cronen arrays a variety of arguments, evidence, and philosophical positions against the idea that a priori codes and knowledge have a privileged and controlling role in the communication process. He does so on the grounds that what this predicts is radically untrue of everyday life: a uniformity of thought and action, a predictability of understanding and coordination; and the improbability (impossibility?) that innovation, individuality, and unconventionality of action and interaction would be anything but rare and dysfunctional. But Cronen argues this one side of The Paradox so strongly that one may wonder whether his view of the human condition really is what he projects in his chapter—that we are constantly at sea in a ceaselessly changing (at least changeable) social world, without hard ground and fixed points of reference to depend on, and relying on communication as our only navigational instrument.

Based on my reading of Cronen's other published work (Cronen, Pearce, & Changsheng, 1989–1990; Pearce & Cronen, 1980), I do not think he has so radical a view. Rather, I think he views a priori codes and knowledge (rules and contexts of interpretation) as providing people with delimited possibilities of understanding and coordination that they bring to the communication process in any instance. In that view, these a priori possibilities of what acts and episodes mean, and how to respond to them, have to be sorted out and one of them agreed on as the communication process unfolds. These agreements may become rigidified over time among specific people or in specific contexts, but not so much as to rule out the possibility of their being changed, at least through therapy or other intervention. If so, although Cronen may abjure theoretical codifications of the communication process insofar as they imply a determinacy he denies, eventually we have to detail the characteristics of such a priori codes and knowledge (delimited possibilities of understanding and coordination) and the principles of their utilization in the communication process. Otherwise, we cannot capture that the process has the constant potential to, and yet only occasionally does, become nonroutine and problematic.

Beach's analysis of "Okay" brings us to the same place Cronen does, but by an entirely different route. Beach also abjures theoretical codifications, and deliberately avoids addressing the theme of this volume in global terms. Instead, he examines the consequentiality of a single token, "Okay," although in a way that I think makes it archetypal: He treats "Okay" as consequential in the strong sense because it functions to perform any of several actions in the communication process that can only be performed by that token as part of that process, and the actions that "Okay" performs make a difference in what takes place between the persons involved.

Although Beach does not and would not frame the matter as follows, his analysis meshes with the more global issue I raise here: No matter how hard one tries to specify the a priori meanings of "Okay," or what several definitions "Okay" seems to have in light of the several uses Beach's analysis shows it has, no list of such a priori meanings can explain what it specifically means in any instance, or how people know what it means in any instance. Do we then say that its specific meaning depends on the activity/situation in which speaker and hearer are engaged, and what relationship and obligation speaker has to hearer in that situation, about which they have prior, mutual knowledge? This seems necessary—Beach's data indicate that people act as if they make such computations—yet following through on that approach is enormously complicated.

First, we could end up with something that would be cognitively overwhelming if we assume that for "Okay," and every other such token, there is a separate formula that computes from its possible meanings and features of the present activity/situation what a specific instance means. A more general and simple formula is needed, perhaps along the lines of the "principles of relevance" I propose in my chapter and elsewhere (e.g., Sanders, 1987). In addition, any such derivational scheme could not be so determinate as to foreclose the possibility of novel, but coherent usages. For example, a speaker may use "Okay" in a way that is dissonant with the present activity/situation (from the hearer's perspective at least). Rather than produce a dysfunction, this could set the stage for speaker and/or hearer to recast (separately or jointly) their understandings of the present activity/situation. Thus, in an interaction (from Varonis & Gass, 1985) involving a nonnative speaker (Caller), Caller phoned a TV repair service mistakenly thinking it was a TV retail store. Caller's inquiry about the cost of buying a new TV was heard by the Clerk as a question about the cost of repairing a new TV; Clerk's questions about what kind of TV Caller wanted to repair were heard by Caller, in turn, as questions about what kind of TV Caller wanted to buy. When Clerk asked about the size of Caller's presumed TV ("[is the TV that you want repaired] seventeen inch?"), Caller evidently heard the question as an offer of a possible TV to purchase ("[can I offer you a] seventeen inch?"). Caller thus replied "Okay" (agreement to clerk's offer), rather than "yes" (affirmation of Clerk's correctness). Clerk paused at that point, indicating Clerk perceived they might be having a coordination problem because "Okay" was the wrong token for agreement in the activity Clerk thought they were in.

The example above clarifies that the production of "Okay" has a coordinating value in social interaction that would be lost in any formula that assigned it a specific a priori meaning under specific a priori conditions. This instance also introduces a significant complication for any such formulae (including ones as general as my "principles of relevance"), namely, that "Okay" is distributed in (partial?) opposition to other affirmation tokens (e.g., "yeah," "right," and "sure").

Elaborated in this way, Beach's analysis implicitly exhibits, even in the behavior of a single token, the interplay between a priori and situated components of the communication process. But Beach does not move beyond his data to confront The Paradox, nor does he address the principles that make it possible for a priori code and knowledge to be utilized without being privileged and controlling.

There is less to say about Leeds-Hurwitz's chapter or my own because both address The Paradox more directly. Leeds-Hurwitz and Sigman, with Sullivan, are expressly interested in The Paradox, although they come at the issue from a starting place opposite Cronen's and Beach's. They originally held that the communication process can productively be examined in terms of its utilization of a priori codes and knowledge (captured under the rubric of *programs*), but are compelled to modify their position on the grounds that: (a) it fails empirically with reference to the case study they examine, and (b) it fails to capture (the strong sense of) the consequentiality of the communication process. I agree with them on both counts, and applaud their willingness to reconsider their earlier thinking. However, their analysis is far more revealing about the necessity for revising their original ideas than about the details of their current, "modified" view—that programs frame the activities in which people encounter each other, but do not fully script or dictate what is said and done. Their present focus on the need to revise their position led them to show that some components of interaction at the basket party are not based on the a priori program but are situated, rather than consider how such situated components arise and are connected with a priori components. Addressing this latter question requires them to provide more particulars about what a program consists of, and to be more detailed and less abstract about what is actually said and done by participants in such speech events as the basket party. As is, Leeds-Hurwitz and Sigman, with Sullivan, set the stage for a concern with, but do not provide direction about, how we might shed light on the interconnection between a priori and situated components of the communication process.

In many ways, my own chapter is a mirror image of Leeds-Hurwitz and Sigman's. Although for some time my work has been about the interconnection between a priori language (and nonverbal) meaning and situated meaning, I have addressed this with an emphasis on the situated, rather than the a priori, aspects of interaction—the local, strategic give-and-take that often unfolds in interactions. My chapter represents a shift toward relying analytically on other a priori components of the communication process besides language meaning—in particular, what I have referred to as institutional *prototypes* of the enactment of role-identities. However, although my data and analysis are more detailed than Leeds-Hurwitz and Sigman's about the presence in social interactions of both a priori and situated components of the communication process, I am no more detailed about what the a priori (i.e., prototypes) consists of, and am only sugges-tive about its influence on situated enactments of role-identities. Thus, D. Bogen (personal communication, November, 1993) inferred from my dis-cussion that prototypes are much more generic and controlling than I had intended. But the question of their power, or even the sufficiency of that construct to carry the analytic burden I give it, is impossible to resolve without more explicitness—something that is more a matter of empirical than theoretical developments yet to come. Hence, my chapter goes no further than the others in this volume in giving direction about how to capture the systematic aspect of the interplay between a priori and situated aspects of the communication process.

I conclude by briefly explaining what I envision when I talk about capturing "the systematic aspect of the interplay between a priori and situated aspects of the communication process." Some progress has been made in this direction in work on language meaning, and I draw on that as an exemplar.

The a priori meanings of expressions of language are primarily speci-fied by systems of rules—derivational rules or rules of inference—that map strings of words (sentences or utterances) onto interpretations. There has been extensive work on three such systems of rules: semantic interpre-tations, speech act interpretations, and inferences of conversational implicatures. My past work (especially Sanders, 1987) took these a priori meanings and the systems of rules involved as necessary, but not suffi-cient, to explain the situated meaning of sentences/utterances. I formu-lated principles of relevance that specified the situated meaning of a sentence/utterance in relation to its sequential place in a discourse or interaction—as a probabilistic selection of one of its a priori meanings that was relevant to the situated meanings already assigned neighboring sen-tences/utterances.

This work is instructive for the larger concerns I have raised here in three ways. First, this work clarifies the level of explicitness needed about the a priori components of the communication process before headway can be made on specifying their principled interconnection with situated components. We need explicitness about those a priori components, and we need some degree of consensus about what they are. Beyond a priori codes, and beyond programs, prototypes, contexts, and other schema about specific activities and institutions, there are cultural factors and various other background knowledge items that are pertinent.

Second, my past work on interconnecting a priori and situated aspects of language meaning anticipates and explains the possibility that situated components of the communication process are fluid (their values may change over time and vary across the persons involved), whereas a priori components are static. Capturing both the static quality of the a priori and the fluid quality of the situated is a requirement and a limiting condition on any principles we may devise about their interconnection.

Third, my past work is instructive because of its principal weakness. My formulation of the interconnection between a priori and situated language meanings is too narrow and restrictive. It is questionable whether the situated meanings of sentences/utterances are restricted to the set of their a priori meanings, as my formulations specify. The analog for this problem would be for semantic rules to specify all and only the alternative meanings of a sentence delimited by the a priori dictionary meanings of its component words, thereby wholly failing to capture the open-ended possibilities of figurative (e.g., metaphoric) interpretations (see Sanders, 1973). For example, Grice's (1975) inferential schema treats the situated meaning of utterances as much more open ended than do my formulations, but at the expense of analytic explicitness and precision. The most notable and important quality of the communication process is that its situated component holds out the potential for creativity, novelty, and innovation. But capturing this potential in a specification of its interconnection with the a priori component is likely to be the most difficult hurdle we have to overcome.

Obviously, the problems and goals of research on the communication process, when it is regarded as consequential in the strong sense, are much different than otherwise. The assumption underlying the considerable work that is being done on the circumstances about which we communicate—the knowledge base for communication, the psychological and practical basis of its effects, and so on—is that the communication process is consequential only in the weak sense. Not surprisingly, the components and characteristics of the communication process have to become our principal concern when we view it as consequential in the strong sense.

REFERENCES

Cronen, V. E., Pearce, W. B., & Changsheng, X. (1989–1990). The meaning of "meaning" in the CMM analysis of communication: A comparison of two traditions. *Research on Language and Social Interaction, 23,* 1–40.

Grice, H. P. (1975). Logic and conversation. In P. Cole & J. L. Morgan (Eds.), *Syntax and semantics 3: Speech acts* (pp. 41–58). New York: Academic Press.

Pearce, W. B., & Cronen, V. E. (1980). *Communication, action, and meaning: The creation of social realities.* New York: Praeger.

Sanders, R. E. (1973). Aspects of figurative language. *Linguistics, 96,* 56–100.

Sanders, R. E. (1987). *Cognitive foundations of calculated speech: Controlling understandings in conversation and persuasion.* Albany: SUNY Press.

Sanders, R. E. (1992). The role of mass communication processes in producing upheavals in the Soviet Union, Eastern Europe, and China. In S. S. King & D. P. Cushman (Eds.), *Political communication: Engineering visions of order in the socialist world* (pp. 143–162). Albany: SUNY Press.

Varonis, E. M., & Gass, S. M. (1985). Miscommunication in native/non- native conversation. *Language in Society, 14,* 327–343.

7

Maps and Diggings

Wayne A. Beach
San Diego State University

In an introduction and overview of the work and substantive contributions made by Erving Goffman to the study of social relationships (see, e.g., Goffman, 1974, 1981, 1983), Drew and Wootton (1988) observed that Goffman recurringly failed to offer details, and thus evidence, of *how* people actually achieve the activities they are claimed to produce. Although Goffman's sharp and altogether intuitive insights drew constant attention to finely textured moments of human existence—most notably the practices and procedures allowing people to organize transsituational involvements and thereby order face-to-face interactions—in the end, readers were left with a conceptually rich vocabulary (e.g., *rituals, frames, facework, remedial interchanges*) for identifying and discerning the patterns of everyday life. However useful Goffman's conceptual frameworks might be for understanding the unique ways humans order their affairs with one another, Drew and Wootton noted that they remain essentially underdeveloped:

> Such concepts are not themselves the endpoints of analysis. Whether people share the interactional concerns identified by Goffman, and whether they orient to such concerns in the manner he suggests, are frequently questions which await further enquiry. Goffman himself rarely went down that road. He was often content simply to indicate the potential relevance and significance of the interactional parameters in question; as a result, the maps he provides of this new terrain are often akin to those one buys on holiday in certain countries—suggestive sketches rather than definitive. (p. 6)

Such a position is by no means a discounting of Goffman's early and significant contributions to both the study of social interaction and its status as a legitimate enterprise within the social sciences. On the contrary, Goffman's conceptualizations continue to resonate throughout contemporary interaction studies, providing useful resources when raising and fleshing out issues, and in these varied ways reveal scholars' intellectual indebtedness to Goffman's work.

Nevertheless, it might be argued that the lack of detail—available only from diggings through inspectable evidence of actual (recorded, transcribed) conversations—is problematic when attempting to validate the resemblances between Goffman's characterizations of actions and how interactants display real-time understandings of the moments in which they are integrally involved (cf. Schegloff, 1988). Simply because such moments are replete with spontaneously generated problems and innovative resolutions designed by and for the participants, inherent to and deeply implicated within the delicate and changing landscapes of the talk at hand, it is not possible to capture the working order of routine interactions by conceptualizing, hypothesizing, or, in other ways, idealizing possible, rather than actual practices, especially when attempting to document their consequences for shaping and being shaped by subsequent and emerging streams of activity. Devoid of a methodology for systematically collecting, analyzing, and reporting on naturally occurring events in ways making ordinary peoples' orientations available to readers for critical inspection, researchers' observations are constrained less by practices employed by speakers and hearers and more by their own descriptive competencies for articulating envisioned worlds.

Such envisionings are the stuff of conceptual frameworks, and they inevitably constitute diverse mappings of interactional terrains. Although maps are often helpful for exploration, they are misleading and inaccurate; they offer essentially incomplete versions of the scenes they are designed to depict. More important, maps are incapable of capturing and thus specifying what people do in everyday settings and involvements, on their own terms, as they methodically and interactionally make available their thoughts, feelings, and understandings of real and determinate circumstances involving altogether practical choices and actions.

In short, there are key differences between maps and actions, between envisioned interactions and embodied talk-in-interaction, between mappings of and diggings through everyday conversations. Planning for and thinking about upcoming trips are only rarely, and then in glossed version, the same as actually getting on the road and adjusting to the omnipresent and unexpected circumstances that each journey undeniably entails.

The chapters by Sanders (chap. 2, this volume); Leeds-Hurwitz and Sigman, with Sullivan (chap. 4, this volume); and Cronen (chap. 1, this volume) each treats interaction/behavioral productions/conversation as central analytic resources for gaining access to the consequentiality of human communication. Each chapter, in its own way, provides transcriptions of actual conversations to clarify, exemplify, and substantiate a priori theories, frameworks, and positions. Sanders offers a neo-rhetorical perspective for understanding institutionally enacted role-identities, Leeds-Hurwitz et al. offer a social communication theory for situating human actions and the structuring of behavioral productions, and Cronen offers Coordinated Management of Meaning (CMM), in which a grammar of conversation is necessary to generate rules of action and context. Yet, and most important in light of the prior discussion, each spends considerably more time mapping out interactional terrains than digging through actual details of conversational data. All three chapters are more preoccupied with providing an extended theoretical backdrop—stipulating the importance of sense making, conversational organization, and various relationships to the consequences of communication—than with offering evidence of the claims being put forth by turning more directly to the real-time details of actual interactional involvements, and how such details reveal resources employed by speakers and hearers in the routine course of creating, addressing, and resolving interactional problems.

By articulating and laying out what a priori assumptions are brought to the data, direct and situated analyses of interactional materials are postponed in each of the three chapters. Yet having provided readers with such elaborate introductions, setting up and leading readers to data segments, when interactional materials are addressed they appear to offer minimal descriptions of participants' displayed orientations. Therefore, questions can be raised about the inherent "goodness of fit" between, on the one hand, the social world as envisioned via a priori theories and perspectives—replete with deeply motivated definitions, assumptions, tenets, and corollaries focusing on roles, rules, programs, and the like—and, on the other hand, how the ordinary people whose actions are described actually go about engaging one another so as to collaboratively achieve social order. Stated somewhat differently, if there is a goodness of fit between what the bulk of each of these three chapters lays out and actual conversational involvements, they by and large remain unaccounted for in the segments of data provided and analyses made of such interactions.

Because too little is done with data too late (and even then observations drawn from the data examined seem to reflect "templated" versions of a priori concerns "pyramided" onto the details of interaction) discovery *per se* appears short-circuited or preempted, which is yet another sense in which mappings can be said to be more suggestive than definitive. This is not to say, of course, that the conceptual frameworks offered by each of these three chapters is not intuitive, insightful, and appealing in its own right, or that some progress in understanding interactions has not been made. Like Goffman, numerous and thought-provoking notions offer heuristic alternatives to prior research and theorizing about communication processes and, particularly with this volume, the importance of consequentiality for understanding what is inherently unique about communicative phenomena. Nor is the argument being forwarded that all inquiries must necessarily employ interactional data, and in the same ways, to forward and refine positions regarding the organization of social interaction. Rather, if interactional data are employed to advance claims regarding the practices and patterns of human existence, there is considerable burden on the researcher to make clear what in the data are germane to certain claims and interactional possibilities: What findings emerged from the data and/or were imposed on the data as a result of a priori theorizing? In any case, readers should be in a position to carefully inspect whatever claims and findings are being made. When little or no interactional data are available for inspection, readers should recognize the inherent difficulties and limitations in talking about a social world by utilizing criteria that may be unrecognizable when faced with actual, naturally occurring events and activities on their own merits.

REFERENCES

Drew, P., & Wootton, A. (1988). Introduction. In P. Drew & A. Wooton (Eds.), *Erving Goffman: Exploring the interaction order* (pp. 1–13). Boston: Northeastern University Press.

Goffman, E. (1974). *Frame analysis.* New York: Harper & Row.

Goffman, E. (1981). *Forms of talk.* Philadelphia: University of Pennsylvania Press.

Goffman, E. (1983). The interaction order. *American Sociological Review, 48,* 1–17.

Schegloff, E. A. (1988). Goffman and the analysis of conversation. In P. Drew & A. Wootton (Eds.), *Erving Goffman: Exploring the interaction order* (p. 89–135). Boston: Northeastern University Press.

8

(Re)Situating Social Communication in Consequentiality

Stuart J. Sigman
State University of New York, Albany

Wendy Leeds-Hurwitz
University of Wisconsin–Parkside

We recognize that the approach taken to explore the consequential character of communication in our chapter, as informed by social communication theory, represents the most conservative research agenda of the four presented in this book. It is conservative precisely because of its unwillingness to relinquish certain notions of a priori resources that communicators "bring" to communication episodes. Although sociocultural rules are inexact predictors of what actually transpires in real-time moments of behaving, and such real-time moments may produce both novel outcomes and revisions of rules, we are nevertheless unwilling to abandon the idea that rules transcend any particular communication event. Given this recognition, we offer here a brief analysis of how our position on rules is similar to and different from that of the other contributors.[1]

We could not agree more with Cronen's (chap. 1, this volume) contention—following Dewey, Mead, and Wittgenstein—that "sense is created *in* communication, not by the adjustment of what we do to a universal grammar or logic." This is the basic motivation for a consequential view of communication processes. However, we question whether rules—the guiding principles and habits for communication—even occasionally are entirely emergent and ephemeral as Cronen implies: "Sometimes after many

---

[1]There are certainly several issues around which this comparative chapter could have been organized. An equally important issue concerns the "size" and "shape" of the time dimension each of the chapters deems relevant for locating communication consequentiality. All four chapters speak to the retrospective and projective features of communication acts, although "how much" and "in what manner" these acts reference time beyond the here-and-now moment is both decidedly different and left unclear by the authors.

trials, but sometimes in the course of making one effort, rules may come into use and dissolve moments later as action emerges in new directions." Although we do not deny that situation-specific accommodations and solutions to emergent problems may materialize (see Sanders, chap. 2, this volume), we question the utility of labeling these as *rules*. Any one-time behavior that is oriented to as meaningful by self and others can appropriately be considered a rule, given this reading of Cronen's work. It seems to us that rules (or scripts, programs, or prototypes) have some wider distribution across persons and situations.

Cronen does not categorically reject *rules*, in the sense that we use the term, but his writing tends to emphasize emergent ones and deemphasize a sociocultural behavioral repertoire or heritage. For example, in summarizing Watzlawick's descriptions of courtship between American soldiers and British women during World War II, Cronen writes: "To understand this situation is not a matter of comparing how often an attempt was made to kiss [an assertion with which we agree], but how the attempt figured in a pattern of conjoint action, and understanding what affordances and constraints were then created for subsequent action." But the fact that courtship problems were found in many of these American–British pairings indicates that not only the "conjoint action" produced by any one soldier and companion must be considered. We must also examine the enduring sociocultural rules—the a priori repertoire—that each participant was trying to enact and maintain.

Similar concerns arise in our reading of Beach's (chap. 3, this volume) study of "Okay" usage in conversation. First, Beach's contribution to the discussion of consequentiality discounts our ability to theorize about it apart from any specific empirical corpus. Second, it situates consequentiality as an observable activity performed by speaker–hearers at junctures made relevant by them during the moment-by-moment unfolding of interaction. Beach rejects a priori psychological and cultural explanations of communication, in favor of studying locally occasioned, context-shaping and context-renewing, jointly accomplished activity. According to this view, "Okay" does not have inherent properties or consequences. Rather, it is during the course of interaction that "Okay" is seen to be used by participants retrospectively (to close off some prior topic, activity, or speakership, and/or to acknowledge receipt of some prior utterance) and/or prospectively (to introduce or transition to some new topic, activity, or speakership), and to establish in its enactment relevant (re)interpretations of previous turns at talk and relevant junctures for subsequent turns at talk. Thus, "Okay" is studied as one of many "locally occasioned resources available to participants for achieving specific and relevant tasks" (Beach, chap. 3, this volume).

The last quoted sentence is ambiguous, however. In what way does conversation analysis treat "Okay" as a resource? What is a locally occasioned resource? We agree with Beach that "speakers may be preoccupied with somewhat different concerns involving very similar matters"—that these concerns may emerge during the course of conversation, and that "resources [may be] invoked to coordinate specific kinds of emerging actions." In our estimation, conversation analysis emphasizes the locally occasioned or emergent problems, resource invocations, and solutions at the expense of the range or repertoire of resources that may be appropriately and/or relevantly employed. Not all tokens may or do accomplish the interactional "work" accomplished by "Okay." Although Beach alludes to other linguistic tokens—"Mm-hmm," "Yeah," and the like—the absence of an explicitly comparative methodology here inhibits our ability to know what "Okay" brings to emergent interaction junctures. Stated differently, we believe that "Okay" is "tailored to the 'spontaneous combustability' of the moment," in part, because of its opposition (and oppositional functioning) with other such lexical items—all of which are contained within some a priori grammar of interaction.

In contrast to Cronen and Beach, Sanders' neo-rhetorical framework fully endorses the existence of some a priori, institutionalized material, toward which participants orient their behavior:

> Given that the institutional aspects of role-identities are prototypes that represent the rights and responsibilities that sufficient enactments have to uphold, not "scripts" that make certain acts and treatment by others obligatory, it falls to individuals to devise acts and secure treatment by others, within the limits of the business at hand and the course of the present interaction, that most approximate the prototype for enacting their role-identity. (Sanders, chap. 2, this volume)[2]

We disagree with Sanders' view of these a priori materials as non-obligatory prototypes. We think that the sociocultural repertoire encompasses a range of moral forces (from optionality, through preference, to requiredness), and that Sanders may have chosen pieces of discourse during which obligatory and unambiguous role-identities may not have been relevant.

Sanders' approach to the prototypes is refreshing on the one hand, and potentially troubling on the other hand. First, we consider the kind of bald-

---

[2]What constitutes "sufficient enactment?" The implication of Sanders' writing is that some number of enactments is necessary for a prototype to be upheld, but certainly the coherence and intelligibility of any one episode is to be gauged in terms of behaviors that orient to (either faithfully or in the breach) the prototype and not the frequency of occurrence. This, and our prior doubt about one-time behaviors alluded to by Cronen, lead us to suspect that researchers still do not have a good handle on what constitutes a rule or pattern.

on statements Sanders offers of the prototypes for superior and subordinate to represent an important awareness of the type of sociocultural knowledge that exists prior to and beyond the particularities of the episodes depicted. As our own chapter attempts to delineate, there is some value in considering the set of transcendent grammars and values according to which participants behave. Second, however, we wonder whether some alternative means to developing descriptions of a priori resources, and ascertaining their relevance in any particular episode under study, should be undertaken. Sanders employs both intuition and the same discourse corpus used for his subsequent neo-rhetorical analysis to develop the prototypes (the latter method potentially resulting in tautologies). In contrast, we use interview data, both before and after each communication episode, to achieve our description of the a priori resources (although the problem of matching interview data with subsequent performance data must be acknowledged). The relative difficulty and value of using these (and other) methods requires serious attention, especially if researchers concerned with communication consequentiality focus increasing energies on performances and their relationship to some transsituational repertoire.

This is the direction that we think demands attention. We find ourselves in the curious position of arguing for a view of consequentiality that acknowledges two principles that are seemingly at odds with the very idea of consequentiality. First, the groundwork for the relevance and meaningfulness of any particular moment of communication is to be found not only in the locally occasioned behavior, but also in the set of prior expectations, constraints, and grammatical affordances with which persons enter into those moments (not all of which are publicly displayed during interaction). Second, to study the consequentiality of communication, we must be willing to examine multiple iterations of an event or event type, not a single event. Without some understanding of what is common and what is unique across events, we will be unable to understand what it is that may and does occur during behaving that "goes beyond" the resources, and is therefore consequential. Hence, in order to know how communication permits participants to travel beyond the limits of those resources, we must study those resources that apparently exist apart from any one interaction episode, and we must study numerous occasionings of each episode. This dual-research track permits us to approach the essential and consequential features of communication.

Author Index

Subject Index

235